PRAISE FOR

THE RIDE OF HER LIFE

Featured in "Feel-Good Books to Brighten Your Summer"
—The Washington Post

"This is a feel-good story in every way, and [Elizabeth] Letts keeps the momentum lively, sprinkling in interesting historical tidbits that enrich the drama. *The Ride of Her Life* is an altogether quirky, inspiring journey that's not to be missed." —*BookPage* (starred review)

"Letts (*The Perfect Horse*) inspires in this miraculous true story of one woman's trek from Maine to California on horseback. . . . Letts's attention to detail and clear admiration of her 'funny, quirky, and bold' subject light up the narrative and make it hard to put down. This story has it all: bravery, determination, and a whole lot of heart." —*Publishers Weekly*

"Heartwarming." —*AARP*

"Letts provides ample . . . historical context, bringing the people [Annie Wilkins] met and the places she visited to life on the page. A longtime equestrian herself, Letts touchingly communicates the connection between Wilkins and her horses. . . . *The Ride of Her Life* also serves up a hearty helping of Americana: Readers will enjoy a glimpse of the country at midcentury." —*The Christian Science Monitor Weekly*

"Thanks to deeply sourced research and her own travels along Wilkins's route, Letts vividly portrays an audacious woman whose optimism, courage, and good humor are to be marveled at and admired. Upbeat and touching, Wilkins's story is the perfect pandemic escapist read." —*Booklist* (starred review)

"Twenty pages of notes and a Bibliography attest to the serious and thorough research by the author who travelled ten thousand miles to research this story. . . . What is so appealing about this nutball adventure is that the reader is taken on a trip across the United States."
—*New York Journal of Books*

"Equestrian Letts (author of best-sellers *The Perfect Horse* and *The Eighty-Dollar Champion*) has documented another fascinating, little-known slice of history. . . . Skillful prose and meticulous research combine to create a rich narrative and captivating character portraits of both Annie Wilkins and the people and places of the 1950s. Considering the popularity of her other nonfiction titles, the latest by Letts is likely to be on many hold lists."   —*Library Journal*

"*The Ride of Her Life: The True Story of a Woman, Her Horse, and Their Last-Chance Journey Across America* by Elizabeth Letts is the feel-good travel/adventure story we all need now. . . . Annie's tenacity and humility will endear her to your heart."   —*Saddle Seeks Horse*

"What sets Letts's [books] apart is her ability to seamlessly weave narrative and research together, creating tomes that are absolute page-turners. She is foremost a storyteller, and flexes her talent once again in her latest horse book, *The Ride of Her Life*."   —*Horse Network*

"Readers who'd love an easy, gentle story that's entirely true will want to cozy up with this one for a long winter's read. *The Ride of Her Life* is so good, you'll never want it done."   —The Bookworm Sez

"Elizabeth Letts's gift is that she makes you feel you are the one taking this trip: selecting your route from a gas station map, enduring awful weather and accidents, hearing the creak of the saddle and the roar of the trucks that pass you by. Best of all, you are the one who sees not a country divided and mean-spirited, but rather one full of people eager to console, to care for, and to celebrate the spirit of a woman who would not give up. This is a book we can enjoy always but especially need now." —ELIZABETH BERG, author of *The Story of Arthur Truluv*

"This poignant, inspiring story is not just about a woman choosing to live instead of die but also about an America that no longer exists. Annie Wilkins will never leave your heart. Her determination and homespun common sense make her a heroine for the ages. And thanks to this remarkable book, she'll never be forgotten again."

—MELANIE BENJAMIN, author of *The Children's Blizzard*

"Elizabeth Letts once again hits it out of the park with this triumphant historical tale of Annie Wilkins, 'the last of the saddle tramps.' A love story on so many levels—from the menagerie that was with her every step of the way, to the kindness of strangers who opened their homes to help Annie complete this ride of her life—this book will tear at your heartstrings from beginning to end. I loved it, and so will you!"

—ROBIN HUTTON, author of *Sgt. Reckless: America's War Horse*

"Annie Wilkins was an American original, and *The Ride of Her Life* gives her the tribute she deserves. Elizabeth Letts has created an indelible account of hope, loyalty, generosity, and sheer grit—and the power of a woman doing something just because she wants to do it."

—MATTHEW GOODMAN, author of *Eighty Days*

"There is sly wisdom in Annie Wilkins's simple journey: Keep faith in yourself and animals, trust in strangers, dismiss all the downers, and always live as if you just received a mortal diagnosis. Letts honors her subjects—Wilkins, 1950s America, and that moment when range gave way to road, and horse to car—with an author's hand and a historian's eye."

—KEN ILGUNAS, author of *Trespassing Across America*

BY
ELIZABETH LETTS

The Ride of Her Life

The Perfect Horse

The Eighty-Dollar Champion

FICTION

Finding Dorothy

Family Planning

Quality of Care

THE RIDE OF
HER LIFE

The Ride of Her Life

•

THE TRUE STORY
OF A WOMAN, HER HORSE,
AND THEIR LAST-CHANCE
JOURNEY ACROSS
AMERICA

•

Elizabeth Letts

BALLANTINE BOOKS
NEW YORK

LIBRARY OF CONGRESS CATALOGING-IN-PUBLICATION DATA
NAMES: Letts, Elizabeth, author.
TITLE: The ride of her life : the true story of a woman,
her horse, and their last-chance journey across America / Elizabeth Letts.
DESCRIPTION: New York : Ballantine Books, [2021] |
Includes bibliographical references and index.
IDENTIFIERS: LCCN 2020048732 (print) | LCCN 2020048733 (ebook) |
ISBN 9780525619345 (paperback) | ISBN 9780525619338 (ebook)
SUBJECTS: LCSH: Wilkins, Mesannie—Travel. | Horsemen and horsewomen—
Travel—United States—Biography. | Travel with horses—United States. |
Overland journeys to the Pacific.
CLASSIFICATION: LCC SF284.52.W55 L48 2021 (print) |
LCC SF284.52.W55 (ebook) | DDC 636.10092 [B]—dc23
LC record available at https://lccn.loc.gov/2020048732
LC ebook record available at https://lccn.loc.gov/2020048733

For Chris

NOT ALL JOURNEYS

ARE ON ROADS

Faith is not the clinging to a shrine
but an endless pilgrimage of the heart.

—**Abraham Joshua Heschel**

Contents

THE RIDE OF
HER LIFE

*A nickname is the hardest stone that
the devil can throw at a man.*

—William Hazlitt

Prologue

H ER NICKNAME WAS JACKASS ANNIE. No matter what else they said about her, everyone agreed on this. She got her nickname when she worked as a stitcher in a shoe factory and was so poor she had to ride a donkey to work. In a 1958 history of her hometown of Minot, Maine, she was described as "one of the so-called characters that provide the humor that makes towns of this type interesting." Some said she had run off as a teenager and joined the circus, become a bareback rider, only returning home when she heard that her mother was sick. Others swore she'd lived in and around Minot all her life, a life that hadn't amounted to much. She'd been married once, at least, and people said she'd sent the man packing when he'd tried to get the title to her farm. Her given name was Annie. Around Minot, Maine, it was Jackass Annie that stuck.

In November 1954, Annie took her dog and got on a horse and started riding. Destination: California. From a modern perspective, her journey seems almost bewildering—imagine trying to navigate without the benefit of GPS, to travel with no cellphone, no credit or debit card, not even a bank account to draw from. In fact, when she first set off, Annie didn't even have the kinds of tools that were available in 1954: road maps, a flashlight and batteries, a waterproof raincoat. Annie headed south, a Quixote in the company of her Rocinante, a run-down ex-racehorse, and her Sancho Panza, a little mutt. Society has called these people by different names: vagabonds and drifters, pilgrims, hoboes, and hippies. She called herself a tramp.

Had she been a man, perhaps her independence, her eccentricities, her free spirit would have won her admirers, but the citizens of Minot, like much of small-town America in that era, valued outward conformity. In the postwar years, women's roles were tightly circumscribed and largely defined by their relation to others—wife, mother, widow. The cult of domesticity was in full swing. A single older woman didn't have much leeway if she wanted to be seen as respectable. The ideal unmarried older woman was devout, docile, and a bit dull. Annie was none of these.

Her real personality—funny, quirky, and bold—had been buffed and sanded in memory to make her appear more conventional, more palatable to those who would judge a woman for any deviation from the straitlaced norm. Forgotten was her fondness for a good party, her two divorces, her stint as a vaudeville performer, the fact that she never set foot in a church. In its place was the respectable Widow Wilkins—folksy, kindhearted, and maybe a bit simpleminded. When I traveled to Minot and met people who had known her, that was how her former neighbors described her. They were proud of their famous citizen. They hesitated to tell me how poor she was, how mean her circumstances, how she'd never been considered part of polite society. They didn't want to say a word against her. What struck me, though, was that in spite of their pride in her grand adventure, folks still remembered her as Jackass Annie. The pejorative had stuck like a burr on a shaggy dog's coat. Annie deserved better.

So this is her true story, and in this story I call her by the name she was born with—just plain Annie.

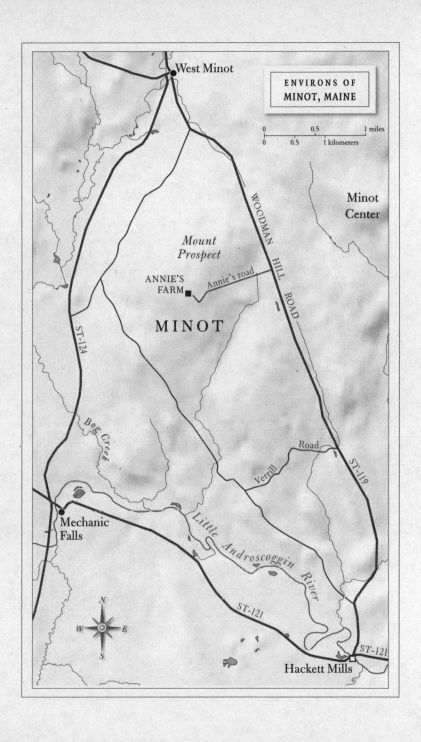

ENVIRONS OF
MINOT, MAINE

West Minot

Minot
Center

Mount
Prospect

WOODMAN HILL ROAD

ANNIE'S
FARM   Annie's road

MINOT

ST-124

Bog Creek

Road

Verrill

ST-119

Mechanic
Falls

Little Androscoggin River

ST-121

N
W   E
S

ST-121

Hackett Mills

ST-121

Winter is not a season . . . it's an industry.

—Sinclair Lewis

———

1954

———

CHAPTER

1

Living Color

THE SUN ROSE BRIGHT over Pasadena, California, on January 1, 1954. All along Colorado Boulevard, people had lined up early, five or six deep, in preparation for the sixty-fifth annual Tournament of Roses Parade. Pasadena's Rose Parade had originally sprung from the flowery imaginations of a committee of boosters who wanted to show off the beauty of California in midwinter, when most of the rest of the country was covered in snow. Now parade floats festooned with thousands of fragrant, bright-hued roses rolled past mop-top palm trees in the sparkly morning sun. But this Rose Parade was like no other. As the debut event of 1954, it was a fitting launch to a year that would mark many important transitions. This year, in addition to the palomino horses ridden by the Long Beach Mounted Police, the display of the crisp crimson-and-white uniforms of the Bellflower High School Marching Band, and the brilliant floats—Gulliver's Travels, Cinderella sponsored by Minute Maid Orange Juice, flamenco dancers in sequined costumes whirling on the Mexican entry—each festooned with thousands of individual fresh flowers, there was an important new addition. Two state-of-the-art NBC television cameras scanned the procession, broadcasting the first live TV colorcast to twenty-one NBC affiliates.

To show this first ever coast-to-coast color broadcast, the Radio Corporation of America had sent out a preproduction run of two hundred of their brand-new color receivers to RCA Victor distributors across the continental United States. A few of the receivers were put into strategic central locations, such as hotel lobbies in major cities, situated so as to attract the most attention for this newfangled invention. On New Year's Day, a few thousand people in selected cities scattered across the country—Omaha, Nebraska, and Wilkes-Barre, Pennsylvania, St. Louis and Toledo, Baltimore and New Haven—were able to see the golden shine of the palominos, the vivid reds and yellows of the roses, the crimson and white of the drum majorettes. Southern California, America's land of perpetual sunshine, a mild and sunny sixty-two degrees that New Year's morning, would never again seem quite so far away. It was a fitting start to 1954—the year the world suddenly accelerated.

SOME THREE THOUSAND MILES AWAY, in Minot (pronounced MY-nut), Maine, it was four degrees Fahrenheit and windy. Sixty-two-year-old Annie Wilkins and her elderly uncle Waldo did not have a color television—or any television, for that matter. They didn't have electricity. Their water came from a pump, their heat from a wood-burning cast-iron stove. It might have been New Year's Day, but there was no holiday from the endless chores that marked their days on the top of Woodman Hill.

The winter of 1953–54 had started out promising enough. Annie believed that she and Waldo were just about to get ahead. A good harvest in '52 had allowed them to invest in livestock—a few heifers, some gilts, and some old hens. Come spring, she calculated, they'd have enough to cover the feed and a bit to spare. All they had to do was make it through the winter. That, however, was easier said than done. Waldo's eyesight was going. He had cataracts, but the hospital said he was too old and weak to risk the surgery.

Waldo had always been a hard worker. When he'd been forced to retire from his job on a road crew for the WPA at age seventy-five, he'd set out to show them that he was not too old to work. He kept up doing day labor, whatever he could find.

But now he was eighty-five and mostly blind. When the snows hit in November, he couldn't see well enough to get to the barn. Too much glare. So Annie had to feed all the animals. He could gather firewood, but he couldn't see well enough to split it. So Annie split the wood. With each passing day, she had to shoulder a larger share of the workload, carrying feed and buckets of water for the animals, cooking from scratch over an old iron cookstove. That New Year's Day saw her standing at the open barn door, looking at the lowering, wintry sky, ticking off the months until spring. But then she chided herself. It was too early to get started on that kind of thinking. A lot of winter remained in front of her. A wriggling at her feet reminded her that she wasn't alone. Her silky black-and-brown mutt sat beside her. He tilted his head, left ear cocked up, as if to say, *What now?* Annie leaned down to scratch him, and he thanked her by edging even closer, his weight a warm pressure on the side of her muddy boot.

Her dog's name was Depeche Toi (de-PESH twah), which is French for "hurry up," a good name for the small bundle of energy with a pointed black nose, always aquiver with the scents of the myriad critters lurking in the Maine woods and fields that surrounded Annie's farm—chipmunks, mice, voles, and lemmings, the occasional snowshoe hare, an abundance of gray squirrels, and sometimes a porcupine. He had floppy ears and, across his chest, a V-shaped bib of white, giving him the air of being all dressed up. Depeche Toi owed his highfalutin French name to the French American boys who lived down the lane. Originally, Minot had been settled by Anglo-Saxons, old English stock, but the nearby twin cities of Lewiston and Auburn, an industrial center powered by the mighty Androscoggin River, had a large French American population, and French was spoken in many homes. Annie thought the name suited him, so it had stuck. She doted on that dog, and he returned the favor. He was never far from her heels, except when he was in her arms or off playing with the stray cats in the barn—he loved cats.

As Annie went about her grueling round of daily chores that January, she had a growing sense of exhaustion. But the sight of Depeche Toi trotting a few steps ahead of her, tail pluming in the air, nose eagerly sweeping in the wintry scent of pine, helped keep her cheer up and her mind off her troubles. Midway through the month, however, she began to feel dizzy and feverish. The doctor said it was flu and she needed to rest. But telling a farmer to rest is like telling her to give up her farm. Someone needed to break the ice on the water buckets. Someone needed to gather the firewood. Someone needed to split the logs. Annie rested when she could, though in a full day of farmwork, that wasn't often. As she trudged from house to barn and back again, she thought about the promise of spring, when the heifers would go to sale and the hens would lay their eggs and the gilts would grow into fat sows. That was how she got along that year, and every year. You had to have hope.

And maybe she would have been able to both keep up with the work and recover from her flu, but a Maine winter is a capricious mistress. Right then, a blizzard hit. It drifted over all the roads and covered the farm more than three feet deep with an undulating blanket of blue-white. At the top of Woodman Hill, they were completely socked in. Annie was too weak to shovel the path to the barn, so she tried to wade through the snow, only she kept slipping and falling. Although she managed to get the animals fed and watered, by the time she got back to the house, she was on the verge of collapse. Each time she inhaled, she felt stabbing pains in her lungs. Her teeth chattered. Her breathing was labored. She needed a doctor.

But there was no way to get help. They were stranded a mile from the main road, and even that road wasn't plowed yet. Of all the 144 miles of roads in Minot township, hers, a dead end, what Mainers called an end road, would be plowed last. She knew the law: main roads and mail routes first, end roads last, except in case of emergency. And this was an emergency, the two of them stranded there inside the silent, white, frozen world, only who would know? By now, she was too weak to get out of bed, and Waldo had neither the eyesight nor the strength to walk the mile to the main road through thigh-high drifts.

She was lying in bed, half-delirious, when she heard shouting voices cut through the quiet. Depeche Toi sprang up and started wriggling in joyful anticipation. The French boys had snowshoed over to see how Annie and Waldo were holding up. After coming in long enough to recognize the dire conditions at Annie's farm, one headed down to the main road to call an ambulance, while the other busied about doing farm chores. A few hours later, Annie heard the scrape of the plow. By the time the ambulance finally arrived, she was so weak they had to carry her out.

When she was in the hospital, the decision was made to send Waldo, who was too frail to stay alone, to a nursing home. The French boys took Depeche Toi back to their own farm for safekeeping. The rest of her animals were sold off to help pay some of her hospital bills. Annie was still bedridden when she got the news that Waldo had passed.

She was the only one left. The last of her line.

You don't know your neighbors until
you've summered 'em and wintered 'em.

—Annie Wilkins

—

CHAPTER

2

Live Restfully

MINOT, MAINE, WAS NOT REALLY a single town but more just an area made up of scattered farms, with several small clusters of businesses within its boundaries. Together, West Minot, Minot Center, and Minot Corner boasted one post office, two grocery stores, four churches, one feed store, one consolidated school, and a single country doctor. Right now, Annie was seated beside him in his big black Packard, bumping up the dirt road that led to her farm. He was giving her a ride back from the nursing home in nearby Minot Corner, about five miles away, where she'd been confined since January.

She had left home during a blizzard but was returning in mud season. The monochrome white of winter had been replaced with a variegated landscape of retreating beige and emerging brown. Mud time was a rhapsody of running water: retreating icicles plinked from rooftops, and melting snow trilled a melody, tinkling into rivulets, harmonizing into burbling streams, crescendoing into the fast-swelling Bog Creek, until it rolled into the thundering Little Androscoggin, now overflowing its banks and crackling with branches and dead leaves.

Earlier that day, worried about leaving the farm alone much longer, she had talked Dr. Cobb into letting her go by telling him she felt just fine. In fact, Annie felt a lot weaker than she was letting on. She could breathe more easily now, but each inspiration felt like inhaling shards of glass. Annie surely hadn't fooled the doctor. Both of them knew the true state of affairs. She'd been treated for pneumonia, but an X-ray of her lungs had revealed a trouble spot—maybe her old run-in with TB acting up, maybe the beginning of cancer. It was too soon to tell. In the early 1950s, the medical community had finally started turning the tide on tuberculosis. Doctors had begun treating people with streptomycin. But the treatment was new, and patients and doctors still feared it wasn't a long-term cure. Tuberculosis was a stealthy killer, lying dormant for years only to rage back again. The common wisdom about surviving active TB still prevailed: fresh air, sunshine, and, above all, rest. Annie didn't get a solid diagnosis—but she did get a prognosis. Two to four years to live.

Dr. Cobb passed a well-kept farm, slowed, and wheeled his Packard off the main road, onto the muddy unpaved lane that led past ragged stone walls, woods, and empty fields. Just a week or so earlier they couldn't have driven; they'd have had to come up from the main road on foot. About a mile up the hill, they arrived in front of Annie's empty house. Dr. Cobb cut the ignition and turned to her. "Remember what I said," he told her. "You must live restfully. Do you understand me, Mrs. Wilkins?"

Live restfully.

To remember a time when she didn't work from sunup to sundown, Annie had to go all the way back to her girlhood—to the few magical years her family had spent in the small town of Jackson, New Hampshire, a picture-postcard-perfect place in the foothills of the White Mountains. Her father had left Maine for Jackson, hoping to find work, and with her mother and father working, seven-year-old Annie had been allowed to go to school in a bright red schoolhouse prettily situated on the road into town. What a life that had been for her, with nothing more on her mind than learning to read and figure. Her time entirely her own. But the schooling time for Annie had been short. She'd left school for good at the end of sixth grade, and she'd worked hard every day since then.

Dr. Cobb was waiting for an answer.

Annie didn't want to tell a bald-faced lie, so she settled on a half-truth.

"I'm not one to pay for advice and then disregard it."

She would not *disregard* his advice; she would keep it in mind. In truth, however, Annie had no idea how she was supposed to live a restful life. The farm wasn't going to take care of itself, and she had to eat. As a country doctor, Dr. Cobb would have known that his prescription was unlikely to be followed. Most likely from pride, she'd turned down his offer of a place in the county's charity home. He must have hoped that Annie had some relations who would step in to take care of her. It was evident that she couldn't survive on the farm, but Mainers are known for being independent, and he wouldn't have wanted to pry. Surely, friends and neighbors would be watching out for her. In any event, he left her there and drove off.

In spite of the awakening nature around her, the farm seemed unlike itself. The barn stood empty—the cows, the pigs, the chickens all gone. The only thing of value they'd left behind was the pile of composted manure next to the barn. Her truest companion, Depeche Toi, was still with the French boys. And, of course, the biggest difference was that her uncle Waldo was gone. He wasn't really her uncle—he'd moved in with them a few years after her father died in 1922, first as a hired hand; later, he'd taken up with her mother, and Annie had started to refer to him as Uncle Waldo. Annie was a grown woman by then, and had lived on her own before moving home to help her mother on the farm. Waldo had been an eager farmer, though not an especially skilled one. Waldo had encouraged Annie and her mother to go into Lewiston to work in a shoe factory, to earn cash to help keep the failing farm afloat. That factory was most likely where Annie had picked up TB. Annie had clashed with Waldo when she was younger—he'd thought that because he was a man, the women should defer to him, and that had never set right by Annie, since the farm belonged to her mother. But Sarah had let him make all the decisions, and Annie had had little choice but to go along. Still, he was a good sort, and for the last twenty years, since her mother had died, he'd been her only human companion.

Although Annie had plenty of grit, the prospect of finding her way from where she stood now—still seriously weakened from her lung troubles, nearly broke, and with an empty barn—would have daunted anyone.

In 1954, a single older woman without family or employment faced few and stark choices. Annie had no bank account, no savings, and no relatives to rely on. She didn't have any siblings or children. And there was no state welfare program for her to draw on, because she had not yet turned sixty-five. Her only significant asset was her farmland—land that had been passed down from her grandfather, and that for three generations had been their family's primary source of wealth.

Yet, as long experience had proven, the farm was always hungry—hungry for seeds and fertilizer, rubber buckets and baling wire, straw and wheelbarrows, chicken feed and seedling plants. Any farmer knew that a farm demanded tribute. In lean times, you had to go off the farm to work, to earn money to put into the farm, in the hopes that down the line, the farm would pay you back with enough left over to allow you to purchase what you needed for the following year—but it seemed that every year something unexpected happened, and just when you thought the farm was about to go into the black, you'd be forced to start the cycle again. Annie had been caught up in that cycle since 1934, when her mother had died and Annie had inherited the farm in the depths of the Great Depression. Somehow, she'd managed to keep it going with an unceasing cycle of on-and-off-the-farm labor. She was a strong woman, and willing, but now it was just her alone, and she was worn out.

At least in the bleak landscape of Annie's new life, there was one spot of joy. You couldn't keep a secret in Minot, Maine, for long. That very afternoon, Depeche Toi came barreling up the road, pink tongue hanging to the side, zipping along as if he were chasing a snowshoe hare, the French boys tagging along behind him. As soon as they'd seen Doc's car passing by, they'd set out to check on their neighbor and to return her pup, who was now fourteen months old. Annie, still walking a little unsteadily, reached out to greet him, happy to let the dog bathe her tear-wet face with his tongue. She buried her face in his warm fur to hide her tears; she was a stoic woman, and wouldn't want to let on how much it meant to her to see her best friend again.

THAT NIGHT, HER FIRST night home, her first night alone, before she went to sleep, Annie surveyed the contents of her small living room. The woodstove was warm, with wood stacked carefully alongside. An oilcloth covered the table. Through an open doorway, you could see her cot, neatly made, covered with plaid woolen blankets and a quilt that bore the tiny stiches of some past female relative with more womanly skills and defter fingers than Annie had ever had. Her light came from a kerosene lantern. Her little home was tidy and warm, but she knew the neighbors whispered about her—living in a shack that was nothing more than an old outbuilding. Her grandfather's big square farmhouse had burned down years ago. All that was left of the house was a grown-over indentation where the cellar used to be. The attached barn, with its corncrib and spacious hayloft, had burned along with it. This building—an old smokehouse, or maybe the icehouse—had been sturdy enough to convert into the home where she now stood, but its clapboard walls still didn't do much against a stiff winter wind. With her feet in ancient woolen slippers, she shuffled to the door and pushed it open a crack, shivering as the cold night air swept in.

Annie coughed, cleared her throat, and coughed again. She ran her fingers through her short gray hair. She squinted up at the night sky. Not a star in sight and a crisp bite in the air that smelled like snow. Her little dog ran outside, circled in the darkness, and then, his business finished, ran back in.

She started to close the door behind him, but on second thought, left it slightly ajar.

Depeche Toi looked at her, his eyes alert and soft.

"I'm leaving the door open for you, buddy."

He gazed at her attentively, as if speaking a silent question: *Why?*

"I just don't know if I'll make it through another night. I don't want you trapped in here with me. If I die, you run down to the neighbors. They'll know something's wrong and come looking for me and I guess they'll not let a little dog starve." Annie shivered at the thought of her own still body, alone in the house, slowly turning cold. She shook the thought away, stooped down to pick up her little mutt, and pressed his warm, furry body firmly against her heart.

"Live restfully," Annie thought. "But how?"

But in this world nothing can be said to be certain,
except death and taxes.

—Benjamin Franklin

—

CHAPTER

3

Tax Money

A FTER A FEW DAYS BACK at the farm, Annie felt a little stronger and started to take stock of her situation. Even after selling off all of her animals, she was still in the hole, without enough cash on hand to settle her debt. And it was the very worst kind of debt: she owed back taxes on the farm. She needed to find a way to do something that was pretty near to impossible: to extract a cash crop from her land when she had no capital, and had only her own highly compromised womanpower to do it. By nature, she was an optimist, and honestly, what else could she be? She spent some time surveying her possible courses of action, of which there were few. Replacing the animals was too expensive. She needed to figure out what kind of cash crop she might be able to plant—especially since she had no money for hired help, or even for seeds. But doing nothing wasn't an option. After running through the scant list of possibilities several times, she decided to stake her entire future on *Cucumis sativus*—or, more specifically, the pickling cucumber.

The land that crested Woodman Hill in the township of Minot had been in her family for three generations. At three P.M. on November 24, 1875, sixteen years before Annie was born, her maternal grandfather, forty-three-year-old George Libby, stood before the justice of the peace in a foursquare white building in Minot Center that served as the Registry of Deeds. Libby had recently returned from a foray out west, to Wisconsin and Iowa, where his father and several of his siblings had gone seeking land and fortune. Having done well for himself in trade, Libby decided to return home and invest in land in his hometown. For the sum of $2,800, Libby purchased 240 mostly wooded acres along the crest of one of the highest hills in Androscoggin County, high above the Little Androscoggin, a tributary of the main river, which ran through the valley to its west. Married, with four children to help him clear the land and cultivate the fields, he must have believed that his prosperity was assured.

George Libby could not have known that Maine's golden age of farming had already passed. The economy that favored small Maine farms had peaked in the 1820s and 1830s. By the 1870s, when Libby bought his farm, the descendants of many of Maine's original settlers had already pushed toward the western frontier in search of more fertile soil. One early Maine settler, Benjamin Tibbetts, who was interviewed in 1877 on the occasion of his one hundredth birthday, bragged that his children, grandchildren, and great-grandchildren had scattered far from Maine—some landing as far away as California.

When the Libby family acquired their acreage, the amount of deforested land in Maine, cleared painstakingly by hand, was already shrinking, with second-growth forest resurging over much of the land that had proven too difficult to farm. The growing season in Maine was short, the weather fierce, and the soil remained stony no matter how much one worked to refine it. The underlying motor of the economy had decisively turned toward manufacturing. The nearby twin cities of Lewiston and Auburn, powered by the Androscoggin River, which flowed between them, were filled with textile mills and shoe factories, crowded tenement housing, and a bustling economy of industrial labor. Farmers, desperate for cash to pay for seeds, equipment, and hired labor, began sending family members into town to work in the factories in order to keep their farms afloat. Twice the labor, in factory and field, did not lead to twice the profit, but the revolving door from farm to paid labor and back to farm became a mandatory way of life for many of those trying to eke out a living from the land.

When Annie was a girl, every small farmer grew corn for canning. They called it "canning gold" because it was a surefire cash crop, reliably producing enough to pay their property taxes. By 1954, the old corn factory had shut down, but there was still a pickle factory over in Mechanic Falls, just a few miles away. The owners would spot you the seed, and then come pick up your cucumbers as you harvested. They paid in cash. So this was the plan Annie settled on in the spring of 1954: she'd spend the summer growing pickling cucumbers. Not restful. But maybe doable. She'd paid off her doctor's bills. Now she just needed a little extra for Uncle Sam.

In Shakespeare's *The Tempest*, King Alonso asks, "How camest thou in this pickle?" He might have asked the same of Annie Wilkins. How did it happen that a sixty-two-year-old woman just out of the hospital could find no better alternative than to stake her bet on pickles? The truth was, though Annie did not know it, she camest in this pickle— almost penniless, with a prognosis of two to four years to live—through no fault of her own. For Annie Wilkins, along with thousands of rural farmers all over America, the early 1950s was not the beginning of a new era of suburbanization but the bitter tail end of a long, steady decline. Annie was the last member of a family of Yankee farmers, descended from people who had fought in the American Revolution, fought for the belief that every man deserved his own plot of land, people who were willing to work ceaselessly in the harshest possible conditions to see that dream through. Annie had inherited that land, her family's tradition, and a strong work ethic. What she hadn't inherited was any money.

George Libby had died in 1902, twenty-seven years after signing that title deed. Four years later, his widow mortgaged their land for $850. When she died, she left her land equally between her two living daughters. One sold it back to the bank for $400. The other held on to it, until she passed it to her sole living heir, Annie Wilkins. Currently, by the county's calculation, the Libby property was worth exactly $54.36: the amount of back taxes due, plus one dollar, the amount that her neighbor had offered in exchange for her land.

THE CUCUMBER SEED PACKS came in the mail. Annie collected empty cans from a pile in the corner of the barn, filled them with soil, pressed three seeds into each, and arranged them so that they would catch the sunlight through the windows. She sprinkled them with water and waited. She watched as the tiny seedlings emerged, pale green shoots, curled as if in prayer, tiny signs of hope, pushing up from dented tin-can planters, her entire future held in their delicate tendrils. She waited for the exact right moment to transfer them to the ground. If she planted too early, a late frost would knock out the entire crop.

For the last few days, she'd been taking the seedlings outside to harden them off. Then, in the first week of June, on a mild morning that followed a cloudy, starless night, she felt in her bones that it was the right time. Annie might have had only a sixth-grade education, but the number of things she knew about her little patch of ground would take stacks of books and years of study for an outsider to learn. She watched for signs: songbirds in May, gnatcatchers when the trees started to leaf out. Clear nights often brought frosts. Two cloudy days in a row or a spring rain portended warmer weather. She looked for rings around the moon, waited until it was waxing, and watched its color to make sure it looked neither sallow nor red. She even checked her bones—an ache in that leg that got crushed in a horse-and-wagon accident years ago always eased up as the frosts ended. The time was right. But she wondered how she would get all the seedlings into the ground—a backbreaking job for a woman alone, much less for one who was still frail from her winter illness.

Around Minot, people looked out for one another. When people needed help, word got around. Just as the French family down the road had helped her out before, somehow people knew that Annie was fixing to plant cucumbers and that she'd need help putting them in.

Almost no one had everything they needed, so people got in the habit of sharing—one farmer had a truck, another had a reaper or a plow; people helped each other put their hay in, and they paid each other back with shares. Annie was grateful but not completely surprised when an old friend from a neighboring town stopped by to check in and promised to help get her seedlings in the ground.

With this neighbor's help, Annie cultivated a sizable plot. The cucumber, being a viny plant that proliferates rapidly, needs a good bit of space. Her friend planted three seedlings per mound, three feet apart, in long, straight rows. Annie followed along behind, kneeling on the dirt, placing her handmade wax-paper cones around each fragile tendril, hoping that the plants would stay warm enough to survive. At first, the entire endeavor looked as if a stiff wind might put her plan to rest.

When her friend left, he wished Annie luck. He'd been kind enough to give her a whole day's work. But this was just the bare beginning. All the hoeing, picking, and grading would be up to her.

These Boston variety seedlings would produce a cucumber that was nicely rounded, with a thin, bumpy skin. The word "pickle" comes from the Dutch *pekel* or the northern German *pokel,* meaning salt or brine. Annie knew that the ideal pickling cucumber was freshly picked, about four to six inches long, and relatively uniform in shape. A good example of the way industrialization had affected farming, pickling cucumbers had been specially cultivated to grow to a size that would fit nicely in a Mason jar.

And if all went well, and her plants weren't attacked by cucumber beetles, or burned by a dry spell, or iced by a late frost, if all went well, she'd signed herself up for a summer of work—picking, grading, hoeing, sorting, every day, over and over again. That she didn't have the strength to do it was immaterial. Annie surveyed her young crop with a combination of hope and resignation. The way she saw it, she and her cucumbers would live and thrive or wither and die, together.

Three weeks after the seedlings went into the ground, each mound was covered with a profusion of vines. The little heart-shaped leaves were a vibrant green, and there was no sign of mildew or the scourge of the cucumber beetle. Annie threw her hoe over her shoulder and headed to the fields, where she weeded around the vines, attacking the fibrous quack grass that wanted to carpet the entire field. As the weather grew warmer, she was starting to feel stronger, but she was still easily winded and couldn't do more than a few minutes of work before she had to stop and rest.

By late July the vines were flowering. By now, the mosquitoes and blackflies were thick over the fields. Annie wore men's dungarees and a long-sleeved man's shirt when she worked, but she spent almost as much time swatting at bugs as anything else. She kept up her routine, out early in the morning to weed, while Depeche Toi chased field mice or napped in the shade. At noon, she leaned up against an old fence post in the shade and split her lunch fifty-fifty with her dog. Her energy kept improving, as long as she paced herself. In the evening, completely pooped, Annie went to bed early, with Depeche Toi curled up beside her.

About two weeks later, she spotted small fruits, like tiny thumbs, sprouting from the flowers. By early August, some of the cucumbers were ready to pick. Annie was able to spend the entire day in the field, relying on their packed lunch and a pail of water to sustain them through the long summer afternoons. If she didn't pick fast, the cucumbers would grow too big, and she'd be paid less money for them. When the light grew too dim to allow her to pick, she carried the cucumbers back to her house, and under the glow of the kerosene lamp she graded them, sorting them into piles by size and shape. Finally, for the first time since she'd returned from the nursing home, she was sleeping soundly, too tired to worry or even think much. Sometimes when she fell, bone weary, into bed, she would remember her doctor's admonition to live restfully, but she couldn't stay awake long enough to dwell on it.

As the calendar turned from August to September and then to October, Annie was still picking cucumbers with Depeche Toi at her side. They'd had a spell of unseasonably warm weather—hitting eighty degrees in early October. The farms at lower elevations had already gotten frost, but the particular location of Annie's hilltop farm kept it a little warmer, and her vines were still producing. By now, the pickle company was paying top dollar, as most of the other farms had already exhausted their crops. The roll of bills she kept wrapped in a rubber band was growing.

When the last of the cucumbers were picked and graded and sorted and carted away, Annie couldn't quite believe it. She had taken Dr. Cobb's orders and turned them upside down. Instead of resting, she'd never worked harder in her life. Yet, miraculously, she was still standing, and most of all, she had amassed over a hundred dollars—enough to make it through the winter. Not enough, however, to sustain herself through the winter *and* set the farm right.

In 1950, twenty million Americans lived on family farms, a number that was still robust, though there'd been a slow decline since the beginning of the century. But the number of farm families was about to go into a precipitous dive, leaving only half that many by 1970. Zoom out ten miles from Woodman Hill and you'd find the cities of Lewiston and Auburn, with their factories and supermarkets, car lots filled with chrome-covered American-made sedans with fat rubber tires, and appliance stores where you could buy televisions and refrigerators, hi-fis and air-conditioning units. Zoom out to a hundred-mile radius from where Annie stood and you'd find highway workers constructing the extension of the Maine Turnpike, a four-lane highway built in 1947 to accommodate the increasing amount of car traffic from Kittery, on the southern New Hampshire border, north to Portland and now being extended all the way up to Augusta. Zoom out even farther and you would find the modern cities along the Eastern Seaboard, connected by an increasingly sophisticated system of highways, clotted with cars and trucks, quickly extending outward to the suburban areas of single-family homes rapidly expanding along the edges of the great cities. Zoom out once more and you'd see a country that had radically changed in the past ten years—a landscape that was quickly moving from agrarian and rural to urban and suburban—and a world that was smaller than ever, thanks to commercial transcontinental air travel.

But now narrow your focus back in to Annie's world, bordered by the familiar lanes she had always passed on foot, on the back of a donkey, or sometimes, when she was lucky, in a horse and wagon. Its boundaries didn't extend far—as far as the small hub of Minot, down to the mill town of Mechanic Falls. Remember, she had no telephone, no television, nothing to tell her that the quiet universe of her farm and her town no longer represented the norm for the rest of the country.

Even if Annie did not have the full picture, she could still see that she was losing the battle to hold the farm, and for the first time in her life, she wasn't sure she wanted to keep up the struggle. She also realized that she had no appetite for living alone. The memory of those frightening days when she and Waldo had been stranded up here was still fresh in her mind.

When she was a girl, Annie remembered, every year, without fail, at some point her mother would stare through a frost-spattered window with a hungry look in her eye.

"You know, we should just quit this place," she would say. "Hitch a horse up to a buggy and head west. Out to California. I would love to see that Pacific Ocean at least once in my life."

At night, quilts piled high on top of her, Annie would imagine that blue expanse of ocean, sparkling under the sun. But there was always something stopping them: plowing to do, chickens to feed, hay to bring in, seeds to plant, another plan to earn a little more money to get them through another day.

Annie had no children, no husband, and her parents were gone. The people who had once populated the small world of her childhood now all lay at rest under the Libby headstone. As she gazed out at the familiar world outside her door, Annie knew that her family's time on this land was coming to an end. Three generations had split wood, sown seeds, mucked stalls, slaughtered hogs, canned preserves, picked apples, loved, toiled, cried, exulted, looked up at the sparkling expanse of stars splattered across a black winter sky.

She'd held on. As tight as she knew how. Hadn't she?

But that was the thing about Maine. Seemed like every year, about this time, people started to talk about leaving. The frost crept in, the jagged V's of Canada geese honked past, the light blue endless summer sky put on its winter coat of gray, the mercury dropped, and the days got shorter, making the familiar slow, silent march toward the deep frozen heart of January. No chance you could think about going then. By then, there'd be drifts of snow up around the eaves and black ice on the roads, fires roaring in fireplaces, crossword puzzles and knitting in the chairs, and you just knew you'd have to stay put and wait for the thaw.

But before that happened—there was always a moment. A moment when people got the urge to leave, when they looked up at the Canada geese and thought maybe they could just go with them.

Her mother never made it to California. Never traveled farther than New Hampshire. Right now, on this cold October afternoon, Sarah Libby Stuart lay in the graveyard at Mechanic Falls, just a couple miles as the crow flies from the doorway of the helter-skelter farmhouse where Annie now stood. Her mother had been gone for twenty years. Annie was well past the age her mother had been back when Annie was a girl— and yet here Annie still was.

But she had some money, and she had her furry companion, and the more she thought about it, the only thing she truly lacked was courage. The courage to follow the plan that was starting to form in her mind.

Horses raise what the farmer eats,
and eats what the farmer raises.
You can't plow the ground and get gasoline.

—**Will Rogers**

—

CHAPTER

4

The Search

> WANTED:
>
> LOOKING FOR A TOUGH HORSE. SEX AND
> DISPOSITION UNIMPORTANT, WITH LOOKS
> I WOULDN'T BE ASHAMED OF, AND WEARING
> THE LOWEST POSSIBLE PRICE TAG.

ANNIE WILKINS SPREAD THE *Lewiston Evening Journal* out on top of the oilcloth-covered table in front of her. She flipped past the headlines: "6 More Accused Communists Arrested," "Four Cases of Polio Confirmed," "Traffic Fatalities Increasing." She skipped over an advertisement for Northeast Airlines—tickets for flights to New York City were available for twenty-one dollars. The supermarket touted modern conveniences such as "tasty, thrifty frosted foods," instant pudding, and Sylvania lightbulbs "for longer evenings." On page 4, there was a floor plan for the "home of the week," a postwar-style suburban house with two bedrooms, a modern bathroom and kitchen, a utility closet for the water heater, and a carport. And just below it, a Maine Electric ad described the latest "all electric home."

As she turned the newspaper's pages, she read about a world that was right outside her door, one she had never had a chance to join. The *Journal* conveyed an America focused on the emerging Cold War, fears of Communist infiltrators, and a buoyant, humming economy, none of which had yet been felt on Annie's rural hilltop. She flipped past the Magnavox and Mercury ads, past the crossword and the funny pages, to the very back of the newspaper, where the classified ads still catered to the needs of rural farm folk—baling wire and chicks, Guernsey cows and hay, used farm equipment. Apples by the bushel (but you had to come to the farm to pick them up). Sometimes, at the bottom of the classifieds, there were small human-interest articles, and today there was a brief article titled "Wheelchair Traveler Dies in California," about a woman whose husband, unable to pay for the health-care treatments she needed, had pushed her in a wheelchair all the way from Boston to California to raise money and attention for her plight.

Most days, the classifieds had listings for puppies and kittens, and livestock for sale—sheep and milking cows, and poultry, too, a going business in the area at the time. But there were few ads for horses. Farmers were more likely to get around in cars and trucks these days. Only a few old-timers still hitched a horse to a plow.

However, on this day, Annie was lucky. Among the ads for musical instruments, refrigerators, electric supplies, and help wanted was a single listing that looked promising: "Saddle horses for sale at all times. We also buy meat horses. Davis Stables Winthrop, 205-4 or 214-1."

We also buy meat horses.

That one sentence was enough to alert Annie that this was the right kind of place. "Meat horses" were the ones that no one but the butcher wanted, the kind that sold cheap.

Since Annie didn't have a telephone and couldn't afford a toll call from a pay phone, she addressed a two-cent postcard to Davis Stables in Winthrop, Maine, a small town about thirty miles northeast of Minot. On its back, she carefully inscribed a brief description of the qualities she was looking for in a horse. She included her home address, walked into Minot, dropped it with Mrs. Slattery at the post office, and waited.

For Annie, the waiting wasn't so bad. She knew nothing of instant gratification. If she wanted to talk to someone, she could write a note and wait for a response, or she could go for an in-person visit, on foot. With her postcard sent, Annie went about her business, figuring that some kind of answer would present itself in due time.

Due time turned out to be about a week, when a young man showed up on her doorstep and introduced himself as Richard Davis, the owner of Davis Stables. A gangling fellow who looked more like a schoolboy than a business owner, he assured her that he was in fact the proprietor and that he had a horse in his stable that was perfect for her in every way. He seemed eager to sell her on this unseen horse's merits—which only made Annie suspicious. The more questions she asked, the more his description of the horse in question seemed to change, like a chimera, always shifting form. But he offered to give her a ride up to Winthrop so that she could give him a try, and Annie figured she could trust her own eyes better than any description.

Richard Davis ran a typical rental stable of the time. During the warm months, he rented hacks to vacationers who came to the Winthrop Lakes region. Davis would buy a horse from pretty much anywhere. He loved horses and would rather give one a home than let it go to the local butcher, who was always looking to buy. But Maine winters weren't a good time for a rental stable. So as much as Annie might not have seemed like a prosperous buyer, he was still eager to find a horse he could figure out how to package to match her needs.

Annie chatted amiably with Davis as they drove toward Winthrop, but just like her uncle Waldo, who always talked more when he was nervous, Annie commented on the weather, the landscape out the window, anything she could think of to mask the fact that she had no idea what she was getting herself into. She hadn't sat on a horse in at least thirty years. Was she about to make a fool of herself? Or possibly lose her nerve? She didn't exactly know what she was looking for in a horse.

What kind would be suitable for her purposes? A sturdy one, for sure, one that was reasonably calm. She had a hip that bothered her with rheumatism, and the last time she had weighed herself down at the drugstore, she'd clocked in at a sturdy 170 pounds on her five-foot frame.

The horses at Davis's stables were ragged-looking, and most were a little thin. Their coats were already grown shaggy, and while the animals were not outright neglected, each one was already becoming a burden to the owner—an expense of hay and grain, shoeing and veterinary care—with no way to earn it back as winter set in.

When they went out to the stables, Davis pointed out a plain, solid-looking fellow. Annie could see that he was a gelding, his color a shade she described as rusty black—a dark seal brown without a single mark of white anywhere on him. Maybe his coat had been shiny in summer, but now it was long and dull, obscuring the angles of a body that appeared strong but a bit too lean.

When they approached, he looked half-asleep, but as he turned his head to regard Annie, she noticed his lively brown eyes. This one was no plug—he had some fight left in him. His long forelock, black between his ears and tinged a rusty red toward the ends, swept across his forehead at a jaunty angle—it reminded Annie of the way the racier village boys used to style their hair when they went out courting. The horse flicked his ears forward, then let them flop to half-mast again as he looked away, as if to say, *I don't need to please anybody.* Proud. A Yankee horse.

But not as proud as all that, because when she pulled a carrot out of her pocket, he let out a soft nicker and reached his head forward, nuzzling it up, sweet as you please, from the palm of her hand.

Davis slipped a halter made of twisted rope over the horse's head, led him out of the stall, and pointed out some of his finer features. According to his teeth, he was "aged"—meaning at least nine years old. He was about fourteen hands (four inches to one hand, so technically he qualified as a large pony). He had solid bones and good depth through the chest, allowing ample room for his lungs; a short back, which is good for a saddle horse; and rounded, muscular haunches—a quality much prized in Maine for plow horses working on hilly pastures.

Right away, Annie got a good feeling. With his coloring, stature, and build, he looked like a local horse, a Maine horse, like the kind she used to see in the trotting races at the county fairs when she was a girl. When Annie mentioned this to Davis, he didn't deny that the horse might have raced a few times, might be a castoff from the track, might have done some trotting in his day. When Annie replied that she needed a quiet horse and an ex-racehorse might not fit the bill, Davis quickly insisted that this one was gentle enough for a baby to ride and had just come straight from a children's summer camp.

Humph. Annie wasn't buying any of it. As far as she was concerned, a horse trader was just one step away from a horse thief, no matter how nice this young man seemed, and unfortunately, Annie knew something about horse thieves. No matter. She didn't need anyone to sell her on it. She was planning to use her own judgment.

The gelding gazed at her with friendly interest, not unlike the way she looked back at him. Both smallish and square, both Maine-bred, both a little past their prime and a bit scraggy around the edges—and both needing a new home. And Annie recognized the flash in his eyes. He was down, but he wasn't done.

His name was Tarzan. Annie remembered the famous movie horse who belonged to the actor Ken Maynard. Seemed like a good name to her.

Davis had saddled the horse up and thrown a bridle over his rope halter. Why not, he suggested, get on and give him a try?

Annie looked Tarzan in the eye, as if to say, *Don't try anything, brother.* She was worried she was going to make a darn fool of herself.

Even though Tarzan wasn't too tall, she didn't think she could heave herself into the saddle from the ground, so Davis led him over to a mounting block. Feeling a bit foolish, she swung a leg over his back, settled her ample backside in the saddle, and kicked her feet, clad in lumberman boots, into the stirrup irons.

Annie liked the view from up here. Tarzan had nicely formed ears, the tips pointing inward toward each other. He stood completely still as she got her bearings and stepped forward only when she gave him a nudge with her heels, letting the reins slide out between her fingers to give the horse a free head. Tarzan stepped right forward as if he'd love nothing more than to go on a long walk. Annie and Tarzan circled the field next to the barn several times before she pulled up in front of Davis.

"I feel right at home," she said.

"When you feel like that on a horse," Davis said, "then he is the horse for you. You could ride ten thousand and not find a better one."

Now Annie worried that she'd made herself a sucker. It was so easy to tell that she was smitten. She clambered off, looked Davis in the eye, and asked, "How much?"

Sure enough, he quoted a price that was steeper than she'd hoped for.

She was gearing up to say no, to tell him this horse was out of her price range, to figure she could keep on waiting, or maybe see if there was another, cheaper one in the barn when Tarzan reached out and nudged his muzzle against her hand.

She turned to look at him, and his two soft brown eyes were studying her with a gentle curiosity, as if he could read her mind.

"He likes you," Davis said, and as if on cue, the shaggy gelding reached over and rubbed his head against her shoulder and took a couple of side steps over, so that he stood next to her.

Annie shrugged, then smiled broadly.

Looked like he'd chosen her. Didn't seem like she had much say in the matter.

Annie had spent some time at the races in her day, and though she didn't consider herself a gambling woman, she'd cast a bet or two, won some and lost some on the Maine trotters. Now she was about to take the biggest gamble of all. She was farm-born and farm-raised and she knew that you didn't bet the farm on a horse, and yet here she was looking at this horse with the intention of doing just that.

Annie named a lower figure, but the wily horse trader could surely see that her heart was already taken. He shook his head as if facing the gravest possible sorrow and started to lead Tarzan away, but Annie held up her hand to stop him. She knew that this was her horse.

It wasn't until she'd parted with a sizable chunk of all her money that she realized she could have asked a few more questions. Had he ever been in traffic, ever ridden along a road? And which part of Davis's story was even true? The part about him being an ex-racehorse or the story of him being a gentle children's horse? She hadn't thought it through. She'd just followed her heart.

This wouldn't be the first time she'd been smitten by a good-looking guy with a sparkle in his eyes. People say that you should ask your best friend's opinion before you go sweet on a fellow, and so now Annie was worried about what her own best friend, Depeche Toi, would think about this tall, dark stranger.

She needn't have worried. When Davis and Annie arrived at the farm, as soon as she pulled the back of the trailer down and unloaded her new horse, Depeche Toi ran right up to Tarzan, and the horse reached down and greeted the little dog with a friendly trumpet of warm air from his nostrils. Depeche Toi responded in kind with a frantically waving tail and a soft pink tongue darting out for a lick. Annie could see that they were going to be friends.

It wasn't until Tarzan was in the barn, fed, watered, given a carrot and three lumps of sugar, had approximately twenty-seven kisses bestowed on the silken side of his nose, and his affable mug was peering over the half door of his stall that Annie began to wonder about what she was doing. The idle dream of riding to California had just gotten a lot more concrete with the addition of four new hooves to the barn. She'd set this journey in motion now, even if she hadn't set foot on the trail yet. It was one thing to idly think about getting on a horse and riding out of town, and a whole different thing to figure out exactly how on earth she was going to make that work. Over the last couple weeks, she'd paid visits to two of her mother's old friends, casually mentioning what she had it in mind to do. One of them had laughed outright at her, telling her she'd be sent up to Augusta if she didn't watch out—up to Augusta, the state psychiatric hospital—because people would think that was where she belonged if she kept spouting such nonsense. Her mother's other friend had given Annie her blessing and said it was just like something a Libby would do. She told a story about Annie's maternal grandmother, who'd once ridden a horse to Bangor and back. But she also told Annie she didn't have to go, that if she needed a place to stay, she could always come live with her.

Annie might be foolish, but she wasn't crazy, and certainly, she'd thought over the pros and cons plenty of times. If she stayed home, she knew exactly what she was in for. She was going to lose the farm, and she'd end up with nowhere to go—a charity case. And if she left? Truth is, she kept looking for some kind of sign, some certainty, a giant message written clear as day, right across the sky. But one thing Annie had figured out in her almost sixty-three years of life was that although you could dip your toe in a pond on a summer day and guess how cold it was going to be, you never really knew for sure until you plugged your nose and closed your eyes and jumped all the way in. The unexpected could always be a shock, but sometimes it was the expected, the predictable, the resigned acceptance of whatever bad thing was coming your way that could end up dragging you down. While she didn't have all the whys and the wherefores figured out yet, it looked like she'd picked her path and was going to keep on walking until she could see round the next bend, and then she'd figure the next step out, and the next one. She didn't know any other way.

Thus settled in her mind, Annie started to get ready. She spent the next two weeks preparing for her journey. She started with Tarzan's tack. She had an ancient artillery saddle, left over from some ancestor who had once owned a riding horse. She stripped the saddle down, removing the hoods and the skirts to make it as light as possible. She mended the stirrup leathers and sanded down the rivets so there would be nothing to rub Tarzan's skin.

The next step was trying to decide what to bring with her. She made a list, continually adding things and then crossing them off. She didn't have many possessions, but since she had no intention of returning, anything she didn't carry with her would have to be left behind for good. She planned to wear several layers of clothing and bring other garments along for spares. She rolled up blankets to sleep in, brought rope to stake out her horse, some tools in case anything broke along the way, a fry pan and a spider to rest it on, a can opener, a ball of twine, and two burlap bags, one filled with hay and one with grain to get Tarzan through the first few days of travel. She had felt-lined lumberman's boots, a navy-surplus coat, and a fur-lined bonnet that had once belonged to her grandmother. And she had two saddlebags she'd ordered from the Sears, Roebuck catalog. She also had some tinned food and a few packs of army rations, but she didn't try to carry all the food she'd need. She planned to stop at a roadside diner from time to time if she wanted a hot meal.

From the last of the cucumbers to the first of November, Annie had been occupied with her preparations, and now she had nothing left to do. October had been unseasonably warm, but the temperature was dropping daily. If she didn't go soon, she might miss her chance—or lose her nerve.

On Thursday, the fourth of November, she realized that there was nothing left to hold her back. She was planning to leave the next morning, rain or shine. She went to bed extra early, and before she snuffed out her kerosene lamp, she slowly wrote the following words in the sixty-cent diary she'd bought for the trip: "I start tomorrow, on Friday, leaving home and friends behind. I go forth as a tramp of fate among strangers."

But then she was too nervous to sleep, tossing and turning, wondering if she was doing the right thing. She found herself still wishing she could have some kind of sign to let her know she was making the right choice. She clambered out of bed and started flipping a coin. Four times out of five it came up heads. Satisfied that the matter was decided, she climbed back into bed and fell soundly asleep.

*I was surprised, as always, by how easy the act
of leaving was, and how good it felt.*

—Jon Krakauer

—

Leaving Home

ON FRIDAY MORNING, ANNIE was up early. Just a faint glow appeared behind Streaked Mountain in the distance, while Depeche Toi circled around her, wondering what all the excitement was about. She pulled on each layer of her traveling clothes with care. The bottommost layer was two sets of long underwear, wool union suits, scratchy against her skin. Over that she wore two men's wool work shirts, a blanket-lined vest, two pairs of heavy men's work jeans cinched at the waist with a leather belt, and waterproof rubbers over her felt-lined boots. Men's clothing, all of it, but the only kind practical to wear on the road. On her head, she wore a fur-lined bonnet with earflaps, pulled down over her short gray hair.

Having spent the last two weeks trying to winnow down her packing list, in the end she'd managed to gather up pretty much everything she owned. She stuffed her pockets full of gear and bundled up all sorts of things—a coffeepot and tin cup, a handful of kindling, matches and oilcloth—inside her bedroll. And once she tried to actually load up Tarzan, it was more of a puzzle than she'd expected. He could wear his bridle right over his halter, with the lead rope knotted around his neck—something else for her to grab on to, she figured. She'd planned to tie everything else she needed to the saddle, but lacking straps, she had to make do with twine. She cinched her blanket roll in front of the saddle and her buckets and feed, her cast-iron fry pan, heavy coat, and extra clothing behind. At last she found a place for almost everything. What she couldn't fit, she had to leave behind.

Depeche Toi was clearly intrigued by this novel spectacle. He sat on his haunches, mouth open to reveal his pink tongue, ears cocked, following Annie's every move.

When all her things were finally secured, there was just a twelve-inch expanse of saddle for her to sit in. She worried that she must weigh at least two hundred pounds now, thanks to her overloaded pockets. Yet for all she carried, she was missing the items a practical person might have thought of first—she carried no road map, no flashlight and batteries. Diners Club had issued the first credit card in 1950, but Annie didn't have one. In fact, she didn't have any kind of bank account. All that was left of her cash, about thirty-two dollars, was deep in a pocket, secured with a rubber band.

She tied a length of cotton clothesline to Depeche Toi's collar while he wriggled and licked her hand, thinking it was a game. Being a farm dog, he'd never been on a leash. Next, she led Tarzan over to an overturned wooden crate, where the horse stood patiently as she hoisted her thick rubber boot into the stirrup, and struggled awkwardly aboard, wedging herself into the small space she'd left open. If he had thoughts about his load or the outlandish garb of his rider, he kept them to himself. She had so many layers on that she felt like a sausage, but at least she was warm. She wrapped the end of Depeche Toi's rope around one hand. In the other, she held the reins.

She nudged Tarzan with her heels and he lurched forward into a quick trot, setting up a clatter from all the gear. Annie grabbed a bit of his mane and held on tight, but Tarzan soon settled right down to a walk. She shifted her weight until she felt secure.

As they walked away, she kept her eyes turned forward—refusing herself a single look back at the place she'd lived in most of her life. She figured she would most likely never see her home again.

But she'd hardly gone a hundred yards before doubts crowded her mind. She couldn't stay on her land, but she didn't have to leave Maine. Her mother's old friend had offered her a place to live. And her bankroll of bills, which had seemed so bountiful a few weeks ago, had already dwindled to the much smaller roll in her pocket. Was she foolish enough to think that she could make it to California when she was starting out with so little money? Her plan was to ride south as far as she could and then start looking for work. But what if no one would hire her— a stranger, an old woman, and dressed in men's clothing to boot? In spite of her earlier determination, it took every ounce of strength she had not to just turn around right now, before she'd reached the main road and made a fool of herself.

Twenty-five months. That's all she needed—until she turned sixty-five and could receive old-age benefits. At that point, she promised herself, she would rest and live out whatever was left of her life in peace. Annie understood that she didn't have that much life left in front of her, and if she didn't make it all the way to California because her time was up—well, she felt she could live with that.

The farm she was leaving behind no longer belonged to her. Seventy-nine years after her grandfather had bought it, almost to the precise date, she'd let it go to the neighbor for exactly what he'd offered: $54.36. He would have let her stay for a while, and not just her mother's friend but others, too, would have taken her in. And, of course, there was Dr. Cobb's offer. She could become a charity case at the county home. But her pride wouldn't allow her to even consider that—or any of the other choices, really. At least this way, she was beholden to no one.

AS THE TRIO HEADED DOWN the road, away from the Libby farm, the gear rattled around her. Tarzan jigged a little, his ears flicking back to listen. Depeche Toi seemed to sense that an adventure was afoot, and he kept running ahead, then stopping when the rope leash caught him with a tug. He seemed surprised, but he didn't fight it.

Her journey began with the accompaniment of a timeless music: the

percussion of a horse's hooves on the dirt, the light staccato of Depeche
Toi's rapid footsteps hitting a contrapuntal beat, the fluting of the few
birds still this far north in the winter, the reedy breeze in the trees, and,
of course, the in-and-out rattle of her not-so-easy breathing and the
steady two-step of her thudding heart.

OF THE IRREGULAR LITTLE GROUP who headed down the hill that
morning, Depeche Toi was the youngest—not yet two years old. Annie had
raised him from a pup, but he wasn't a dog with a pedigree. His silky coat
and keen intelligence indicated that he might have some spaniel in him,
though his legs were short in proportion to his body, suggesting that a bit
of dachshund could be in the mix. He was certainly no citified purebred,
accustomed to heeling along on a sidewalk wearing a rhinestone collar. He
was the result of a stray coupling, and Annie had taken him in when the
neighbor boys were giving away puppies from the litter. Since birth, he'd
been allowed to roam free. The occasional car that lumbered slowly up
their end road posed little danger to him. He'd had unfettered access to
miles of pastures and woodlands, muddy bogs and fresh rivulets, a paradise for dogs, though he'd heel right to Annie's side whenever she called
him. Still, she didn't know exactly how he'd react to traffic on the road.
She hadn't given much thought to how many miles a dog could walk in a
day. Annie had spent most of her life getting around mostly on foot. In her
world, dogs and horses and people all walked, as far as they needed to.

The next youngest of the trio was Tarzan. Davis had said that he was
at least nine years old, based on his teeth, but Annie figured he was probably older than that. He'd come to her with no pedigree or story of where
he had been, other than the one cooked up by Davis. He'd no doubt been
passed from hand to hand a few times before ending up as a riding hack.

Tarzan's color was what horsemen would call dark brown with black
points—"points" referring to his legs, mane, and tail. As Annie had immediately noticed, he had not a single white marking anywhere. His
head was set well on his neck. His deep brown eyes were free of discol-
orations, with a bright devil-may-care expression. He was compact and

well-muscled for his size, with flat withers, and strong shoulders that sloped gently at a forty-five-degree angle. His disposition was both calm and lively—he walked forward with a good pace. Around the barn he'd had an agreeable temperament, and he'd seemed to have settled well into his new home. But that was before Annie took him on the road.

Tarzan may have come to her without history or family tree, but most of his heritage was written right on him—plain as day to anyone who knew how to read the story of a horse. The first time she saw him, Annie had been struck by his similarity to the kind of trotters she had encountered at country fairs as a girl, and that's not surprising. Tarzan's conformation and color showed strong clues that he carried the blood of New England's native horse breed: the Morgan, a lineage prized for its versatility. These animals could pull a heavy load, work the hilly and rocky New England fields, and carry a rider on long journeys. By the early part of the nineteenth century, the Morgan-type horse was prominent in Vermont, New Hampshire, Maine, and Massachusetts. She may not have realized it, but for a long-distance ride, Annie couldn't have done better than to choose a Morgan.

The eldest member of this odd trio of travelers was Annie herself. Born in 1891 in Mechanic Falls, the small mill town just a few miles from her grandfather's farm, she had to rely on her mother's memory for her birthday, because Annie had been born at home and had never been issued a birth certificate. She knew she was a Libby—the surname is one of Maine's most common—but she didn't know that generations earlier, her ancestors had come over to Maine from England to work in the fisheries. In *The Libby Family in America,* written in 1882, the author, a distant relation to Annie, described the Libby clan as being generally undistinguished by power or wealth, but neither paupers nor criminals. He described a clan that was honest, neighborly, generally engaged in manual labor, and "contented with the enjoyment of present happiness." Annie had a strong sense of what it meant to be a Libby. She believed that her family stood for a tradition of pride, hard work, and self-reliance.

Annie's forebears had arrived in Maine in the seventeenth century, 150 years before the American Revolution. In the early years of the republic, the area around Minot, Maine, was a hotbed of populist fervor. Poor settlers, many of whom were ex–Revolutionary War soldiers, believed they had the right to claim any unoccupied land they were able to settle and clear. But Maine's interior, which had been home to Woodlands Indians for twenty to thirty thousand years, was sparsely settled by colonists. The British Crown had laid claim to the land and distributed vast landholdings to British allies. Much to the anger of many patriots, these land claims survived the Revolution, and the descendants, wealthy absentee landlords, tried to force settlers to pay to acquire the titles to the land the locals believed they'd come to own through the sweat of their labor.

For decades after the Revolution, determined squatters continued to fight, although the landlords eventually prevailed. Still, the memory of how hard they'd struggled to acquire land lingered through generations of Mainers. Settlers to Maine in the seventeenth and eighteenth centuries effected enormous changes upon the land they farmed. Over the course of about two hundred years, they deforested vast swaths of land, then worked to clear the soil of the stones that were heaved up by the freezing and thawing cycles every winter. The chopped-down trees were used for building, but primarily to feed the settlers' nearly insatiable need for heat in Maine's extreme climate. The long stone walls that crisscrossed southern Maine, as well as much of New England, were silent testaments to this herculean labor.

In some ways, Annie and her horse, Tarzan, were uncannily alike. She, too, was not tall, rather rounded, had a spirited disposition and a high tolerance for hard work. Like a Morgan, she had been born and bred in New England. And had she known the story of the Morgan breed's great progenitor, Figure, she would have certainly been struck by similarities between Tarzan's ancestors and her own. Figure, the original Morgan, belonged to a poor singing master named Justin Morgan. The Morgan breed's foundation stallion first won fame for his strength in pulling giant logs to clear fields. Like the mighty Figure, Annie's own people had toiled in these fields, pulling up rocks to make walls and clearing the very land that Tarzan, Annie, and Depeche Toi passed by as they headed toward the main road, about a mile away.

Annie's dirt end road led down a series of gentle slopes. As they started off, Tarzan's ears were at half-mast, flicking back and forth as he accustomed himself to the creaking ropes, squeaking saddle leather, and Annie's somewhat labored breathing. He started off a bit slow, even stopping in his tracks once and turning his head to look at her, as if wondering whether she really meant that he was supposed to keep walking with all this load. Annie jiggled her seat bones in the saddle, pressed her heels down to get the feel of the stirrups.

They hadn't gone more than a quarter of a mile before Annie tried to readjust her weight in the tight spot she'd left herself in the saddle. In doing so, she accidentally dislodged the fry pan, which she'd tied to one of the saddle rings. The heavy pan clattered to the ground, startling Tarzan, who did a little hop-skip forward, which loosened the ties on her blanket roll, unfurling its contents onto the ground. She pulled Tarzan to a halt, dislodged herself from the saddle, and slid to the ground with a thump. She retied the blanket roll, rehung the fry pan from a piece of twine secured to a ring on the saddle, and then made a full circle, tightening every single tie, while Depeche Toi perched on his haunches, watching her and wagging his tail in encouragement. Now that she was all set again, she faced the puzzle of how she was going to get back on the horse. Up at the house, she'd stood on a wooden box to mount. Surveying her surroundings, she spotted a sawed-off tree stump. Annie led Tarzan over to the stump, stepped up onto it, and, after a bit of negotiation, got her stirrup close enough that she could jam her toe into it and swing herself aboard. Triumphant, she wedged her bottom into the saddle, nudged Tarzan into a walk, and then held her breath. Fortunately, this time, everything seemed to hold.

Finally, what Annie called "the hard road" came into view. Maybe if in that moment Tarzan had whirled around and headed back up the hill, she'd have let him. But the horse clattered onto the pavement without complaint, and Depeche Toi trotted happily alongside, so that Annie didn't even have a moment to second-guess her plan.

Minot, Maine, was behind her. Ahead was the rest of her journey.

If I'd asked people what they wanted,
they'd have said faster horses.

—attributed to Henry Ford

—

CHAPTER
6

Cars

ANNIE, TARZAN, AND DEPECHE TOI clopped right down the middle of the narrow two-lane road, heading toward the small hamlet of Hackett Mills, about four miles away. Shortening Depeche Toi's rope around her right hand, Annie steered with her left. When the occasional car passed, she veered toward whichever side of the road had a wider shoulder, not thinking much about whether she should travel with or against the flow of traffic—since there wasn't much. Annie, being accustomed to life as a pedestrian, didn't think of the roads as belonging to cars first and foot traffic second. Still, the ungainly trio must have raised an eyebrow or two among the few drivers who passed. Because even in Androscoggin County, Maine, in the 1950s, the typical mode of transport for most people was, without question, the automobile.

The area around Minot was considered scenic—a region of low hills and abundant lakes and rivers. The town of Poland, a few miles past Hackett Mills, was famed for the healthful water bottled at Poland Spring, and just up the road in Hebron, the state had constructed a sanatorium— a place for people with tuberculosis to rest and take in the healthful air. The roads Annie was familiar with were meandering two-lane affairs, shaped around the contours of the land. She was old enough to remember when traffic was all horse and buggy or on foot. She vividly recalled the coming of the automobile—it had seemed a fad at first, until it stuck.

For the American automobile, 1954 was a banner year. That year, the average price of a new car was $1,700, costly enough in 1950s currency that most people bought on a payment plan. Nearly seven million cars were produced in the United States in 1950 alone—and during that decade, the automobile industry exploded, producing a new car for every third man, woman, and child in America. By the end of the decade, one in six American workers was employed in car manufacturing. In contrast, the equine population plunged drastically in the same decade, the number of horses in America falling by half. Animal husbandry expert M. E. Ensminger wrote in 1951, "In this streamlined mechanized age, the relentless wheels of progress are steadily replacing man's good friend and stout companion, the horse. Today, there are fewer horses in the United States than in any year since the Civil War."

Cars were certainly a common sight around Minot, but there were still plenty of people of Annie's acquaintance who couldn't afford one. When Annie set out on her journey, she knew that they'd be sharing the road with cars, but it's unlikely that she understood just how *many* cars.

At Tarzan's pace, it took Annie about an hour to reach Hackett Mills. Although the village's namesake mill was gone, a small cluster of buildings remained—a feed store, a small grocery store, and a row of clapboard houses. To reach the village, Annie was planning to cross the Little Androscoggin River over a wooden bridge she'd traversed countless times on her way to the nearby town of Poland. But as she rounded the corner and the bridge came into sight, she was surprised to see the old wooden one gone, replaced by a wide concrete construction— perfect for cars, although, unlike the old bridge, not designed with pedestrians in mind, and certainly not horses.

When Annie approached the bridge, a couple of men were milling about on the other side, watching her as she headed toward the concrete expanse. Unlike the road's bumpy asphalt, the concrete of the bridge was slick under Tarzan's hooves. He seemed tentative as he started off, and about halfway across, his front foot skidded; his head jerked up and he spun around, almost unseating Annie, who managed to stay on only by grabbing a hunk of his mane and holding on for dear life. Her twine-tied load began swinging wildly, thumping and rattling, which frightened the horse, making the situation worse. Depeche Toi sprang into action. Jumping right in front, he crouched down, barking loudly. Annie was too busy clinging on to tell her dog to quit it. But it wasn't necessary. Tarzan stopped whirling and stood still, responding to the little dog's admonition. Annie resettled herself in the saddle and tugged on the parts of her load that had almost shaken loose, trying to gulp back the tears that were forming and retain whatever was left of her dignity.

Meanwhile, the two men had crossed the bridge and caught up with her. With no more than a grunted hello, one grabbed Tarzan's bridle and the other stood alongside the horse, and with their help, Tarzan hesitantly continued. When they reached the other side, the two men helped Annie rebalance her load, and inquired where she was headed. Too embarrassed to say "California," she named the town of Upper Gloucester, about twelve miles south of Minot. They made no further comment, and relieved that she'd survived this first mishap, she headed on down the road.

The rest of the morning passed without incident. Cars that drove by slowed down and gave the trio a wide berth; the drivers around Minot were accustomed to seeing pedestrians, animals, and slow-moving farm equipment along the side of the road. Annie and her companions were passing through countryside that was mostly wooded—black willows and silver maples, red maples and speckled alders. By now, the foliage was off the trees, and the side of the road where they walked was matted in old yellowed leaves. There, she saw brambles of bright red berries clinging to leafless vines. She passed square white farmhouses with traditional attached barns, and newer houses—compact postwar Cape Cods. Through the windows she could sometimes glimpse the flicker of a black-and-white TV.

It took a while for Annie to figure out the best way to handle Depeche Toi. Twice he wrapped himself around a telephone pole, and Annie had to stop and reverse-circle the pole to get herself free. She tried keeping the rope short, but then he tugged. When she let it go longer, she had to watch that he didn't dart into the road when a car sped past. As they went along, however, he seemed to gradually get the hang of it—he liked cruising into people's front yards, and sometimes he tried to race off after a squirrel, but most of the time he trotted along a half-length ahead of Tarzan, his tail waving like a frond on Palm Sunday.

Annie planned to travel the twelve miles to her friend's house and spend the night there. Only by midafternoon, Upper Gloucester was still a good way off, Annie ached from sitting in the saddle for so long, and she thought her horse and her dog needed a rest. She spotted a woman outside her house and asked for some water, but the woman insisted that Annie stop to rest and water her animals, and invited her to come inside for a proper lunch.

After giving some water and hay to Tarzan and sharing her own food with Depeche Toi, Annie followed the plump middle-aged woman inside, grateful that a total stranger would share a meal with her.

"You'll like California," the woman said.

"Have you been there?" Annie asked.

"No," she replied, "but a car broke down outside our house last year and the people were from California. They were very nice."

Her husband soon joined them, and the couple was so friendly that Annie felt a little surge of hope. She had a lot of faith in the kindness of strangers, even though so many people had told her that times had changed. Everyone, it seemed, was afraid of something—burglars, strangers, Communists. To hear some people tell it, you'd think that outside the handful of folks you knew personally, the United States of America was just one big stretch of people who'd slam the door in your face as soon as they'd say hello. She didn't believe it. She'd set out to test that idea, and right now, as she set out again, she figured she was two nice strangers down, with hopefully many more to go.

Not far past the spot where she'd paused for lunch, Depeche Toi was trotting along beside her. He'd been tugging on the rope, and so she'd let the line all the way out to give him some room to roam. He had just trotted into the yard of a house near the side of the road, nose in the air, tail floating like a flag, when a large muscular dog bolted from behind the house, snarling, heading straight toward Depeche Toi. Before Annie could even figure out what to do, her little dog had disappeared, darting directly under Tarzan's belly. The horse snorted, then reared up, his hooves flailing. Annie was almost flung off, but managed to hold on. The big dog slunk back into the yard. Although Depeche Toi resumed his lively trot as if nothing had happened, Annie wrapped the rope tighter around her hand. She'd not thought of the danger of other dogs. Just one more thing to worry about.

At least one thing Annie did not need to worry about was the friendship between her two four-footed companions. Depeche Toi had calmed Tarzan during his panic on the concrete bridge; then Tarzan had reared up to chase away the aggressive cur. Annie admitted to herself that her main role in both near misses had been managing not to fall off. She decided to give herself credit for that anyway. They were starting to work as a team.

It was late afternoon when they reached Upper Gloucester, and by then Annie was grateful for a hot meal and a comfortable bed, a stall in the barn for Tarzan, and a comfy spot near the fire for Depeche Toi. Her friend, an old acquaintance of the family, pretty much told Annie she thought she was crazy, but she didn't try to discourage her—just pressed a few dollars into her hand and insisted that she take a roll of hay from the barn.

The next morning, Annie was so stiff that she didn't want to get back in the saddle until she'd had time to walk out her kinks. She led Tarzan down the main street. He had so much hay piled up behind the saddle that he looked completely lopsided. By the time she reached the southern edge of town, she had limbered up enough to mount up again.

Before an hour had passed, they'd reached the turnoff onto the main highway. This was the last time Annie would see a familiar face. From here on, she was truly heading out among strangers. Decisively, Annie turned Tarzan onto the main road that headed south from Lewiston to Portland.

In 1954, there was only one stretch of four-lane highway in the state of Maine. During its early years of statehood, Maine had lagged badly in road building, and even in the mid-1950s, there were vast portions of the state, particularly in the northwest and inland, that lacked any paved roads. Early travelers in Maine had been transported largely by waterways—the patterns of settlement following the many rivers, inlets, and tributaries that spread inward from the state's long coast. In the nineteenth century, railroads began to lattice the state, connecting the smaller, more rural communities with the transportation hubs. Prior to World War I, the areas of Androscoggin and neighboring Oxford County had done a booming business exporting apples. Hearty varieties such as the Northern Spy and Baldwin were harvested in the orchards, taken to train depots by horse and wagon, and transported by rail to Boston, where they were packed into barrels and shipped across the Atlantic to Liverpool, England; from there, they were sent out to the English market. The entire trip for the apples, from start to finish, could take almost two months. Fortunately, apples could weather such slow transit, but Maine farmers struggled to export other crops because of the difficulties with transportation.

In the early part of the twentieth century, roads in Maine were strictly seasonal affairs. Most roads became impassable during the spring mud season; when snow covered the roads in winter, they were traversed on runners by sleds and sleighs. One Minot resident remembered riding sawed-off logs all the way down Woodman Hill as a mode of transportation. The one thing you couldn't do in winter was drive a car.

The first attempts to keep Maine's roads clear during the winter came in the 1920s, as motorized snowplows cleared roads and salting prevented ice from forming. Of course, even by the 1950s, those who lived on rural roads, like Annie, could be snowed in for more than a week—and in more remote areas, for much longer.

But in spite of—or perhaps because of—its transportation limitations, Maine was early in adopting the modern "superhighway," meaning a limited-access road of four or more lanes. The first stretch of the

Maine Turnpike was opened in 1947. As the first superhighway built after World War II, running from Kittery, at Maine's southern border, to Portland, it was only the second modern toll highway in the entire country (after the Pennsylvania Turnpike, which opened in 1940). When it was new, the Maine Turnpike featured the most up-to-date design: four wide, clearly marked lanes divided by a wide grass median, which was an innovative safety feature at the time. The highway was so well designed that a motorist could safely travel at a speed of sixty miles an hour. The *Portland Press Herald* dubbed the new turnpike "The Mile-a-Minute Highway."

THIS MILE-A-MINUTE HIGHWAY WAS such a success that the Maine Turnpike Authority had approved Maine's largest infrastructure project—the turnpike extension—which would expand the highway north as far as the state capital of Augusta, passing over the Androscoggin River at Lewiston. A crew of two thousand workers had begun work on the extension in the spring of 1954. The transformation would be swift. By 1956, just a year after the extension was completed, the turnpike authority would estimate that the road had already carried more than three million cars.

The passengers cruising along these twentieth-century superhighways zipped along fifteen times faster than Annie did—her nineteenth-century pace was about three to four miles per hour. In fact, this development—the exponential difference between the speed of car travel and foot travel—was a surprisingly recent phenomenon. When the Maine Turnpike Authority had been formed, in 1941, it had taken almost all day to travel by car over the roughly forty-five-mile stretch between Portland and Kittery. Before the turnpike had been built, the main thoroughfare was Route 1, which hugged the coastline, stopping to cut through the middle of every tiny town along the way, following the twists and turns of the natural contours of the land, and crisscrossed by bridges more suitable for foot travel than two lanes of cars. While mid-century automobiles could motor along at speeds much greater than three or four miles an hour, the roads had proved an impediment to speedy travel.

Annie's destination for her second day on the road was the town of Gray. When the turnpike extension was completed the following year, a car would be able to travel from Lewiston to Gray in under half an hour. The turnpike was being built just parallel to the road that Annie and her two companions walked along, and right now, that state road, a two-lane highway, had to accommodate all of the traffic that would soon be diverted to the turnpike. Annie didn't know anything about the turnpike construction, but she found herself venturing along the right-hand side of a road where cars whipped past her at high speeds, passing her with a rush that left her rolled-up blankets flapping, her ears ringing, and her horse skittering dangerously close to the vehicles tearing by her. At one point, Depeche Toi got tangled up in his rope, and seeing her predicament, a driver pulled over. A man got out to assist her.

"You really shouldn't be on this road," he said. "It's too dangerous."

He helped unwind Depeche Toi, who had managed to dart around Tarzan enough times that he had gotten the horse hog-tied.

"I'm turning off at Gray," Annie said.

"That's about three miles up the road," he said, and told her to be careful until then.

But when Annie got to Gray and turned onto a more minor road, not only did the traffic not abate, it got worse. She didn't realize that even the smaller road was being used to detour traffic around a stretch of turnpike construction.

The road narrowed, and woods grew on both sides. Now there was no shoulder to speak of, and the cars seemed to pay no heed to Annie and her four-footed crew, neither slowing down as they passed nor giving them a wider berth. Annie was keeping as far to the right-hand side of the road as she could, but with the shoulder so narrow, she had no choice but to stay on the pavement. They were rounding a curve when she saw an oncoming passenger car swing into her lane to pass a slow-moving vehicle, followed suddenly by a truck with a load covered by a tarp. Screeching around the bend too fast, the truck swung completely into the opposing lane, trying to pass both vehicles. As it did so, the truck careened dangerously close to Annie and her animals—the flapping canvas so close it almost whipped Tarzan right in the face. Tarzan spooked and took off into the woods, with Annie just managing to hang on. Thank heavens Depeche Toi had darted away from the traffic, not toward it. But Annie's entire body was shaking. An inch or so more and that truck would have plowed right through the three of them.

Annie had had a previous experience with this kind of collision. Many years ago, she'd been driving a horse and wagon by the side of the road when a car had run into her. Her leg had been broken so badly that it had taken almost two years to heal. She wasn't hurt now. Just shaken. But the roar and splinter of a car crashing into her came vividly back to her.

It wasn't only the number of cars on the road that increased exponentially during the first half of the twentieth century. So did the number of traffic fatalities. From the moment cars were introduced onto American roads, the number of traffic deaths began a relentless march upward, a trend that peaked in the 1960s and 1970s, and finally began to decrease in the 1980s and later, due to the development of better automobile safety features in tandem with better road design. In 1954, as Annie set out, traffic fatalities were a common occurrence and a cause of great public concern. Cars were dangerous, but ways to make them less so had not yet been found. Modern highway design, such as was being pioneered with the Maine Turnpike, was still in the future for most of the country's roadways.

As Annie, Tarzan, and Depeche Toi headed toward California at their own animal speed, the cars they would share the road with were fast, heavy, numerous, and lethal. That ache in her leg, that bone that predicted the weather, had already given her a taste of what could happen when humans and machines shared America's narrow old country roads.

Be not forgetful to entertain strangers: for thereby
some have entertained angels unawares.

—Hebrews 13:2

—

Strangers

H ER SECOND NIGHT ON the road, she got lucky. She stopped
near dusk to ask for water, and the couple in the house offered
her a bed for the night, as well as a place in the barn for Tarzan. She
recognized from their voices that they weren't local people, and, in fact,
they told her they'd moved up from Massachusetts. Strangers. Kind
ones. In the morning, they gave her a plate of eggs and bacon and wished
her well. By eight, she was back on the road.

If Annie had embarked on this journey just twenty years earlier, she
would have had a lot of company on her travels. As a self-described "tramp
of fate," she was part of a grand American tradition of itinerants who hit
the road looking for work. The word "tramp" comes from a Middle Low
German word meaning to walk with heavy footsteps, to stamp. First
commonly used in America to describe the long, arduous marching un-
dertaken by Civil War soldiers, it later came to be used more often as a
noun. A person who traveled from place to place looking for work along
the way was a tramp, and the first time tramps became visible in large
numbers was after the Civil War, when former soldiers, unfitted for normal life, took to the road. By the 1870s, during a major worldwide reces-
sion, tramps had become a familiar part of modern industrial life. Aided

by the vast network of railroads, homeless itinerants were seemingly per-manent fixtures of the landscape—their numbers peaking again after the First World War, when returning soldiers added to their ranks. During the Great Depression, the number of homeless people in America sky-rocketed. Called hoboes or tramps, these predominantly white and native-born men seemed to be a permanent part of the American landscape.

But after World War II, when the economy expanded and new hous-ing was built, the number of homeless people fell to the lowest point since the Civil War. The American tramp or hobo, long a familiar sight in American cities and towns, long a staple of American folklore, had become so scarce that he was turning into a figure of some nostalgia.

Annie differed from most tramps in one important way: she was a woman. Among the ranks of American hoboes and tramps, women had never been represented in significant numbers. She was certainly aware of this. She never explained exactly why she chose to dress in men's clothing on her journey. It was likely a simple matter of practicality and a way to be comfortable on the road, but it did lend her a certain air of anonymity and, probably, protection as she passed.

She was heading south on her third day when she was pulled off the road by Tarzan, who bunny-hopped sideways, startled by a passing truck. She was sitting there in her saddle, adjusting her belongings and gathering her wits, when she realized that she was being observed. An elderly man, clearly a farmer, was mending his fence line and had seen the whole thing.

"There's terror on the road these days," he said. "I can see you know horses, and from your outfit, I'd say you might be looking for work."

Her fear of a moment earlier fell away. She'd been so worried that she'd have trouble finding work—and now, just her third day on the road, here was someone offering her a job. But something about the way he was speaking to her made her guess he hadn't figured out the truth—so she pulled off her hat. Though she'd cut her gray hair short before she set off on the road, still, with her fur bonnet off, there was no mistaking it.

"Why, you're a woman," the farmer said in surprise.

Would he be so eager to hire her now? He assured her that it didn't matter. "It looks like you can handle a horse better than most men," he said. "I'd be happy to put you to work."

Annie politely declined, knowing that she still had money to spare. She was too close to home to stop here. If word got around that she'd just moved a couple of towns over, people would think that her story about riding to California was just cover for leaving town out of shame. As Emily Dickinson, a fellow New Englander put it, "Luck is not chance— / It's Toil." Annie wasn't hoping for luck or wishing for charity. She planned to earn her own good fortune. Nevertheless, her journey did rely on a certain amount of neighborliness. She needed shelter for her horse and a place to sleep, even if in the stable with the horses or out in someone's damp, cold pasture. She would accept people's hospitality, but only if freely given. She might have to ask, but she wouldn't beg. Annie had the graciousness to receive gifts, accompanied by a fierce determination not to be a burden.

In her life, Annie had often faced hardship: backbreaking labor, frozen fingers, illness, loss, loneliness; on the other hand, as a denizen of rural Maine, she had inherited a homegrown strength, as substantial and weighted as the granite stone walls that stood like silent testaments along the roads she traveled.

Well aware that she was not descended from the educated or the wealthy, the distinguished or the lettered, still, Annie knew who she was. She was a Stuart and a Libby. She saw her people as those who had been near the great events of history, the helpers, the accompanists, never the great leaders in the history books but the solid citizens who came along to do their duty. The Libbys had helped settle Maine, and one of the Stuarts had driven an oxcart that transported a fine specimen of white pine to build the mast of the ship that John Paul Jones sailed during the Revolutionary War. As she passed through Maine, Annie would interpret a certain expression on someone's face as possibly a family trait. She saw the Stuart in a stranger's clear blue eyes, the Libby in someone's adventuresome spirit. Everyone she encountered might be a distant cousin. She felt that her people were everywhere, and because of that she couldn't fully be a stranger.

This feeling of deep connection was becoming less common in this postwar period, which, for many Americans, was a time of increasing xenophobia. In 1952, Congress had passed the McCarran-Walter Act, reinforcing racially based quotas introduced in the 1920s, in part due to anti-Semitic bigotry and fears of communism. Senator Joseph McCarthy had whipped up the fear of Communist infiltrators with his inflammatory rhetoric. "Man the watchtowers of the nation," he scolded. "Be vigilant day and night." Being vigilant was generally the opposite of being neighborly. In a world of connection, bonds of friendship and kinship made every stranger a potential acquaintance. The world of vigilance suggested the opposite: every stranger might bring danger.

With each step she took away from Minot, Annie was moving farther away from the people she knew. Closer to home, she'd felt like a traveler, but as she got farther away, she became something else, a wanderer, a stranger—in fact, perhaps she could most accurately be described as a pilgrim. The Christian theologian Richard R. Niebuhr wrote, "Pilgrims are persons in motion—passing through territories not their own— seeking something we might call completion, or perhaps the word 'clarity' will do as well, a goal to which only the spirit's compass points the way." Annie was becoming a pilgrim. From here on in, she would be dependent on the kindness of strangers.

Around three in the afternoon, the shadows had grown long on their third day on the road, and Annie started thinking she should look for a likely place to pass the night. She hoped to find a farmhouse with an empty barn out back. She knocked on several doors. At the first couple of houses, she saw someone peering through the window, but no one answered the door. At the third house she tried, a woman opened the door and listened, but after looking at Annie and her menagerie, she said that she couldn't invite her in because she'd closed up most of the house to save money on fuel. Annie explained that she didn't need to come inside—she was hoping to sleep in the barn. Still the woman said no.

"In these parts, women don't sleep in barns," she said.

By now, it was getting late, and Annie politely insisted that she just needed a place to spend the night—even a spot to camp out would do.

Finally, the woman relented and gave Annie directions to one of her fields, saying that there was a stream that ran through it that her horse and her dog could drink from. Annie didn't mind sleeping outside—she had planned for that. As they entered the field, Tarzan let out a good whinny—perhaps hoping there were other horses about, although none answered. She pulled off his saddle and bridle and all of his cargo, and the horse was so relieved he shook himself thoroughly, pawed the ground, and then lay down to roll. Annie fed Tarzan and fastened two blankets over him to keep him warm. Depeche Toi was so tired that he settled his nose on his paws and fell asleep. She had to wake him up to feed him. After they'd all eaten, she stretched her bedroll out and lay down under the stars, and fell sound asleep.

Sometime later, she was awakened by the low sound of Depeche Toi's growl.

"Keeping holding that dog," a man's voice called out. "We're officers of the law."

Annie held tight to Depeche Toi, who didn't stop growling.

"We have the owner's permission to be here," she called out, her voice unsteady.

After a few minutes of confusion, Annie's heart stopped thudding wildly as she realized that the officers hadn't come to arrest her for trespassing. The woman who owned the field didn't think she should be out at night. She had called the police, hoping they could find her a place to stay—and she'd offered to keep Tarzan overnight in her barn.

It was after midnight and Annie was aching from exhaustion when the squad car pulled up in front of 305 Windham Center Road—a spacious two-story white clapboard house with black shutters, elegant in its contours, set well back from the road. A porch light glowed a warm welcome, and while the second-story windows were dark, cheery lights still shone from inside the first floor.

A smiling woman opened the door, looking not the least tired in spite of the late hour; she greeted Annie and invited her in. The house was mercifully warm. The woman thanked the police officers and, taking no

notice of the time or the condition of Annie's clothing, warmly welcomed this total stranger inside.

ANYONE WHO KNEW NELLIE BENNETT would not have been surprised by her response to Annie's unexpected arrival. A woman of
inexhaustible energy and good cheer, she was the mother of five, ranging
from eleven to not yet two, who ran a nursing home in their house, providing care to elderly and bedbound patients. She was aided in this endeavor by her husband and beloved partner, Dr. Laurence Bennett, but
her day started and ended with caring for him as well. Dr. Bennett had
lost a leg in a horse-and-wagon accident at age nine. Eventually crippled
by arthritis, he was now immobilized and unable to maintain even a sitting position. Nellie wheeled him about on a specially equipped bed that
allowed him to attend to patients while lying flat on his back.

Nellie awoke at five every morning, and never went to bed before
one A.M. And Dr. Laurence Bennett was also a source of strength in the
family, in spite of his physical weakness. After his lower leg had been am-
putated, his family had him fitted with a wooden leg, but his parents did
not know that a prosthesis must be readjusted constantly to accommodate
a growing child. Laurence put so much strain on his growing body that he
began to develop curvature of the spine and severe osteoarthritis. By dint
of his will, he not only made it through college but also fulfilled a childhood dream to help others by graduating from medical school. By that
time, however, he was so afflicted that he found it almost impossible to
keep up with the demands of being a practicing physician.

Nellie Pleasant had grown up in Gorham, Maine, where she'd trained
as a nurse. She was working as a private-duty nurse when a young doctor came to check on his patient. He was a handsome fellow with a smile
that curled to show his sense of humor, a shock of longish brown hair
that gave him the air of a romantic poet, and a walrus-like brown mus-
tache. Nellie was instantly smitten, and the two fell in love.

When he proposed, she happily accepted, even though she knew that she was marrying a man whose severe disability would require her constant help and care. The pair decided that the best use of their combined talents would be to open a nursing home in the spacious nineteenth-century farmhouse that had been in the Pleasant family since it had been built.

That a husband and wife who were already raising five young children while coping with severe disability and a grueling work schedule would be the first to open their doors to a complete stranger in the middle of the night was not surprising—once you got to know them. They were admired around the community for their kindness and generosity of spirit. Their children and all of the nursing home patients were already settled and asleep, but the Bennetts were waiting up for Annie and had set some soup to simmer on the back of the stove for her arrival.

After the long day and the unfriendly encounters, capped by the shock of finding police flashlights glaring in her eyes, Annie was especially touched by the hospitality she received at the warm, rambling home. When Annie learned of Dr. Bennett's accident, she shared with him the story of her own horse-and-wagon accident. Unlike him, the only aftereffect she'd suffered was her leg's uncanny ability to hint at upcoming weather.

Dr. Bennett was attentive. He inquired after her health, and when Annie shared that she'd been sick in a nursing home for several months the previous winter, he seemed concerned. His wife tilted his wheeled bed up so that he could listen to her lungs and take her temperature and pulse. Annie marveled at the gentle touch and bedside manner of this physician who could not heal himself but was still eager to heal others.

After Annie was fed and warm, Nellie gave her fresh towels so that she could wash up and showed her to an empty bed in the large room where some of the elderly patients were sleeping. Annie ended her long day of trials with a full stomach in a comfortable bed, and Depeche Toi, who had eaten a generous bowl of food, now jumped up on the bedside next to her, rested his chin on his paws, sighed contentedly, and fell asleep.

The next morning, Annie woke with the sun, but Nellie and Laurence Bennett were already up, and soon the house was filled with the chatter of children getting ready for school. Annie joined the family for breakfast, and once most of the children were off, Nellie offered to drive Annie back to the barn where Tarzan was stabled, just a mile down the road.

Annie thanked Mrs. Bennett and promised to write to her from the road, but Nellie lingered as Annie packed up, as if she had something on her mind.

"Some people don't approve of what I'm doing," Annie ventured.

Nellie looked relieved to have an opening.

"My husband called your doctor in Minot—Dr. Cobb," she said. "So, now we know all about you." They had learned about her diagnosis, and that her doctor felt that she should definitely not be on the road, and that he was holding a spot for her in the county home.

"Courage isn't everything," Nellie said. "It's just one thing."

Annie reflected on Mrs. Bennett's words. And truly, just a few hours in the Bennett home had been enough to reveal that Mrs. Bennett knew a thing or two about courage, and Dr. Bennett, too. How much courage had it taken for Annie to walk away from her problems? It had taken a lot. But how much more courage did it take for the Bennetts to face every day with strength and good cheer? Certainly, much more.

Nellie lingered as Annie busied herself getting ready to leave, but she said nothing further. When they arrived at the farm down the road, the barn creaked, the air filled with the quiet sounds of animals moving in straw. Tarzan waited for Annie to feed him and then load him up. Depeche Toi had wandered off and was sniffing at something in the corner of the barn.

Right now, Annie was a three-day ride from Minot, still in her home state of Maine. She had her horse and her dog, some money, and her lungs were holding up so far. She could call it quits today, turn around, and head toward home, full of tales about her little adventure. Wouldn't most people think that was the sensible thing? She could take her spot in the county home or move in with her mother's elderly friend—it was no better or worse than the future that was expected for her. Should she give up her outsized yearnings? Should she swallow her pride? Should she accept the fact that she was just an old woman whose time had passed, from whom nothing surprising or new or vivid was expected?

But Annie knew that whichever way she turned—south toward New Hampshire or back toward home—she faced the same set of obstacles. She had a bad pair of lungs, no home, little money, and not much promise of a long life. At least this way, she was taking charge of the situation instead of just letting fate push her along. She was too young to be cooped up in an old folks' home while she still had breath and fight in her, and too proud to accept charity when she was sure she could still do some work. Courage is just one thing—but right then, it was the only thing she had.

"I'm feeling a lot better now," Annie said, turning to look at Nellie more directly. "The fresh air seems to help."

An emotional look flitted across the doctor's wife's face. She placed her hands on Annie's shoulders and gave them a squeeze. "Then you *must* go," she said, and Annie was surprised to see tears in her eyes.

As Annie rode away, heading south, she turned to see Nellie's car motoring the opposite way, to her home, where she spent her days bound by so many ties—to a man who couldn't walk on his own, to children who needed her, to patients who were too weak to care for themselves. She couldn't leave even if she wanted to. Annie knew she didn't want to, but wondered if maybe sometimes she wished she could.

When people were kind to Annie, what could she do to repay them? She hadn't been sure. But now she knew. She could send letters back from the road to all the people she met along the way, the homebodies, the stuck people, the people who might wish that for once they could drop everything just like she had. Maybe, Annie thought, they wouldn't want to pay such a high price as she had—unwell, alone but for her animal friends, homeless, penniless—but hadn't all those things also made her free?

That was when Annie realized that she wasn't just riding for herself—she could carry other people's hopes and dreams along with her. As she steered Tarzan along the side of the road, she added Nellie Bennett's spirit to her load.

Be thine own palace,
or the world's thy jail.

—**John Donne**

—

CHAPTER 8

Jailbirds

THE THREE COMPANIONS WERE almost a week into their journey when Annie, Tarzan, and Depeche Toi found their way to the town of South Sanford, Maine. When they'd arrived on the outskirts, Annie had asked if anyone knew where she might find a rental stable where she could board her horse for the night, and a passerby had suggested that she could try the fairgrounds on the south side of town. That had sounded just about perfect. She figured she'd sleep in the straw herself, but when she found the night watchman, he offered to give up his cot if she'd watch out for the midnight delivery of a racehorse that was being shipped in, so that he could go home and sleep in his own bed. This seemed like a fair deal to Annie, so she settled Tarzan into a real box stall. Depeche Toi ran off to make friends with some barn cats, and after accepting the delivery of a beautiful black stallion, Annie slept soundly in the cot, not waking up until the sun rose the next morning.

Now into her seventh day of travel, since she and Tarzan were both well rested, she decided to push on—hoping to make it before sundown all the way to South Lebanon, the last town in Maine. Tarzan's head was up and his eyes were bright, and Depeche Toi had grown accustomed to the lead and hadn't shown the slightest sign of being footsore, in spite of the fact that he had taken more steps than any of them.

Hopeful that they'd soon leave Maine behind—and she would feel as if her journey had begun in earnest—the trio pushed forward without any worries. The weather was cold but dry, the skies were gray, and Annie was moving along so well she didn't start looking for a night's lodging until late afternoon, when she realized they were still some distance short of South Lebanon. By then, she'd happened to hit a stretch of road that was fairly deserted. When she passed a couple of farmers walking along it, she asked them for advice. They suggested that she turn off on a side road, because there was a big farm with a barn up that way.

Annie soon came to a lovely farm with a big barn, just as they'd described, but though she pounded on the door, no one answered. She was unsure what to do. Should she push farther up this side road or head back to the main road and keep traveling south? Then she remembered the farmers telling her that there wasn't much up ahead, so she continued on the side road. Surely she'd come to another farmhouse before long.

Unfortunately, she continued to have poor luck. At the first house, a porch light came on and she saw someone looking out the window, and at the next house, no one answered even though she could see lights on and people moving around inside. At the third house, the person just grunted no, before slamming the door in her face.

Annie was close to tears—they were headed up a side road, off in the wrong direction, and after trying and being turned away at no fewer than seven houses, and spending almost two hours, she felt she had no choice but to turn back the way she'd come from and try her luck on the main road again. She could feel Tarzan's weariness under her seat. He walked steadily, but the spring was missing from his gait, and though she'd stopped by the side of the road to feed him earlier, she knew he must be eager to shed his heavy load. Even Depeche Toi, who never seemed to slow down much, had given up all of his detouring and was plodding quietly behind her.

At long last they arrived back at the house with the big empty barn she'd first tried. She went back up to the door, and this time she pounded and hollered. Finally, a light came on, and a man answered the door, looking none too happy. By now, it was well after ten o'clock at night.

Annie apologized and explained that she'd been on the road for almost fourteen hours straight and needed a place to rest. The man offered his barn for the animals and said that someone would be along shortly to take her to a place where she could sleep. Exhausted as she was, she'd have preferred to stay in the barn, but she was grateful for his help. By the time she had Tarzan and Depeche Toi unloaded, watered, fed, and settled, she was so bone weary she could hardly stand.

When the animals were set, the man asked Annie to get into his car. "I'm taking you back to South Sanford," he said. "I called the police station. I hope you don't mind sleeping in a police station."

"I'd have just as happily slept in the barn," Annie said. She was trying to make light of it, but she was worried. She didn't see why she had to go all the way back to where she'd spent the previous night. Were they planning to lock her up? There were laws against vagrancy and trespassing. The man seemed friendly enough, although surely he couldn't be happy that she'd pounded on his door in the middle of the night. In her heart, she thought of herself as a lady traveler, a woman on a journey. She had money in her pocket and the desire to work if she needed to. But she hadn't stopped to think too hard about how other people might see her. Now she was about to find out.

"Well, I couldn't have that," he answered. "I can't have people gossiping about me letting a woman sleep in my barn."

At the police station, the officers told her to sign the police register and then led her toward a cell. As she passed by, a slurred voice called out to her from one of the cells, "Are you in for being drunk?"

"No, I'm in for being sober," Annie replied. Her mouth was dry, and she had a queasy feeling in the pit of her stomach.

The police officer nodded to the spartan accommodations. A cot, bare but clean. A toilet. A concrete floor, bars, and no windows. Annie entered the cell utterly dispirited. Is this, she wondered, where her grand plans had led her? Sure, she'd had ups and downs in her life, but she'd always been a law-abiding citizen. Now, a week on the road, and look where her crazy ideas had landed her. Shoulders drawn up tensely, staring at the bleak prospect in front of her, she waited to hear the steel bars clang shut and the lock click behind her. Instead, she heard the officer's friendly laugh. She turned around and saw him smiling. "You're our guest," he said. "We'll bring you a hot breakfast in the morning."

Once she knew she wasn't going to be locked in, Annie didn't mind sleeping in a police station—she'd been born in a jail, as she liked to tell it. When the town of Mechanic Falls, where Annie began her life, had lost its jail in a fire, Annie's mother and father had stepped up, leasing out some rooms in their house to serve as a makeshift prison. Annie's mother cooked the meals, and her father served as the warden. She didn't remember much about it, as she'd been so young.

Police stations had long offered overnight lodging to itinerants. In the 1850s, one of the earliest functions of newly formed urban police departments had been to furnish temporary shelter for homeless men. As that century progressed, it became common for police departments to provide overnight rooms and meals. By late in the century, this kind of lodging was so common that one historian estimated that some 10 to 20 percent of families had a member who had spent a night in a police station. Annie's father, who had often traveled while looking for work, could well have been one of those people.

And indeed, Annie's night in the police station was uneventful. In the morning, the farmer who had boarded her horse retrieved her in his car and drove her back to Tarzan. His sister had packed a lunch for Annie and Depeche Toi to take on the road. Any sign of unfriendliness had vanished in the light of day.

But it turned out that Annie had gotten more than a night's rest at the South Sanford jail. She had also gained a reputation. An enterprising reporter with the *Portland Press Herald* had seen her name on the police blotter and gotten curious.

That morning, Annie and her animal companions hadn't been on the road for more than an hour when a car drove up alongside her and two men and a woman got out. They introduced themselves as reporters and asked if she would mind answering a few questions. Pulling up her horse, Annie patiently answered their queries, at least the ones she didn't think were too personal or too political; she had no opinion on the Army-McCarthy hearings, and she kept mum about Eisenhower. She said she thought the Cold War was the one they fought every winter in Maine. But they seemed mostly interested in asking about how many layers of clothing she was wearing—Annie said she thought she looked like a frog on a lily pad—and about what had prompted her to take to the road. Annie was matter-of-fact. She explained that she'd been ill and had lost her farm. By the time they were done with their questions, Tarzan and Depeche Toi were restless and she was eager to get on with her journey.

"You know, if we keep standing here talking, I'm not getting any closer to California," she told the reporters, who soon got back in their car and drove away. Annie didn't realize that this brief encounter would turn out to be her first truly lucky break.

Annie and her companions ambled along, heading toward South Lebanon. Tarzan stepped right out, as if he knew that they were soon going to reach their first milestone in the journey: the New Hampshire border.

But about four in the afternoon, Annie had another surprise. A car drove up behind her and pulled over. A man got out and introduced himself. He was from the AP wire service. Could he ask her a few questions and take some pictures?

The words "AP wire service" meant nothing to Annie, and she wasn't eager to be delayed again, but she liked to be cordial, so she steered Tarzan off the road and answered all of the young man's questions, most of which were similar to the ones she'd already answered. Then she waited patiently while he took what seemed like an interminable number of photographs of her—on the horse, on the ground, and even packing and unpacking her load. When they were finished, he told her that she was only a few miles from South Lebanon and that he'd arranged a place for her: a private home for her to stay in, a box stall for Tarzan, and a hot meal at a local restaurant. Just for answering some questions and letting him take her picture a few times? Annie felt like she'd gotten a pretty good deal.

The next morning, Annie, Tarzan, and Depeche Toi left South Lebanon well fed and rested and unaware of the newfound audience for their journey.

Tarzan's hooves rang hollow as they came to the small bridge over the Salmon Falls River that marked the border between Maine and New Hampshire. The day was cloudy and the river appeared still, a milky gray in the middle but black along the edges from the shadows of the overhanging trees. A few orange and yellow leaves still clung to the shrubs closer to the water level, and their colors were mirrored back. The three companions had been on the road for just over a week, and as they clopped across the short bridge, which marked their departure from Maine, they had traveled a distance of eighty miles.

Annie felt a great deal of pride and satisfaction at reaching this milestone—their first state line. What she didn't know was that a newspaper wire service travels much faster than a horse does. While they'd been strolling along at four miles an hour, her image and story had been dispatched to hundreds of newspapers.

People all over America were learning about the woman, the horse, and the dog who were trying to cross America.

ABOUT A HUNDRED MILES NORTH of the state border that Annie had just crossed, in the small town of Whitefield, Maine, a woman slipped a letter into her house's mailbox and flipped up the flag. The envelope was addressed, in her perfect penmanship, to:

> Mrs. Annie Wilkins
> c/o General Delivery
> Springfield, Massachusetts

On the surface, Mina Titus Sawyer did not resemble Annie Wilkins at all. Mina was elegant and feminine. She favored belted A-line dresses that showed off her slim figure, calfskin pumps, and velvet-trimmed poodle coats that kept up with the latest fashion. Her shiny brunette bouffant had turned a silvery gray, but her face was mostly unlined, and her blue eyes reflected a keen intellect. As a young woman, Mina had shocked the locals by driving fancy Ford cars around the tiny town of Whitefield. Her uncle owned a dealership down in Portland, and he figured that a pretty young woman being seen tooling around behind the wheel was the best kind of advertisement for his cars.

These days Mina was a newspaper reporter who specialized in writing human interest stories and regional lore about Maine. On November 13 she was reading her newspaper when she found the AP wire story about Annie Wilkins, and it immediately struck her fancy. She chuckled at the fact that Annie described her farm as "the old rockpile" and delighted in the detail about how Annie had embarked wearing four layers of pants.

In fact, Annie and Mina had more in common than met the eye. They were born the same year. They'd both grown up on rural farms and had gone through difficult times during the Great Depression. Both had lost their fathers when they were young—Mina's father, many years older than her mother, was a veteran of the Union army. Both women had been raised in households that had to save every single penny and find creative ways to make ends meet.

But their biographies diverged in one important way. When Annie had turned twelve, her parents had made her drop out of school to help on the farm. Mina's mother had kept her in school. After graduating from high school, Mina had worked as a teacher in a one-room schoolhouse, then headed to Colby College, one of Maine's premier institutions of higher learning, graduating with a degree in English literature as a member of the class of 1912, at a time when few women attended college, fewer still rural women from single-parent homes.

Mina took a lively interest in many things—and the story about

Annie, her dog, her horse, and her impossible quest caught the journalist's attention. Perhaps it was because for all of Mina's education, her love of reading and writing, and the thrill of seeing her byline appear in the newspaper, she had never had a chance to travel. In 1932, unmarried but possessing the deed free and clear to the home she'd inherited from her mother, and moved by the terrible economic hardship she saw all around her, Mina had traveled to a Maine orphanage and adopted a daughter. Mina loved abundantly and collected living things around her—not just a new daughter and, later, a husband but also an ever-changing number of adopted and stray animals. Horses, dogs, cats—all found a safe place and loving care in Mina's home.

In spite of this abundance, however, Mina had never left the state of Maine, never been south of Portland. So she'd long ago learned the pleasures of armchair travel, and one of the books that had particularly fascinated her was *November Grass,* by the author Judy Van der Veer, about living on a rural ranch east of San Diego. Mina loved reading Van der Veer's descriptions of the natural world, but what a different world California was from her small Maine town. Mina could imagine the scented sagebrush, the fog rolling in over the hilltops in thick gray waves from the Pacific, the golden eagles and hawks soaring through the canyons, then rapidly streaking downward to catch their prey. Mina had written to Miss Van der Veer, and they'd developed a correspondence. That was how Mina traveled: with books and with her long, handwritten letters, each one in an envelope carrying a three-cent stamp, slipped into the mailbox at the end of her hollyhock-lined driveway.

Today, in November, the hollyhocks were long gone from Whitefield as Mina posted her letter to Annie Wilkins, care of General Delivery in Springfield, Massachusetts, the address Annie had mentioned in the article. Mina's request was simple: Could Annie keep in touch with her during her journey? Mina wanted to write about Annie as she made her way west, and to make her more newsworthy to Mainers, she'd sent along a letter from Maine's governor to deliver to the governor of Idaho, a message from one state famed for its potatoes to another.

WHILE ANNIE LIKED TO say that she was a lifelong Mainer, it wasn't entirely true.

In 1893, James and Sarah Stuart, a day laborer and his wife, left the small mill town of Mechanic Falls, Maine, in search of opportunity, with their two-year-old daughter, Annie, in tow. Their decision to move that year was not arbitrary, coinciding as it did with a severe national financial panic. Banks closed; factories were unable to pay their employees' wages. As one observer described it, "Never before has there been such a sudden and striking cessation of industrial activity. Mills, factories, furnaces and mines all shut down. Hundreds of thousands of men were thrown out of work."

Annie's parents were among the thousands searching for work in dark times. The family ended up about fifty miles due west of Mechanic Falls, in the small town of Jackson, New Hampshire. Situated at the base of the White Mountains, with the summit of Mount Washington rising in the distance, the area was so beautiful that it drew painters from the White Mountain School of painting. The town green was ringed by stately white grand hotels, a casino, and a group of cottages that catered to tourists coming in by rail. A red covered wooden bridge on the road into town was so popular with young lovers that it was dubbed "the honeymoon bridge."

James Stuart found steady work at the Goodrich Falls Electric Company, a power plant built by wealthy investors who'd needed electricity to operate one of New Hampshire's earliest ski lifts. Annie started attending school in Jackson's red cedar one-room schoolhouse. For a child of working-class parents, she had a good life in Jackson. In the late nineteenth and early twentieth centuries, larger towns, like Lewiston, adjacent to Minot, were crowded with people living in tenements. Diseases such as TB and polio were rampant among children, and many youngsters roamed the streets unsupervised while their parents worked in factories. The fight for temperance was raging, the movement to prohibit alcohol gaining strength due to the tolls of men's drunkenness on women and children's welfare. At that moment in her life, Annie was in the luckier portion of American children. In 1900, only about half of the country's children were enrolled in school. In fact, at the time, about half of the state of Maine did not have any schools at all. But like most girls born into families of limited means, Annie would not stay in school long.

The life of a New England girl, a daughter in a working-class, non-property-owning, wage-earning family, offered limited opportunities. She could enter service, working as a domestic; she could work in a factory if, as a woman, she was able to find a position; she could pick up seasonal labor on farms—again, whatever work was available to a girl; and, of course, she could get married and begin the drudgery of keeping house.

At twenty-one, Annie found herself in Windsor, Vermont, in front of a Methodist minister, saying her wedding vows to a man named Peter Robinson, presumably unaware that he'd recently completed a stint in a Rhode Island prison. Where they'd met, how their courtship had unfolded, the story of their romance, were things even her friends never knew. She took off with him to Massachusetts, where he trained animals for the vaudeville circuit. She even took a turn in vaudeville herself. Adopting the name "Mesannie Mabel," she performed as a recitationist, telling stories about backwoods rural life. She didn't make much of a mark, but she perfected her deadpan sense of humor. Three years later, Peter Robinson was arrested for horse thievery and thrown back into jail. Annie divorced him on the grounds of "extreme cruelty," hers becoming one of 142,000 marriages ending in divorce in 1919 America. She took back her name, moved back in with her parents, and never spoke of that marriage again. She found work shoveling snow to clear roads, selling fruit, stitching shoes in a Lewiston shoe factory, cutting down trees on her grandfather's land, and doing whatever else came her way. If she'd ever had a chance to better herself, that chance was now over.

As Annie reached the end of the bridge and crossed into New Hampshire, she was returning to a state where she'd spent some of the best moments of her life. She wondered where the journey would lead her this time.

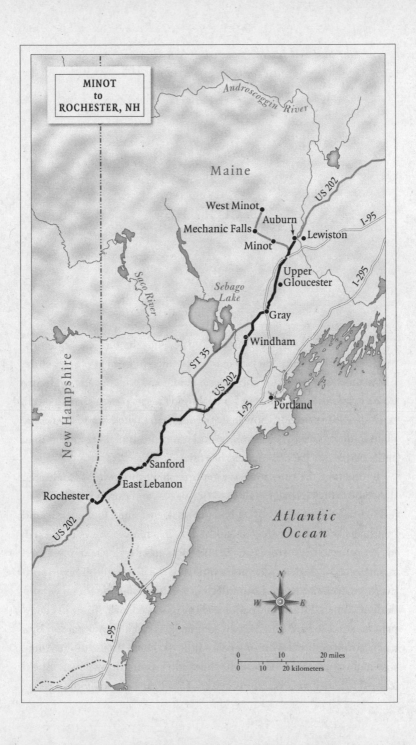

MINOT
to
ROCHESTER, NH

Androscoggin River

Maine

West Minot

Mechanic Falls

Auburn

Minot

Lewiston

US 202

I-95

Upper
Gloucester

Saco River

Sebago
Lake

Gray

I-295

Windham

ST 35

US 202

New Hampshire

I-95

Portland

Sanford

East Lebanon

Rochester

US 202

Atlantic
Ocean

N
W   E
S

0   10   20 miles
0   10   20 kilometers

Our battered suitcases were piled on the sidewalk again;
we had longer ways to go.

—Jack Kerouac

—

CHAPTER

9

Veterans

THE FIRST LEG OF Annie's journey into the Granite State progressed without much to mark it as different from her time before.
She planned to proceed as she'd done in Maine, knocking on farmhouse
doors to ask for shelter for her horse, hoping to sleep in the barn as well.
She'd been surprised by how many people had invited her to spend the
night in their houses, but Annie would never presume to count on that,
and a barn—or a jail cell—suited her fine.

By the time the threesome was approaching the town of Rochester,
they'd been on the road for close to two weeks, and they were starting to
feel like veterans. Depeche Toi had grown accustomed to the leash, and
he usually trotted a few feet ahead of Tarzan's hooves, his ears perked,
his eyes alert to his surroundings. The horse and the dog had developed
an intricate pas de deux—no more did Depeche Toi tangle them up with
his rope. And Tarzan trod carefully, never letting his little friend get underfoot. When Tarzan jumped, he always jumped away from his companion, never toward him. But the gelding *was* still jumpy—startled by a
truck backfiring, a car whizzing past a little too close. All too often, Annie
was almost unseated—although she hadn't been thrown yet. She'd
learned to anticipate his actions better; if she heard a loud motor bearing

down, she steered him off the road, tightened her reins, and stroked him on the neck to calm him down while murmuring, *Whoa there, buddy, take it easy, it's all right.* Still, she noticed that he seemed to show the ex-racehorse side of himself more often than the "gentle enough for a baby to ride" part.

Still, her mount more than made up for his mild case of skittishness by his sheer dependability. Like the American-made Timex watches that were manufactured in large numbers and heavily advertised between 1952 and 1954, Tarzan seemed completely unfazed by his long days of travel and the heavy load he carried. Timex's ad campaigns focused on the watch's ability to withstand harsh conditions and still work, and popularized the slogan "It takes a licking and keeps on ticking." Tarzan was just like the Timex and other mid-century American-made products: Rugged. Solid. Durable. Dependable.

By late afternoon, Annie had made it to Rochester, where she'd heard there was a fairgrounds on the far side of town. That was when, to Annie's great surprise, some policemen and a troop of Boy Scouts met her and escorted her through their streets. Together, the small parade progressed through the center of town, crossed the old stone bridge over the Cocheco River, and walked straight down Main Street. Rochester was a classic midsized New England town. She rode past the big brick library, the bronze statue of a local hero, and the perfect village green, with its old-fashioned hexagonal bandstand. All the way, to her astonishment, people lined up along the street, waving at her.

Tarzan was remarkably undisturbed by the hubbub. He clopped along, looking around with interest, but managed not to make any sudden moves. Depeche Toi seemed to enjoy the attention. He trotted alongside Annie and Tarzan with his black nose in the air and his tail fluttering like a flag on a summer day. Annie didn't know what to make of all the attention. Had all these people really come out just to watch them walk by? But she wanted to rise to the occasion, so she grinned and waved and called out hellos as she passed. As Annie remembered it later, she "looked like Buffalo Bill's wife, and felt like Lindbergh must have felt." The Boy Scouts offered to accompany her as far as the fairgrounds, but

Annie insisted that she'd go on alone—the boys no doubt needed to be getting on. So they gave her directions, and Annie thanked them and continued on her way.

Eleven-year-old Eleanor Blaisdell was playing out in the yard of her family's home when she spotted a brown horse clopping down the road in her direction. On board was an older woman dressed in thick clothing. The horse was laden down every which way. Hanging off his shoulders were burlap bags tied with string, and slung across the front of the saddle was a big old woolen overcoat. The woman aboard was friendly and greeted Eleanor's wave with a hearty hello.

"Can I pat your horse?" Eleanor asked shyly. She was one of those horse-crazy girls who got near one whenever she had the chance.

"Why sure," the woman said. "If you can help me find the fairgrounds. I'm looking for a place to bed my horse down for the night."

The fairgrounds were right around the corner. They could walk there in just five minutes. Eleanor volunteered to show her the way.

Eleanor wasn't afraid of strangers. Such a notion had never occurred to her. She knew everyone in the neighborhood—and this woman, she could tell right away, seemed familiar; she was "country," just like her own mother and grandmother. Eleanor was fully capable of walking to the fairgrounds, even though it was almost dark, without asking for permission. She just needed to be home in time for supper.

Immediately noticing the girl's attraction to Tarzan, Annie slid off, right then and there, in front of the house, and hoisted Eleanor into the saddle. Grabbing hold of the reins, Annie marched alongside, following the girl's directions as they turned right on Brattle Street and right again on Lafayette.

Before long, the arched gateway to the Rochester Fair Grounds rose up in front of them.

"Come back to our house when you're all done," Eleanor said. "You can have supper with our family." Eleanor didn't worry about inviting an unexpected guest to dinner. She knew her mother would set an extra plate at the table on a moment's notice.

Cold Spring Park, on the southern edge of town, had hosted the

Rochester Fair since 1874. The ornate Queen Anne–style gateway, with its faux turrets topped with pennants, had been struck by lightning and destroyed by fire in 1938, but in 1954, a new sign topped the gateway that led to a spacious grounds that included an oval track for the always popular trotting races. There was a gabled wooden farm exhibit building with red doors, white clapboard sides, navy trim, and an eight-sided glass cupola crowning its roof. Although the area had once been largely farmland, newer suburban neighborhoods had sprung up in recent years, so now the fairgrounds were surrounded by small houses with conventional suburban yards. The Rochester Fair attracted visitors from all over the region. Tragedy had struck during the fair earlier that very year. One of the horse barns had burned to the ground, killing five of the trotters who were there to compete in the harness races. Now the remaining stables stood empty. When they reached the gate, Eleanor turned around and skipped home, her Dutch boy haircut bouncing, to tell her family that they would have an unexpected visitor for dinner.

As soon as the trio passed through the pretty gateway, Tarzan began to jig a little. He raised his head and looked around with interest. Annie wondered again where her equine trail mate had been before she'd taken him home. She'd visited a place or two in her day, and she imagined her four-footed friend had, too. Did the fairgrounds remind him of his racing days? But Tarzan's secrets stayed with him. That was the thing about animal friends—they wouldn't bore you with stories of their old glory days, like some people would. Some of Annie's own glory days had been spent at small county fairs like this one. She wondered if she and Tarzan would have talked each other's ears off if they'd known each other's language. Instead, they remained in companionable silence as she unloaded him and settled him into a roomy box stall; meanwhile, Depeche Toi made the rounds of the empty stables, no doubt hoping to find a barn cat or two to befriend.

When Tarzan was settled, Annie whistled for Depeche Toi, and they headed back to the Blaisdell home. There, supper was waiting for her: roast chicken, mashed potatoes, green beans, and apple pie.

The Blaisdell house at 86 Pine Street had been built in 1934. It was cozy and compact, a modern house for a modern family. The small home had three bedrooms, including one for Eleanor's grandmother, to whom the house belonged. Upstairs, Eleanor shared a bedroom with her younger brothers, aged nine and six. Across the hall, her mother and father shared with her youngest brother, who was only two. One bathroom, a living room, and a kitchen rounded out the house. The front porch faced the sidewalk, and the small garage was a separate structure in the rear.

Ruth and Willard Blaisdell represented the kind of family that Annie's parents must have hoped to become. Ruth had been born on a farm on Temple Mountain, in southern New Hampshire, into a life much like Annie's own. As a child, she had walked ten miles down the mountain to a one-room schoolhouse, then come home to a house that was heated by a woodstove and lit by kerosene. By the mid-1950s, there were hundreds of thousands of people all over America who, like the Blaisdells, had traded in the hardship of running a farm for a suburban life.

Many people born in the first part of the twentieth century had, in the course of their lifetime, gone from having few modern conveniences to owning a TV in a well-furnished, electrically lit living room. A woman who lived on a farm just outside Rochester described her home's accommodations in the 1930s:

> The so-called bathroom was no bathroom at all. It had no running water, no tub, no lights, and no furniture of any kind. There were no towels, no soap, no medicine cabinet, and no heat. Our so-called bathroom was a three-hole affair, one large one, a medium one, and one tiny hole. We could use the one that fit us best, but it was not wise to use the big one because it would be a disaster if one fell in! At night when we were upstairs in our bedroom and nature called, we had to make quite a trip to go to the toilet. We had to go down the stairs, through the living room, through the kitchen, and through two storage rooms before we finally came to our destination.

But by the 1950s, life had changed for all but the most rural folk—people like Annie Wilkins.

When Ruth was ten, her father passed away and her mother decided to leave the family farm and find a place in town. In one generation, the Blaisdells moved from farm to town, emerged from poverty, and built a middle-class life. But Ruth and her mother had not forgotten their country roots. The family sat around the dinner table as the three women swapped stories of living on a farm, while Depeche Toi slept at Annie's feet, perking up whenever the children slipped scraps to him. That night after dinner, instead of working hard at farm chores, as Annie and Ruth would have done, the whole family sat on the sofa in their wood-paneled living room and watched the Magnavox black-and-white television set, a scene right out of *Father Knows Best,* the popular show about an idealized suburban family that debuted in May 1954. Annie was fascinated by this new way to treat children—allowing them relaxation and recreation, instead of putting them early to work. She firmly believed it was better than the way she'd been raised.

SOUTH OF ROCHESTER, ANNIE enjoyed a welcome respite from traffic. Route 202A meandered off from the main thoroughfare, Route 202, running roughly parallel, but it was much quieter. She passed the occasional farmhouse and a white church with its high steeple. As they walked in the quiet, with Tarzan's hoofbeats punctuating the silence with a rhythmic muffled thumping on the leaf-strewn shoulder of the road, Annie thought about her father.

He'd been a determined man with a strong desire to make his way in the world and an unflinching work ethic, tempered with a healthy dose of sometimes misplaced optimism. He was willing to work hard, learn new skills, and do whatever he needed to do to keep his family clothed and fed. Yet he never managed to make any real progress—perhaps because his family had remained within a hundred-mile radius of the place they'd started out and had kept to small towns where employment opportunities were limited and tended to be dominated by single industries. When that industry failed, the jobs got tight. When a man lost his job, he might be forced to move along to find a new one. In this, they were no different from thousands of other families who lived in the mill towns of New England—towns that were already struggling in the early part of the twentieth century. There always seemed to be the promise of another place where life would be easier, but in order to get there, you had to go there, and moving far away took money. So, somehow, no matter how much Annie's family traveled, they never seemed to get anywhere.

In fact, they did make one full-blown attempt to bust loose from the orbit of small New England industrial towns that had trapped them in poverty. In 1920, after several good years of steady work in the New Hampshire town of Grafton, her father had earned enough money to purchase a Model T car, and the three of them, her parents and Annie, now twenty-eight years old, took off for Florida. But what should have been a great adventure turned into a nightmare. Annie's father died suddenly en route, leaving Annie and her mother unemployed and stranded in Pennsylvania. In 1920, two women, one widowed, one divorced, with few marketable skills and both effectively homeless, were overnight turned into bums. Their car disappeared—perhaps sold, or maybe too damaged for them to keep driving it. To get home, Annie and her mother had to work their way back up the coast, stopping to do odd jobs, picking fruit and doing other kinds of farm labor. Somehow, 1924 found Annie back in Grafton, New Hampshire, getting married a second time. This time, as an older woman with limited marital prospects, she married Frank Wilkins, a widowed day laborer twenty years her senior. When her grandmother died a few years later, leaving the Minot property to Annie and her mother, Wilkins tried to convince Annie to deed her portion of the inheritance over to him. When she refused, he ran off, and she hadn't seen him since. Annie and her mother finally made it back to Minot together, and until now, Annie had never had another chance to travel.

But here she was, on the road again, hungry to complete that unfinished journey. She was feeling her father's spirit nearby, although he'd been gone for more than thirty years. Still, she remembered something he'd always said: "Keep going and you'll get there." Simple enough, even though it hadn't worked for him. She thought about how he had looked as they took off south in that old Model T with the crank, full of dreams for the future. Hope, adventure, and unexpected things, good things, it seemed, were always just about within grasp; all you had to do was have faith and keep going. She'd learned that from her father, even though he'd died trying. But he'd never made her doubt that it was worth the quest.

*Television has proved that people will look
at anything rather than each other.*

—**Ann Landers**

CHAPTER

10

Face in a Box

ANNIE, TARZAN, AND DEPECHE TOI had been on the road for three weeks when people started telling her that Manchester, New Hampshire, was just up the road a piece. Given that she was traveling without a map, she never knew exactly how far she would get on any given day. And she'd already concluded it'd be better to avoid having any set itinerary, since she never knew exactly what to expect. She'd also learned that "just up the road" meant different things to different people. So far, she was following the advice of folks she met along the way. Everyone seemed happy to provide her with suggestions, and most often people would give her the name of a town she could probably make before sundown. Most of the time they'd also provide the name of a family who might be willing to take her in or tell her about a rental stable or fairgrounds that could have a stall to let. So far she'd managed not to get lost by sticking to main roads and stopping passersby to see if she was headed in the right direction.

Annie was now traveling southwest along New Hampshire Route 101, a narrow two-lane road that meandered past small farms, ponds, brown meadows, and barren trees. But as the day progressed, the houses grew closer together. She was reaching the outskirts of Manchester. Although Tarzan and Depeche Toi both looked chipper, Annie was tiring, and feeling a bit of rheumatism in her hip. She didn't want to start hitting a lot of traffic when she was worn out in case Tarzan started getting fresh.

In 1856, when Walt Whitman published "Song of the Open Road," he described the experience of a nineteenth-century traveler moving from the countryside into the city: "You flagg'd walks of the cities! you strong curbs at the edges! . . . You gray stones of interminable pavements! you trodden crossings!" Ninety-eight years later, Annie's experience would not have been so different from Whitman's. From the quiet country lanes of rural New Hampshire, she, Tarzan, and Depeche Toi entered Manchester, a twentieth-century city with a nineteenth-century soul.

Straddling the Merrimack River, Manchester became a mighty industrial center and the most populous city in the state on the strength of its access to waterpower. In the early nineteenth century, Samuel Blodget, a financier, lawyer, and well-known patriot, had arrived in the town then known as Derryfield and decided that its location was the perfect place for a large industrial city. In 1807, he opened a canal-and-lock system that allowed vessels to bypass the Amoskeag Falls, thereby facilitating passage to Boston. In 1809, the first water-powered cotton spinning mill was built on the western bank of the Merrimack River. The Amoskeag Mills grew rapidly until Manchester became one of New England's largest company towns. In 1935, in the depths of the Depression, the Amoskeag Mills finally folded, but not before leaving an indelible imprint on the city and its several generations of textile workers.

As Annie reached the city outskirts, the sun was getting low. A large group of people was flowing out from a new-looking Catholic church, and the spectacle of Annie, Tarzan, and Depeche Toi clip-clopping down the street immediately attracted the crowd's attention. A few people started pointing at her—that was the lady on horseback they'd seen in the newspapers! The churchgoers swarmed around her, asking for autographs and calling out friendly hellos. Annie dismounted and began happily greeting the parishioners. After a while, the parish priest approached her. He offered a blessing, a ten-dollar bill, and a Saint Christopher medal to hang around her neck—Christopher being the patron saint of travelers.

Russell Foster was driving down High Street near the church in his 1952 green Plymouth station wagon, with its distinctive rounded form, white rims, and chrome features. *Suburban* was inscribed in curly chrome script near the driver's door. His pretty wife, Muriel, was seated beside him with the baby in her lap, and in the backseat were their three small boys. Russ, at the wheel, was a handsome man with prematurely silver hair and a smile on his face. He was curious about nearly everything, and tonight, he wanted to know what all the commotion in front of their parish church was about. He didn't see Annie, her horse, or her dog at first, completely surrounded by people as they were. Muriel didn't think to stop Russ, even though she was surely in a hurry to get home and get the children fed and bathed and into bed. They had plenty of things to do besides pulling over to the side of the road, but she was used to her husband and knew that when he got enthusiastic, there was no dissuading him.

When Russ discovered that the crowd had gathered around a woman and her little dog and horse, and that this unlikely trio of travelers was on its way across the country, and that it was almost dark, he did what came naturally to him: he started to think about how he could help. She needed a place to stay and a place to bed down her horse, but they were less than a mile from downtown Manchester, and she'd find no stable near here.

Russ Foster had been brought up in an altruistic family. When he was growing up, his father, a successful surgeon, had founded the Manchester hospital, while his mother had been in charge of the local YMCA. Young Russ had been a musician and a cutup, flunking out of college before his father had insisted he get his act together. Russ had then done his father proud, graduating from Dartmouth and becoming a high school math teacher.

So Russ took charge. He went to speak to the priest and said he wanted to help. He offered to find a stable out toward East Candia, back in the direction Annie had come from, to keep the horse overnight, and said he and Muriel would take Annie home to supper. She was happy and relieved at the offer. She'd been so busy talking to people she'd hardly noticed that it was almost dark—and Manchester was bigger than she'd imagined. No way she'd get through this big city and out to farmland on the other side before nightfall.

Before long, a man with a truck and trailer came to pick up Tarzan. Annie offered to go along to help get him settled, but the man told her it wasn't necessary. When Annie and Depeche Toi at last climbed into the backseat of the Plymouth, the boys' eyes went wide at the sight of their new visitor, especially the dog, and they quickly scooted over to make room for them. But Annie felt abashed. Clearly this nice family had plenty to do without looking out for her as well. She was worn out from a long day's ride in the cold. Her hip was aching, and she was happy to be in the back of this warm car, though she worried that she was adding to this young mother's burdens. She hastened to tell her hostess not to worry—she'd be out of their hair first thing in the morning. But Muriel told her absolutely not. She insisted that Annie stay for at least two nights. "Your horse is tired, and you need a rest, too," she said, making it clear that she'd brook no further discussion on the subject. "Just a little vacation."

Unexpectedly, tears sprang to Annie's eyes. She fingered the Saint Christopher medal hanging around her neck.

"Why, what's the matter?" Muriel asked.

Annie wasn't sure how to explain it. She was so touched by Muriel's graciousness. "It's just that I've never had a vacation in all my life," she said.

The Foster home was small and tidy. A white house with a peaked roof, it had just three bedrooms inside. Russ and Muriel shared one, and the four boys were divided between the two others. The oldest boy was six, the youngest a two-month-old baby whom Muriel had to contend with as she hurriedly prepared for the stranger in their midst. The home was modest—they had no TV and so watched only during weekend visits with the boys' grandparents, who lived in the same neighborhood.

But in spite of the small home and the big family, they were determined to make Annie feel welcome.

It was Friday, so Muriel prepared fish for dinner. Annie was friendly and warm with the boys, pulling the four-year-old into her lap and regaling him with stories. Her deadpan humor, combined with her Down East burr, played off the father's exuberance. Pretty soon, Russ moved to the family's upright Baldwin piano and began to play. He was a natural—he loved show tunes and ragtime, as well as pop songs. The kids had learned early on to join in. Meanwhile, word of Annie's arrival in town had gotten around. The local television station, WMUR Manchester, which had debuted on the air only a few months earlier, called and asked if Annie would come in for an interview the next morning.

Long after Muriel had settled the baby, tucked in the boys, and cleaned up the kitchen, with Annie pitching in to help, she made up a bed for their guest on the living room sofa.

In the morning, Russ accompanied Annie on the five-minute walk to the WMUR-TV studio. Annie had not only never seen the inside of a television studio, she'd only seen TV a few times, mostly in the homes she'd visited on this trip. She hadn't even seen a movie in years—the last one had been a silent film. So when she was ushered into a small room and seated in a chair for an interview with a newscaster, she felt perfectly at ease—she loved to talk, and this was just one more conversation. But about halfway through, Annie looked up and realized that her own moving face was being projected onto a small screen. Shocked, she stared straight at the camera and couldn't think of anything else to say for a while. Still, she had no concept of just how far her image would travel anytime that camera was rolling.

Television crossed a critical threshold in 1954, the first year that more than half of American households owned a set. In just five years, the television had changed from an esoteric gadget to a central part of American life. In Manchester at that time, there was only a single station, so whatever happened on Channel 9 (WMUR) soon became the talk of the town. The power of television to set the dialogue—to quite literally tune everyone in to the same channel—was just beginning to be understood. And right then, in New Hampshire's largest city—population eighty thousand—the attention was so firmly planted on a sixty-two-year-old woman, her horse, and her dog, that the mayor decided to invite Annie and Tarzan to appear in a parade that was happening the following day. At first Annie said absolutely not. She'd had enough trouble with Tarzan being scared of trucks with flapping canvas on them. What would he do in a parade? And even more, she was worried that she looked like one of the horribles. It was an old tradition in New England to have clowns bring up the rear of every parade. The clowns always came in two waves—first the happy ones, followed by the ugly ones, the latter known as "the horribles." But she found out that this was not at all what they had in mind. The mayor of Manchester wanted Annie to lead the parade— or not quite lead; she'd follow him, as he headed the parade in his car. He'd even arranged to have Tarzan trucked back into town to meet her.

The Fosters lived on Chestnut Street, just a few blocks from Manchester's main drag, Elm Street, which cut straight through the center of town. The parade started up at the corner of Webster and Elm and proceeded past the F. W. Woolworth's five-and-dime, past the big white façade of the Amoskeag National Bank, a remnant of Manchester's company town days, past Hillsborough Drugs, with its sign displaying a big red R_x and a Coca-Cola logo to advertise the soda fountain inside, toward city hall, the three-story brick-and-granite Gothic Revival building whose big clock tower greeted everyone driving through the center of Manchester, until it reached Victory Park, where there was a memorial to the 176 Manchester soldiers who'd lost their lives in World War I.

That year had been a special one for the city's traditional November 11 Armistice Day parade. In September 1954, thanks to an effort made by a Kansas congressman, the holiday had been renamed Veterans Day to honor all returning soldiers. The horrors and deprivations of the World War II era were starting to fade from people's memories, replaced by a new feeling of nostalgia; people were missing the intense feeling of national solidarity and purpose that had characterized the war years. Not surprisingly, one of the most popular films in the fall of 1954 was the

Bing Crosby vehicle *White Christmas,* with its sentimental reminiscence of the war and its bittersweet and melancholic title song.

Not only were the 1950s a time of increasing societal alienation and a newfound suspicion of colleagues and neighbors, but the new technologies of the decade were changing the world in ways that people had not yet assimilated and didn't fully understand. In 1954, Bell Telephone introduced the brand-new rotary dial telephone. It replaced the personal connection of an operator's voice with the technological buzz of the dial tone. There was a sense that an old way of life was passing, and not just passing but actually being destroyed. Along with the joyful rush to the future was a fear that the familiar world of small-town America was on the cusp of changes that would irrevocably alter its familiar ways of life.

That aside, nothing embodied mid-century patriotism like a parade. With its marching bands, men—and a few women—in uniform, flags waving, and ice cream cones dripping, a parade was always a spectacle, always an event to look forward to. And so as people flocked downtown to watch their newly minted celebrity parade through town, the Foster family lined up with the rest of the crowd to watch the parade go by. The boys thrilled to the lines of shiny cars with city dignitaries waving through the windows. When Annie came by, to the boys she looked like a giant figure, a hero aboard her shaggy brown steed. They waved proudly, so thrilled that they had met the woman who was riding at the head of the parade—they would never forget the experience.

At the end, Annie was surrounded by well-wishers, people who'd seen her on television and had come out wanting to meet her and to wish her luck on her journey. Many had brought presents for her and her companions. She gratefully accepted a blanket for Tarzan, and one for Depeche Toi. Strangers gave gifts of clothing and cash, and cans of food to slip into the burlap bags she carried. Sadly, she had to say no to the offer of a pair of silk pajamas. She'd never seen anything so soft in her life, but she didn't think they looked rugged enough to wear on the road; she'd stick with her wool union suit.

The following morning, a police car escorted her to the edge of town. The officers requested that she not travel after dusk, for safety's sake, then bid her goodbye, and Tarzan strode forward, catching the scent of the countryside and picking up his step. The route out of Manchester soon turned from the clang and clatter of city life to a bucolic scene of woods and fields and intermittent farmhouses. By eleven o'clock on November 21, she and her two four-footed friends were back to what Walt Whitman called "the cheerful voice of the public road, the gay fresh sentiment of the road."

But the day did not remain pleasant. When Annie had set off from Minot, there had still been a bit of Indian summer lingering in the air, but now a cold, steady rain started to fall. Several times cars pulled over to ask if she needed some shelter. In answer, she quipped, "I've got on two union suits and I'm not salt and pepper so I won't melt."

She was trying to make it to the town of Milford. Someone in Manchester had given her the name and address of a family there who had offered to put her up for the night.

Around two in the afternoon, a farmer and his wife approached her and offered her a place in the barn for Tarzan and a cot for her to sleep on.

"I'm headed to Milford," Annie said.

"You won't make it that far before sundown," the farmer replied. He assured her that it would be better to come off the road, as there weren't many houses on the stretch that lay ahead. She hadn't covered more than five miles so far that day, but she decided to accept his invitation rather than get stuck when the sun started to set.

Certainly by now Annie had realized that her being in the newspapers and on TV had made people aware of her journey. But as she rode along the side of that country road, cold and wet, she didn't think that anyone in the world knew or cared where she was, except for Depeche Toi, who had finally agreed to ride out this leg of the trip on the saddle in front of her, tucked underneath her coat.

As it happened, Annie was wrong. A reporter at *The Springfield Union,* having read in the Manchester paper that she was planning to swing through his southern Massachusetts city to pick up her mail, had called up to the police department in Milford to see if she'd arrived there. The police in Milford had gone out looking for her, hoping to escort her through town, but had seen no sign of her between Manchester and Milford. They assumed that she'd stopped off along the way somewhere and were not concerned. When the reporter filed a story stating that Annie and her traveling companions had gone missing somewhere along the route, it started a minor furor. Readers of *The Springfield Union* had been following her story for over a week now, and it wasn't just the woman they were concerned about—what about her horse and her dog? How were they faring as they got farther from home and the weather turned cold? One woman wrote to the paper suggesting that the citizens of Springfield should take up a collection to pay her transport to California. There was a groundswell of concern for her horse's welfare.

Annie, Tarzan, and Depeche Toi stayed put for a couple of days until the weather cleared. As Annie packed up Tarzan, thanked the farmer, and set off again toward Milford, she was unaware of a less than favorable article that had run that morning in *The Springfield Union*. The last sentence read, "If and when she arrives here, she will find Charles B. Marsh, prosecuting officer of the ASPCA, waiting to see her."

A canter is the cure for every evil.

—Benjamin Disraeli

—

Horse People and Dog People

S HE WAS HEADING SOUTH, like the flocks of migratory birds, but the birds had gotten a head start on her. The winter solstice was only a few weeks away, and there was no mistaking the feeling in her formerly broken leg bone. As she passed through the small town of Brookline, New Hampshire, past the classic white clapboard church with the steeple, she approached the Brookline General Store. When she reached its doorway, a friendly clerk ran outside and offered her chocolate, a snack for Depeche Toi, and grain for Tarzan.

The snack gave the three of them enough stamina to continue without taking a lunch break. Neither Tarzan nor Depeche Toi showed any signs of fatigue, and soon Annie spotted a metal road marker announcing that she was entering the township of Townsend, Massachusetts.

Her third state! In spite of the sign, there wasn't much to see, but after a few miles she passed through the small hamlet of Townsend and continued south along Route 13. Right here, the road ran alongside a three-hundred-year-old property known as the Peabody farm. It was quiet; the occasional car rumbled by, though she didn't see any people. But about three miles south, just north of the village of Lunenburg, she was surprised by an elegant young woman who emerged from the side of the road and asked if she could take a picture. She started snapping before Annie could respond. Wanting to be obliging, Annie said "Whoa" to Tarzan and called Depeche Toi, who had run up to the woman in a friendly manner and started sniffing her boots. She was young—surely not thirty yet—and slim, with blond hair, a sharp nose, and a wide grin; Annie judged her very beautiful. And although she was dressed for a walk in the woods in November, Annie could tell from the cut of her clothes and the poshness of her accent that she was no ordinary country woman. She introduced herself as Jean Lane, adding, "I've been waiting for you. I was hoping you'd join me for lunch."

"Well, the fellow in the store up the road gave me some chocolate . . ." Annie said, but Mrs. Lane insisted that chocolate was no lunch. Jean, as she wanted to be called, knelt down to pet Depeche Toi, then stroked Tarzan on the nose and commented on his sound-looking legs and excellent conformation—noting that he looked as if he could be an ex-trotter. Annie warmed up to her fast.

Even though Annie had been determined to make good time today and not get stalled too much by people stopping to talk to her, the invitation proved irresistible. Jean was both friendly and kind, and she seemed genuinely interested in Annie, her companions, and her voyage.

As they headed down the road together, Annie still in the saddle, Jean told Annie that she'd been following her story and was so happy to meet her. It turned out they had much in common—Jean loved both horses and dogs. She had attended school in Waterville, Maine, and had first learned to ride there. She loved trotting racers, and most important, she raised huskies—Jean Lane was one of the foremost women sled dog racers in the country. She loved Annie's boldness and sense of initiative, loved that an older woman wasn't afraid to go off on an adventure—and, of course, she felt an immediate affinity for Annie's traveling companions.

During their lunch at Jean's home, Jean plied Annie with sandwiches, hot coffee, and pie. She had fresh ground hamburger meat for Depeche Toi. She wanted to know how the dog was handling all the walking. He was sound asleep, stretched out on his side on the plush rug, but Annie said that so far, she hadn't had any trouble with him at all. He seemed to be going along just fine.

After lunch, Jean walked Annie out to the kennels to see her dogs; she explained that the handsome, thick-furred, blue-eyed dogs were Siberian huskies and Alaskan huskies. They wagged their tails in a friendly manner at Depeche Toi, but Annie's dog kept his distance. Jean talked about how she trained her animals and fed them, and she explained that more than any kind of training, she relied on a feeling she'd get about a dog, that the dog wanted to *go*. This struck Annie as sensible—Depeche Toi had always been eager to go, and that hadn't changed one bit.

When they parted, Jean pressed her phone number into Annie's hands and told her not to hesitate to call if she ever ran into trouble, and Annie explained that she'd be picking up mail when she got to Springfield, in case her new friend wanted to write. Jean Lane was everything that Annie was not: young and educated, affluent and sophisticated. Yet Annie sensed something in this woman. Under her conventional young-lady demeanor, there was an impulse to adventure, a sense of barely suppressed desire—a fire that drew her to trotters and sled dog racing, to fast paces, bone-cold days, and an icy wind in her face.

Jean sent Annie off with a bag of apples for Tarzan, a bag of bones for Depeche Toi, and, for Annie, a promise to keep in touch. Before she rode off, Annie recited a couple of stanzas of her favorite poem, "Thinking," attributed to an obscure poet named Walter Wintle.

> If you think you are beaten, you are;
> If you think you dare not, you don't.
> If you'd like to win, but you think you can't,
> It's almost a cinch you won't.
>
> If you think you'll lose, you've lost,
> For out in the world we find
> Success begins with a fellow's will—
> And it's all in the state of mind.

As she rode away from her newfound friend, Annie threw Jean's spirit into her saddlebag—another woman's hopes and dreams riding along with her.

A week or so later, she was about five miles north of the small town of Spencer, Massachusetts, when she was startled by the sight of a group of some fifteen people dressed in riding tweeds, scarves, and field boots, mounted on horseback, riding toward her along the opposite side of the road. As they got closer, they yelled out a greeting. "You must be the Widow Wilkins," one called out, using the name they'd been reading in the newspapers. "We've been waiting for you!"

Tarzan whinnied and Depeche Toi wagged his tail at the sight of the approaching riders—the first people on horseback the trio had seen since their departure.

"Waiting for *me*?" Annie was not surprised that someone would call her a widow—it was a form of politeness, a sign that they saw her as a respectable woman—but she was baffled by the fact that they seemed to know her name.

"We've come to take you to your next stop," their leader announced. Annie was impressed by the sight of the handsome bays, browns, and chestnuts.

"We're from the Brookfield Riding and Driving Club," one of the riders added. "We have stables for your horse, and our members Mr. and Mrs. Roland Hamlett have invited you and your dog to spend the night with them."

Tarzan picked up his step and raised his head, and Depeche Toi stayed close alongside his companion as the group of horses enveloped them. Annie's solitary trek had suddenly turned into a group ride.

In the 1950s, although the farm horse population had declined, horseback riding for sport and entertainment was reaching a peak. The people who joined Annie that day were completely unlike her—they kept their well-groomed horses in a stable, and they rode in arenas and along bridle trails in the beautiful countryside of central Massachusetts. But a love for horses transcends all boundaries, and Annie felt instantly at home with this gaggle of friendly riders.

The first stop was the Brookfield Riding and Driving Club, where the members had prepared a box stall for Tarzan, full of fragrant fresh straw. Annie untied his load and brushed his coat until it shone. Depeche Toi, meanwhile, had gone off on an expedition.

Stella Hamlett was waiting to pick up Annie in her automobile, and when Annie slid into the seat, Depeche Toi happily hopped in alongside her. The Hamletts had cooked a festive dinner for Annie, and it seemed as if they had invited half the town of Spencer to come meet her. The raucous party stayed up half the night drinking wine, while Annie regaled them with stories of her previous long trip—when she and her parents had headed to Florida, and how the brakes had gone out on the Model T when they were wheeling around a horseshoe curve on Massachusetts's Mohawk Trail, and recited several poems from memory, including her favorite, the Walter Wintle poem.

The Hamletts were impressed by how Annie could recite this and other poems from memory. When interviewed later for the local paper, Stella Hamlett said, "She's a wonderful woman. We'd like to adopt her. It seems like she's been pretty lonesome for a long time."

Stella Hamlett herself was an experienced harness horse driver. The next day, when Annie mentioned that Tarzan had probably spent some time pulling a sulky, she suggested hitching him up to her buggy and seeing how he liked it. Annie was a little skeptical—Tarzan wasn't the calmest horse in the world when it came to wheeled contraptions—but Stella promised she wouldn't force him into anything. As they put the harness on him, Tarzan stood so patiently that Annie guessed he'd probably worn one in the past. Responding to Stella's expert driving, Tarzan clopped all over town, quiet as you please, revealing a hidden talent. They didn't want to tire him, so they cut the jaunt short, and soon he was rubbed down and blanketed, and cozy in the big box stall that had been set aside for his use.

The next day was a rest day for the travelers. Wanting to show Annie around the area, the Hamletts drove her to visit the village of Sturbridge, an authentic colonial town, then took her to dinner at a nearby restaurant. Annie enjoyed herself so much that she tried to ignore the fact that she wasn't feeling well. Her cough had taken a turn for the worse. What would she do if she got sick again? If she got too sick to ride, she risked repaying her hosts' kindness by becoming a burden. She decided to hit the road again early the next morning, in spite of the cough.

As the sun was rising, she rose, got dressed, and packed up her things, but the Hamletts wouldn't hear of it. They had called a doctor to come round to see her, and she could not set off before he did. After his visit, the message was clear: Annie wasn't going anywhere until she was on the mend. She could hardly believe that these kind people, strangers just a few days earlier, were taking care of her as if she were kin.

Two days later, the doctor pronounced her well enough to travel on. Back at the Brookfield Riding and Driving Club, the members had gathered to see her off. Annie discovered that they had reshod Tarzan's front hooves with brand-new rubber shoes to keep him from slipping if the road got icy, and now they presented her with a waterproof horse blanket to carry with her on the road. And that wasn't all: some of the people had brought one- and five-dollar bills, and a local florist had even sent over a bucket of pink carnations.

Meanwhile, all of her doings had been reported in *The Springfield Union,* including an unsigned editorial that mockingly suggested that Annie's stopover in Spencer meant that perhaps she wasn't serious about making it to California and only wanted to socialize along the way. But that mean-spirited opinion hadn't dampened the enthusiasm of Springfield's chamber of commerce. Its members were sending a truck to pick her up, and they had arranged for her and Tarzan to ride into town in style.

The whole life of an American is passed
like a game of chance.

—Alexis de Tocqueville

—

CHAPTER

12

The Checkered Game
of Life

THE CITY OF SPRINGFIELD, MASSACHUSETTS, had developed a
fever of interest in the woman they'd been following under the
new moniker "the Widow Wilkins." Ever since first entering the pages of
The Springfield Union, Annie had been covered in the city's morning
and evening papers. People were taking sides about the wisdom of her
journey: some thought it was a grand adventure, while others saw it as
imprudence and folly.

Springfield's proud citizens felt they had every right to pass judgment. Nicknamed "the City of Progress," their home was a twentieth-
century industrial success story, so prosperous that it had attracted a
tide of new immigrants, who had tripled its population in the past fifty
years. Springfield was now the fourth most populous city in the Northeast. Its downtown was graced with monumental buildings and softened
by more than four acres of dedicated parkland within the city limits. The
home of the Springfield Armory, which had produced the Springfield
rifle, carried by Union soldiers into the Civil War, the city was known as
a center of precision metalwork.

Unlike the planned company town of Manchester, New Hampshire,
Springfield had a diversified economy and had pioneered in many fields.

It was here that Merriam-Webster printed and sold the first widely distributed dictionary of American English. Here, too, Goodyear was the
first company to mass-produce vulcanized rubber. Springfield's Indian
Motorcycle operation was the first American company to manufacture
gasoline-powered bicycles, and adopted citizen James Naismith invented the sport of basketball.

Because she considered herself a tramp of fate, Annie might have felt
a certain affinity for one of Springfield's biggest homegrown industries.
The Milton Bradley Company's eponymous founder had started the
company when he'd patented a board game entitled "The Checkered
Game of Life." Formerly the owner of a lithography company, Bradley
had lost a fortune when he'd commissioned and printed a lithograph of
Abraham Lincoln just before Lincoln decided to grow a beard, render-
ing Bradley's investment worthless.

While Bradley's Checkered Game of Life was almost certainly, according to historian Jill Lepore, a copy of a game printed earlier in London, his American version was a hit, and it spawned an entire board
game industry. Bradley's original version of the game reflected his Puritan New England outlook. The object was to lead a prudent life, which
would result in a happy old age, and this was to be achieved by avoiding
temptations—intemperance and gambling—as well as pitfalls such as
poverty and suicide. All of this, Bradley's rules implied, could be attain-
able with sufficient effort. Early printed directions for the game put it
this way: "It is only by constant and renewed exertion that the lost
ground can be regained."

When the Great Depression dried up the market for board games,
the company teetered on the brink of bankruptcy and had to pivot to
fabricating airplane parts for the war effort. But by 1954, Milton Bradley
was back to making perennial favorites such as the Uncle Wiggily Game
and the Raggedy Ann Game. And the year Annie rode into town, the
company introduced two new games, both reflecting current preoccu-
pations. One was called Swayze—a current events quiz game named
after John Cameron Swayze, whose *Camel News Caravan* (sponsored
by Camel cigarettes) was the first TV news broadcast to include live

footage. The second was called Game of the States: Who Sells the Most from Coast to Coast? Advertised as fun and educational, it was themed around the idea of a road trip. Not surprising: the journey of American life was increasingly being envisioned through the metaphor of car travel.

In 1960, Milton Bradley would introduce a new version of its original bestseller, calling it "The Game of Life." In this revised edition, each player's game piece would be a car, complete with slots to insert pink and blue pegs, representing a mother and father and boy and girl children. Along the way, people would make choices—for example, college or career—and accumulate not just money but also insurance and stock certificates, aiming for the final destination: a suburban dream home in a swanky neighborhood known as Millionaire Acres. By the end of the 1950s, the transformation from life as a moral journey to life as a car trip would be complete.

But right now, in mid-November 1954, the life's journey that Springfield had become obsessed with was that of Annie Wilkins, her cast-off horse and mongrel dog, and their improbable trek to California.

And it wasn't hard to understand why Americans were finding her so appealing. In spite of the country's postwar economic prosperity, newspaper headlines seemed to bring fear at every turn. Since April, the country had been transfixed by the Army-McCarthy hearings, and now Senator McCarthy was being tried for censure for accusing the U.S. Army of harboring Communist infiltrators. So much bad news. As Annie rolled into town in the backseat of a car, with Tarzan following behind in a horse trailer pulled by a truck, she and her critters gave people something else to talk about.

Annie didn't know it, but when she had announced to the media in Manchester that she was going to be stopping in Springfield, she'd done herself a good turn. The story had caught the eye of the president of Springfield's chamber of commerce, Ted Jarrett, a man who always had his eye out for ways to get his community into the news. Now that the press was buzzing about Annie and her companions, he wanted to harness some of that energy to promote goodwill for his city. Even before she'd arrived, there had been more than fifteen articles in the local papers discussing her doings in great detail, and since there were already concerns in the air about the humane treatment of Tarzan and Depeche Toi, he decided to avoid the spectacle of having the trio wade into Springfield's congested traffic.

Fortunately, Joe Bolduc of nearby Chicopee had been following Annie's exploits in the newspaper. Bolduc worked at Springfield's Indian Motorcycle company, and he loved both motorcycles and horses. He had a truck and a horse trailer, and was the sort of person who liked to step up when he saw an opportunity to be of service. After announcing in *The Springfield Union* that he admired her courage and spunk, he drove his truck and trailer straight up to the town of Palmer, where Annie had spent the night, to offer Tarzan a ride.

Like all American cities, Springfield had once been filled with livery stables, but by 1954, most of them were gone. Peter Hogan, however, still had a stable full of horses and other animals behind his business, the Liberty Ice and Fuel Company, just a mile from downtown. And when he learned that the traveling rider needed a place for her horse to stay, he offered to put Tarzan up.

The Hogan homestead had once been out in the country, but the city had grown up around it, and now it was the heart of a close-knit neighborhood of Irish immigrants known as Hungry Hill. The Hogans had found frozen gold in the surface of the pond on their family farm, harvesting large chunks of ice, which they packed in layers of sawdust in their icehouses and eventually delivered to addresses in Springfield or shipped by barge down the Connecticut River as far as New York City.

When ice reaches a thickness of two inches, a man can safely walk across it. When it is four inches thick, it's stable enough to ride a horse across, and when it reaches a depth of six inches, a wagon hitched to a six-horse team can drive onto its surface without worry. The Hogan stables had once housed the work horses they used to harvest the ice and the cart horses that pulled their delivery wagons. The ice-harvest season began around January 10, when the pond's ice could be ten to eleven inches thick and they could cull one or two cuttings. It took about a month to fill the icehouses, and normally the ice would last until August or September.

At one time, ice wagons, their blocks of ice insulated in sawdust as they circulated among homes and businesses all over America, were just part of the vast cacophony of horse-powered transportation that characterized cities in the late nineteenth and early twentieth centuries. The fruit peddler and the junkman, the milkman and the horse-drawn trolley—they filled every city and alley with the clatter of iron-shod hooves on cobblestones or concrete. But between 1900 and 1930, both the business of ice and the horses that were indispensable to its harvesting and distribution were replaced by changing technology. The use of Freon gas in refrigeration quickly made the old icebox obsolete. And trucks began to replace the horse and wagon.

The Hogans' business had survived by transitioning from ice to fuel, and the farm was still in the family. They loved animals, and their stable and pastures were an unexpected oasis of calm so close to Springfield's congested downtown. Bolduc dropped Tarzan off at the Hogan stables, and Peter Hogan promised to look after him well.

Annie, riding with Ted Jarrett in his expansive Ford sedan, was headed with Depeche Toi to much fancier digs. Mr. Jarrett had informed Annie, with much fanfare, that she would be the guest of honor at Springfield's Highland Hotel. "It's not our biggest," he said. "But we consider it our best." Jarrett drove right into downtown Springfield, to the triangle district at the corner of Hillman and Barnes Streets, and pulled up in front of the four-story brick edifice.

The Highland's entrance was on a corner; above it rose a round tower with a bright red, white, and blue flag fluttering from its roof. Designed to house the wealthiest visitors at a time when downtown was every city's most elegant hub, the Highland was the antithesis of the anonymous L-shaped motels that began to proliferate in the late 1950s. With its grand banquet rooms, its long corridors, and, most of all, its lack of a parking garage, the Highland reflected a time when most hotel visitors arrived to a new city by train. Before long, these kinds of accommodations would begin to fall on hard times, as more and more travelers looked for cheaper lodgings on the outskirts of cities, but in 1954, the Highland Hotel and downtown Springfield still put on a good show.

When Mr. Jarrett cut the engine in front of the entrance and Annie saw the giant lettering that spelled out "Highland Hotel," she was struck dumb for a moment. Here she was in her fur-lined bonnet, her red plaid shirt, her men's dungarees, and her rubber boots. She could see the hotel valets, in their gold-trimmed uniforms, swinging open the plate-glass doors for men in well-cut suits and women wearing dresses and elegant coats, stockings, and shiny calfskin pumps. She had stayed in a hotel once—on a childhood trip to Boston with her grandfather. She'd never forgotten it—the most wondrously fancy experience she'd ever had in her life. Until now.

She clutched Depeche Toi, almost afraid to get out of the car. But Mr. Jarrett had already jumped out and was swinging her door open. He handed the keys to the valet and ushered her through the Highland's doors, into the glimmering lobby, where the hotel's maître d' rushed forward to greet her as if she were a long-lost friend.

Annie could hardly get a word out. She was acutely embarrassed and self-conscious. She had remembered the hotel in Boston as a palace, but it paled in comparison to the stately chamber where she now found herself. Soft music seemed to be seeping out of the walls, thick Oriental rugs were piled on the floor, and plush chairs stood in groups, ready for a weary traveler. Every surface amenable to elbow grease—brass, marble, hardwood, and glass—winked and gleamed under the lobby's massive chandeliers. Across its opulent expanse, the shiny brass elevator doors whooshed open and shut, as men in somber dark suits with fedoras stylishly set crossed the lobby, as if each one had a secret mission. In the midst of all this, Annie felt like a piece of flotsam caught in the eddies of Bog Creek during a spring rain. Not another woman was wearing pants—much less dungarees and boots. Depeche Toi seemed a bit awed as well, first clinging close to Annie's heels, then whimpering to be taken up into her arms. With her furry beast's heart pressed up against her own, she felt her courage return to her. She was not normally shy, and she didn't even mind being the center of attention, but right now, she felt completely out of place.

Jarrett said goodbye, and the porter, carrying the rucksack where she kept her clothes, led her onto the elevator, then down a long hallway to a well-appointed room with a private bath. In the bathroom's full-length mirror, she looked at her own reflection with amusement: her shock of gray hair was an unruly mop when she pulled off her cap, and her clothing was flecked with horsehair and smudges of dirt. Unlike Annie, Depeche Toi seemed to have no doubts about whether he belonged here. After sniffing every corner of the room and seeming to find it satisfactory, he leapt onto the pristine brocade bedspread, put his nose on his paws, and promptly fell asleep.

Annie washed up, and for the first time since she'd started her journey, she wished that she'd brought along a dress. She was hungry, but she didn't want to go to the dining room the way she looked. The phone in her room kept ringing, but she never thought to pick it up. A while later a knock came on the door; she opened it to find the hotel manager standing there.

"We're afraid you're going to miss dinner. The dining room closes in an hour."

"I can't come to the dining room," Annie confessed. "I've just got my traveling clothes. I don't have anything appropriate to wear."

The hotel manager tried to reassure her, insisting that she was welcome to come in her dungarees, but Annie said no so vehemently that he gave up. Would madame be interested in room service?

Annie scanned the menu and eventually chose the cheapest thing she saw—a bowl of mock turtle soup for forty cents—and ignored his entreaty to add something else to the order. But when the room service valets wheeled a cart into her room, it was laden down with what seemed like a dozen covered dishes—a feast with so many courses that Annie felt dizzy just looking at it.

"It's all on the house," they insisted.

Annie and Depeche Toi sat down to a meal the likes of which she'd never had before: roast beef and potatoes, warm rolls and butter, asparagus tips with hollandaise sauce, and a velvety custard for dessert.

Depeche Toi seemed to figure out life as a hotel dog, as if he were to the manner born. After a single trip outside, she just let him out the door. He trotted to the end of the hall, where the elevator man greeted the pup and took him down to the lobby. Depeche Toi headed out the plate-glass doors, and when he was finished with his business, he came right back inside, trotted across the lobby into the elevator, and rode like a prince back up to the fourth floor, where he found the correct door without help and scratched on it. Annie swung it open to let him back in—amazed at her country dog's citified manners.

The next morning, Annie woke up early, hoping to get into the dining room for breakfast before many diners were there, but her plan didn't work out at all. While she and Depeche Toi were breakfasting, Mr. Jarrett arrived with a posse of reporters and cameramen, and soon Annie was the center of attention. Still, she was getting over her self-consciousness and starting to enjoy herself.

Mr. Jarrett had a full day planned for her. Her first stop was the Springfield Post Office, to pick up her mail. As much as she had enjoyed the attention she'd been receiving on the road, she still wondered if anyone from back home would have thought to write. She'd been sending letters home, telling stories about her travels, so if she arrived at that post office and not a single person had thought to send a letter back, she knew she would be hurt and disappointed. But when she arrived at the general delivery window in the company of Mr. Jarrett, the postal clerk handed over a fat pack of mail.

The first thing Annie saw was a large, heavy package. She recognized the return address. It was from Jean Lane of Lunenburg, the beautiful young woman with the dreams and the dogs. Opening the package, she was delighted to find a thick sheaf of folded notecards. On each notecard's front was a photo of Annie, Tarzan, and Depeche Toi—it must have been one of the shots that Jean had taken of them by the side of the road. Inside were the words of the Walter Wintle poem. Tucked into the package was also a note from Jean with instructions for Annie. "Don't stop to work," the note read. "You can autograph these notecards and use them to raise money to help you reach sunny California. You can do it!"

Besides Jean Lane's big package, Annie found, to her amazement, letters from people she didn't even know—invitations from all over the country, as far away as Texas and Florida, inviting her to come stay. Best of all, among those letters were several from folks back home. To those who mattered to her most, she wasn't forgotten.

Depeche Toi seemed to enjoy staying in a hotel and riding around in cars, but Ted Jarrett now had to tell Annie that their next stop was the ASPCA office on Chestnut Street. Annie knew nothing about the furor that had sprung up. Nothing about the op-eds, or the concerns that her voyage might be cruel to her two animal companions. She had always loved animals—she liked them better than humans, truth be told. So instead of being ashamed, Annie was delighted and grateful that a veterinarian was going to take a look at Depeche Toi and make sure that he was coping with his journey.

Upon their arrival, the staff's attitude toward Annie was friendly but formal. She sat in the waiting room stroking her dog, who seemed agitated by the sights and smells at the animal shelter. Jarrett no doubt knew that if Depeche Toi showed any signs of strain, the ASPCA would likely insist that she call off her trip. He was certainly prepared to use that eventuality as another publicity opportunity—it had taken Annie weeks to ride as far as Springfield, but Jarrett knew that he could send her and her horse and her dog back to Minot in a single day's drive, all the while highlighting Springfield's humane treatment of animals.

The veterinarian started by asking questions, focusing on how Annie kept her dog out of traffic. She explained that she kept him on a leash but that more and more, he was spending part of each day riding along with her, in front of the saddle. The vet inspected Depeche Toi carefully, paying special attention to his paw pads, which, he explained to Annie, would be taking a lot of wear and tear. In the end, he declared Depeche Toi healthy, and no worse off for their several weeks of travel. He suggested that perhaps the dog could be fitted out with leather boots to protect his paws along the journey, and Jarrett perked up—he knew just the place that would surely be happy to outfit the dog with custom boots and donate them (thereby getting some free publicity).

Jarrett phoned up the newspaper reporters again. Once they'd arrived, they all headed over to the T. J. Regnier harness factory to measure Depeche Toi for custom-made boots, while the reporters took pictures and scribbled notes. Next, the crew headed over to the Liberty Ice and Fuel Company, where Dr. Snow, a horse veterinarian, and Charles Marsh, a prosecutor for the ASPCA, were waiting with Tarzan. Marsh began to ask Annie questions: How far did they ride each day? Where was she stabling the horse along the route? What kind of food was she offering him, and what did she do about water? When was the last time the horse was shod?

Annie answered his questions patiently, explaining that she was making about fifteen miles on the long days, but most days less, that she was carrying feed, got water from natural sources like streams, although more often from filling stations, and that while she'd expected to camp out some, Tarzan had bedded down in a stable every night since she'd left.

Dr. Snow, frowning, looked over every inch of Tarzan. He peered inside his ears, checked his teeth for sharp points that would interfere with feeding, and the corners of his mouth for lesions from rough handling with the bit. He looked at his eyes and inside his nostrils, across his chest and down his sides, to make sure he bore no marks from whip or spurs (Annie, of course, traveled with neither). He slid his hand down each one of the horse's legs for signs of swelling or blemishes. He felt up along the withers and under the girth for sores. He picked up each hoof and examined it minutely.

Dr. Snow made so many notations in his notebook that Annie started to worry. What if Tarzan wasn't up to the journey? What would she do then? She had gotten so used to this new life on the road that it was painful to imagine returning to Minot, her tail tucked between her legs. And by now, she and Tarzan and Depeche Toi had developed a deep bond, a wordless connection, fellow wayfarers together in a great big world of strangers. If she had harmed Tarzan, overburdened him, asked too much of him, she didn't think she could forgive herself.

At last Dr. Snow put his pencil down and looked up at Annie, Peter Hogan, who owned the barn, and Ted Jarrett.

"New shoes," he finally pronounced. "The horse needs rubber shoes in back, and we'll reset the ones in front. They're not quite right. Beyond that, this is a sturdy horse, and he looks terrific. Got some Morgan in him, if not full-blooded Morgan, I'd say. Those horses are strong. Good luck on your journey!" he added cheerfully.

Now everyone in the stable was beaming, except Depeche Toi, who had run off to explore, and Tarzan, who seemed oblivious to all the ruckus he had nearly caused. In parting, the vet advised Annie against riding her horse anywhere within the Springfield city limits and informed her that they'd arranged a ride for the trio: they'd deliver them across the border to Windsor Locks, Connecticut.

The next day, the headlines about Annie blared in *The Springfield Union*. "Doctor Pronounces Widow's Horse Sound!" declared one. And in the editorial section, a writer said,

> Mrs. Annie Wilkins of West Minot, Maine, her dog Hurry Up, and her horse Tarzan have made their stop in Springfield and departed points west. . . . At first secretly, and now publicly, we envy Mrs. Wilkins for her intrepidity and for the way she is going about her trip. . . . She's not selling anything. From all outward signs, she is just a woman going from one place to another at her leisure, unperturbed by the fact that they're so far apart.

On Annie's last day in Springfield, there were so many well-wishers lined up in the hotel to see her off that it took her a full hour just to cross the lobby. She held Depeche Toi and posed for what seemed like a million pictures featuring his new leather booties. Ted Jarrett gave her a ride to the Liberty Ice and Fuel Company, and Annie felt a jolt of joy when she spotted Tarzan looking out over his stall door, whickering when he saw her. Depeche Toi jumped out of her arms and ran to reunite with his companion. Tarzan responded by reaching down with his nose to blow a friendly greeting back to the dog, who appeared elegant in his brand-new boots.

Depeche Toi wasn't the only one with new shoes. The veterinarian from the ASPCA had sent out a farrier to take care of Tarzan, so that he'd be ready to hit the road even if they ran into ice—which, at this time of year, they inevitably would.

Joe Bolduc loaded the horse into his van, and Annie, Tarzan, and Depeche Toi headed out of Springfield. At least this time, Annie had landed on the very best square in Milton Bradley's Checkered Game of Life: happy old age.

The only man who makes money following the races
is the one who does so with a broom and shovel.

—Elbert Hubbard

———

CHAPTER

13

Odds

IF ANNIE WILKINS HAD been planning her schedule to maximize publicity and subsidize her trip, she'd have lingered in Massachusetts, where all the attention had brought her a lifetime's worth of local invitations. Convinced that her recent brush with fame was both novel and fleeting, however, she was thinking not about ways to raise her profile but about how to advance ahead of the winter, which was fast closing in.

Joe Bolduc had offered to drive her all the way to Windsor Locks, but Annie was itching to get back on the open road. As they reached the southern outskirts of Springfield and the buildings scattered and the traffic thinned, Annie thanked Bolduc for his kindness and insisted that she resume her journey on foot. The weather was cloudy and cold, and here, there were piles of snow along the sides of the road.

It was the first of December. The route Annie and Tarzan followed from Springfield wound leisurely southward, following an ancient path alongside the banks of the Connecticut River. The longest river in New England, spanning 410 miles, the Connecticut starts along the Quebec border in New Hampshire, then forms the border between Vermont and New Hampshire before passing through Massachusetts and Connecticut, until it empties into Long Island Sound. In the words of Henry David Thoreau: "He who hears the rippling of rivers in these degenerate days will not utterly despair." In just a few short years, once the interstate was built, hugging the shores of the Connecticut in many places, the organic experience of traveling along the river would be lost, replaced by barriers of concrete and the well-engineered logic of professionally designed roads. But for now, the footsteps of Annie and her companions followed along a peaceful byway, accompanied by the whispers of the river and the ghosts of the many fellow foot travelers who'd passed this way for centuries.

Annie, Tarzan, and Depeche Toi were still about five miles north of the town of Windsor Locks, headed toward the bridge at Warehouse Point, which would take them to the west bank of the river, when they approached a filling station with a small café attached. The owner emerged, waving at Annie—he'd read in the paper that she was headed in his direction, and so he'd set aside some oats for Tarzan and fresh ground meat for the dog, hoping she'd pass this way.

Pleased by the friendly greeting, Annie rode into the filling station parking lot, looking for a telephone pole where she could tie up her horse and find him a bucket of water.

Just then, a fancy-looking car with New York plates pulled up by one of the gas pumps, and a man jumped out of the car and called out her name.

"I've been looking for you, Mrs. Wilkins," he said. He introduced himself as Henry and asked if she'd be willing to join him for lunch.

"Newspaperman?" she asked. Annie was beginning to be familiar with the type.

"Television," he said. "I drove all the way up from New York City to find you."

He handed her a card that read *Toast of the Town*, then regarded her with eyebrows raised and an expectant look on his face. This variety show starring Ed Sullivan had been on the air since 1948, but since Annie didn't own a television and almost never watched one, the name meant nothing to her. She shoved the card into her pocket without a second glance. The man took her ignorance in stride. He repeated his offer: Would she let him buy her lunch?

Over a hot meal in the café, the TV producer laid out his plan. He asked if Annie was familiar with Walter Devine, an ex-marine from Portland, Oregon, who had been bicycling around the country for three years, trying to visit every state capital.

"Never heard of him," Annie replied.

"But you don't seem to be sponsored by anyone," he said. "Nobody set you up to do this?"

Annie explained that she'd come up with the idea entirely on her own. She didn't go into the details—the illness, her money problems, or why she'd felt that she had no other choice.

"Well," the man replied, "we'd like to sponsor you. All you have to do is come down to New York City for an on-air interview."

Annie was interested until he explained that they didn't want her to arrive until right before Christmas.

"Christmas?" It was the first of December—Christmas was still three weeks away.

Annie barely gave it a moment's further thought. "I thank you kindly, but I think I'll just keep heading on my way," she said. "I need to put more miles between me and winter." The TV man told her to hang on to his card and call if she changed her mind. But Annie had no intention of heading to New York City. By the time their meal was finished, the café owner had given the oats to Tarzan and the ground meat to Depeche Toi—and even better, he said he had called a friend in Windsor Locks who had a big barn where Tarzan could sleep.

Located roughly halfway between Springfield, Massachusetts, and Hartford, Connecticut, the town of Windsor Locks had been settled on the precise spot on the river where larger riverboats had to be swapped for smaller ones. In 1827, a series of locks and canals was constructed to facilitate the passage of barges along this stretch of the river. The canal destroyed the waterfalls that had powered a large grist mill, so the mill's owner switched to manufacturing paper, in order to take advantage of the canal's expedited access to the large markets of New York and Boston. By 1857, Windsor Locks boasted the largest paper mill in the world.

During the nineteenth century, the town's riverfront had been designed for industry. The tracks of the New York, New Haven and Hartford Railroad ran along its banks. Factories and warehouses lined both sides of the river, allowing the town's products to be loaded onto barges and sent down the waterway toward New York City. But like other cities in New England, Windsor Locks had seen its economy devastated by the Great Depression, and by the diminished importance of rivers for transport. The town might have faded away, but in 1940, fortune struck. The U.S. Army selected 350 locations in which to install air bases for training during World War II. One of them was Bradley Field, which was situated just on the western edge of town. More than fifty houses were torn down to make room for the base. Property values rose. By 1954, the town's future no longer lay with the economy of the river—it was now wedded to that of the airplane.

Annie and her crew arrived in Windsor Locks in the early afternoon. When she reached the outskirts of town, a Norman Rockwell background of neat houses with white picket fences, she began to look for a policeman, but she was almost in the center of town before she found one. She handed him the paper, and he looked at the scribbled name on it. The officer disappeared into a phone booth, made a call, and not long after, a man rolled up with a truck and horse trailer. Chester Reed introduced himself and confirmed to Annie that he was happy to put Tarzan up on his farm. He'd arranged for Annie and Depeche Toi to stay with one of his neighbors, Gertrude Austin, a local schoolteacher, who lived not far from the Reed farm.

The largest undeveloped piece of property remaining in Windsor Locks had been in the Reed family for over a hundred years, and it had historical roots that traced back to before the American Revolution. Once Tarzan was comfortably settled in the barn, Reed took Annie for a tour of his ninety-acre property—he wanted to show her an old one-room red schoolhouse that was the location of a legendary American first. Chester Reed explained that in Puritan New England, the celebration of Christmas had been banned, the Puritans disapproving of the twelve days of drinking and revelry that marked traditional Christmas celebrations. In 1777, a German mercenary named Hendrick Roddemore was captured at the Battle of Bennington, while fighting on the side of the British. As was customary at the time, prisoners were distributed to help provide labor on local farms. Roddemore was working for a Puritan family on what would become the Reed family farm when, homesick at Christmastime, he put up a pine tree inside his small laborer's cabin and decorated it with candles. According to tradition, this was America's first Christmas tree.

That evening, Gertrude Austin and Chester Reed took Annie to dinner, along with a group of locals, at the Ashmere Inn, a three-story brick building with several wings, crowned by a cupola with a view north and south along the Connecticut River. It was Windsor Locks' grandest edifice. In honor of Annie's Maine roots, the inn had prepared a lobster dinner.

Leaving the Reed farm the next morning, Annie was given a folded paper gas station map—the first of many she would come to rely on—marked to detour her around the next big city, Hartford. She had now traveled more than two hundred miles pretty much avoiding main roads, but as she moved south in Connecticut, she was headed toward the margins of America's largest metropolis, New York City, and the closer she got, the more major roads had been developed. She needed to stay off them and keep to back roads as much as possible. And she was determined not to dally much longer, given the continuing banks of snow along the side of the road. The weather was taking a decisive turn toward winter.

From Windsor Locks, she headed to South Windsor, where she spent a night on a tobacco farm, then proceeded to the town of Farmington, southwest of Hartford, where Gertrude Austin's mother was expecting her. From there, she passed from town to town, each person sending her along to the home of a friend or relative.

About a week after leaving Windsor Locks, she was south of Waterbury when she noticed a bright red, flashy car, probably, she thought, a Cadillac Coupe de Ville. Annie wasn't very good at recognizing cars at a glance, but she could see that this one was designed to flaunt its charms. While such a speedy-looking specimen might have been expected to whiz right past, this one slowed down and gave the trio a wide berth. Annie waved to the driver and watched his car disappear around a bend.

She was hoping to make it as far as Danbury by nightfall, but Tarzan needed a rest, and she was getting cold—the temperature was dropping. Depeche Toi showed no sign of fatigue; still, Annie wanted to get some food into his belly, so when she saw a diner with a lot of trucks parked outside it, she turned in with her horse and tied him and Depeche Toi to a pole that she'd be able to keep an eye on through the diner's plate-glass window.

Annie always ordered soup for lunch—it was usually the cheapest and most filling thing on the menu. When the steaming bowl was placed in front of her, she was disappointed to see that it was a bit thin, but the hot broth was satisfying. As she ate her soup, she noticed that the same flashy red car she'd seen earlier had just turned in to the parking lot.

The man who slid out from the driver's side had a ruddy face with a deep suntan—unusual for this time of year. He headed straight over to Tarzan. Annie was alarmed, but she had learned that Depeche Toi seemed to know right away when people were friendly, and as the man approached, Depeche Toi began to wriggle and wag his tail.

The man was clearly interested in her horse. He walked all around him, looking his four legs up and down and lingering at his head. If Annie hadn't known better, she would have thought he was fixing to buy Tarzan—or could he be another official from the ASPCA coming to see how the horse was faring? Only he sure didn't look like a veterinarian or an inspector for the ASPCA—not with those gold rings on his fingers.

The suntanned gentleman was still standing near Tarzan when Annie finished her soup and went outside.

"He's not for sale," Annie said.

"Can't say that I blame you," he replied. "He's a sound one. How old?"

"Aged. That's all I know."

The man squinted and tilted his head. "At least fourteen," he said. "Trust me. I'm an expert on horses. Do you really intend to ride him to California?" he asked. His manner was friendly, but he definitely seemed to have more than a polite interest in the answer.

"The Lord willing," Annie responded.

An appraising smile spread across his face. "I've been waiting to meet you and get a good look at this horse," he said. Obviously, they could both see that he was getting as good a look as he wished. All the same, Annie hadn't figured out what else he wanted, and he wasn't tipping his hand.

"I've been offered ten-to-one odds that Tarzan won't make it to the coast."

Her horse flicked a lazy ear back at the sound of his name, but seemed unimpressed with the man—shiny car and gold rings notwithstanding.

Annie placed a hand protectively on her horse's shoulder. "He'll make it," Annie said. "Unless we hear the Pacific has gone dry. He wants to wash his feet in it."

The man laughed. He'd read about that in the newspapers down in Florida, he said. Annie would have thought it impossible that anyone in Florida would even know she existed, but she'd already received letters and invitations from people down south, so she knew that her story had already traveled that far.

"So, I've got some advice for you," he said. "Take it easy. Go slow. Take your time."

Made sense to her.

He added a caveat, however. The load Tarzan was carrying was too big for a single horse. While he might be all right for the time being, he'd never make it through the mountains out west.

"Get a pack horse," he said. He handed her a card with a Waterbury telephone number and told her that she could call him if she ran into any kind of trouble.

Annie was outside Danbury the next day when a state trooper pulled up alongside her. He'd been out looking for her so he could escort her into town, where she had an invitation from another one of Gertrude Austin's friends. While they were talking, Annie mentioned the fellow in the red car and showed the trooper his card.

He laughed. "That's one of the biggest gamblers on the East Coast," he said. "Sounds like he's got a lot of money riding on that horse. He's usually down in Florida at the racetracks this time of year."

The next morning, Annie was back on the road, hoping to make it as far as Brewster, New York, a few miles into her first state beyond New England, when a truck pulled up with a horse van attached. The woman behind the wheel introduced herself as a horse trainer from Brewster and offered them a ride.

This was the closest Annie would get to New York City, and she was surprised by how many horses there were in and around Brewster. Tarzan needed another set of shoes, so she waited for a couple of days for the farrier to have time to tend to him. The next day's ride took her to the far side of Brewster, to Shrub Oak, where she and Tarzan had been invited to spend another comfortable night in a high class hunter-jumper stable.

The ride across Connecticut had been almost strangely easy, but the words of the gambler kept rattling around in her ears, like dice rattling in a cup.

Annie kept thinking about the man's words: *ten-to-one odds.*

When she had set off on this journey, a question of odds hadn't even been in her vocabulary. She had come up with a plan—scrape some money together, get a horse, find work when the money gets low—but she'd never thought of it as a gamble. Annie's motivating factor was faith. She *believed* she'd make it. And if she didn't? Well, you don't always get what you want in this life. When she'd been alone on the farm, setting off to grow her pickling cucumbers, she'd had hope—hope that the future held something for her; but she couldn't have quite said what.

Odds, though—that was a different story. What were her odds? It was hard to even know how to respond to the question. The best answer she could give was that she aimed to try.

*Avoiding danger is no safer in the long run
than outright exposure. The fearful are
caught as often as the bold.*

—Helen Keller

———

CHAPTER

14

Party Time

O N DECEMBER 10, ANNIE and her traveling companions rode
out of Shrub Oak, New York. Her plan for that day was ambi-
tious: to traverse Westchester County and cross the Bear Mountain
Bridge to a riding stable near Bear Mountain State Park that the folks in
Brewster had told her about. The entrance to the bridge was eleven
miles from Shrub Oak. Annie was making good time. Tarzan had spent
every night in a barn, and their journey had been a series of pleasant ten-
to twelve-mile hops. She was hoping to cover about twenty miles today,
a reasonable demand for a fit horse. Tarzan was well rested and well fed
and had a new set of shoes, just ordinary metal ones this time. Depeche
Toi, as always, was ready for anything.

The sun was barely up in the sky when they left, heading west, across
Westchester County on Route 202. Traffic was heavier than she'd seen
up north, but not too bad, and the roads were mostly quiet. It was early
afternoon when they reached the entrance to the bridge—the toll operator told Annie that pedestrians passed free and waved her through. The
two-lane Bear Mountain Bridge, opened in 1924, had enjoyed a brief
moment of glory as the world's longest suspension bridge, before it was

surpassed, only nineteen months later, by the Benjamin Franklin Bridge, which connected Camden, New Jersey, to Philadelphia.

Annie had ridden across a lot of bridges so far—but none like this, a giant suspension construction that spanned a major river. Remembering her near mishap on the very first bridge she had crossed back in Maine, she decided that she'd be best off dismounting and leading the horse across. She slid off Tarzan, landing with a bit of a harder thump than she'd intended. He turned to look at her with an expression that read, *What now?* but gave no resistance as she proceeded to lead him onto the bridge. When they reached the center of the span, the view over the Hudson was magnificent, and the three of them stood for a moment, taking it in. But Annie didn't linger long because a light drizzle was falling and she thought she was still at least several miles away from the stable where they were headed. By the time they'd crossed the bridge, the rain had turned to sleet, and she hoisted herself back on board, knowing that they'd make better time if she let Tarzan set the pace.

The trio headed south on a narrow road, squeezed up against the sheer granite face of the cliffs that ran along the river—on a surface that was now slick with ice. Tarzan lowered his head and picked his way carefully along, and Annie was afraid to hurry him for fear he'd slip. There wasn't much traffic, but the cars that did pass roared by at an alarming speed. Even if they'd wanted to give Annie and her horse some space, there wasn't enough space for them to do so—she wondered if the motorists noticed them, so fast did they zoom past without even slowing down. Annie looked around desperately, hoping she could find somewhere to get off the road—but there was nowhere to go. The sun was sinking, and the pavement was getting icier by the minute.

Each time she heard a car rushing up behind her, she gripped the reins tighter and hoped for the best. As they were moving slowly along a narrow, steep section of road, a loud rumbling crescendoed behind her. Over her shoulder, she saw an out-of-control truck fishtailing down the slope, coming straight toward them. Depeche Toi ran underneath Tarzan; then Annie felt her horse shudder as a blow sent a searing pain through her lower leg. The sickening feeling recalled her long-ago horse-and-wagon injury.

When the truck was past, Tarzan stopped in his tracks, shaking. Annie needed a moment to get her wits about her. She slid down from the saddle and took a tentative step. Her lower leg hurt, but she didn't think it was broken. Depeche Toi was unscathed, and Annie scooped him up. He gave her nose a lick. Tarzan was still visibly trembling. She stroked him and murmured soft words as she looked him over to see if he was hurt; her stomach did a somersault when she saw that he had a sizable gash on his gaskin, the upper part of his hind leg. Taking a closer look, she could tell that the cut was superficial—and it wasn't bleeding too much. She coaxed him to take a few steps forward, and he didn't limp. He was scared out of his mind, but maybe, hopefully, he wasn't seriously injured.

She reached down into her pocket and fished out a couple of sugar cubes she'd snatched from a diner up the road, and he nuzzled them out of her palm. She brushed his long forelock aside and looked into his deep brown eyes. All this time, Tarzan had seemed invincible. To realize that he'd been hurt struck Annie right in the gut. The truck driver had pulled over to make sure she was okay, but once he'd been assured that she was unhurt, he got back into the truck and drove away without offering any further assistance, leaving the three companions alone on the narrow, slippery road. It was now almost dark and still sleeting. By her calculations, they were nowhere near their destination.

Annie stood by the side of the road, half-hoping another car or truck wouldn't come racing around the curve and half-hoping someone *would* show up—someone helpful. She was paralyzed, trying to decide what to do next, with no good solutions at hand. But after a few minutes, she realized that she had no choice: there was no way to escape the spot she had put herself, her injured horse, and her little dog in. She could turn around or she could keep going, but either way, she'd be by the side of the road, with dark falling and sleet coating the ground. And isn't this just how life is anyway? You could plan, but you couldn't control much, except your own two feet and which way you chose to point them. Annie gave Tarzan a reassuring stroke on the neck and allowed Depeche Toi to jump down from her arms, and then the three of them continued along that narrow, icy road in the dark. The flash of headlights temporarily illuminated them as the cars whizzed past, so fast that Annie could hear the roar and the slick sound of wheels on ice. The road looked black, and the way they were dressed, there was nothing to make them stand out from the gloom. No one slowed or stopped to ask about them. On they trudged, hoping that around some bend they would see a welcoming light.

And isn't that what hope is? Not a wish, not a specific thing that you pray will be delivered to you, but merely an expectation that whatever dark, sleety side of the road you might find yourself on will not last forever.

BY THE TIME ANNIE saw a small house in the distance, it was inky dark. She led Tarzan right up to the front stoop and knocked on the door. After a few minutes, a porch light came on, and a man opened the door a crack and listened skeptically to her story. Annie thought she was going to be turned away, until she saw the man's wife appear behind him in the hallway. "Isn't that the woman with the horse that we read about in the papers?" she said. At least the man opened the door wider at that point and heard Annie out. Finally, grudgingly, he said he'd telephone the police in the next town and ask them to help her find a place to stay. In the meantime, she and her animals could wait in the garage.

Annie didn't mean to be ungrateful, because the garage, though unheated, was at least out of the weather, but they waited there for about two hours for the police car to show up. The officer told her that she was nowhere near the stable she'd been shooting for, in Nyack. Instead, he had found a stall for Tarzan in a nearby stable, and now they had to wait for the feed-truck man, who had been awakened, to come pick them up and take them over there. It was very late by the time Annie finally got Tarzan settled into an empty stall, piled up her gear, fed Depeche Toi, and told him to keep an eye on her belongings. She was chilled to the bone. The stable owner demanded that she pay cash up front to rent the stall. Annie pulled the tack off Tarzan, got him settled and comfortable, and cleaned up the cut on his leg, which didn't seem to be bothering him too much.

Her own leg was a different story. It was black-and-blue from knee to ankle and hurt even more now than it had before—maybe because she was letting herself think about it. The stable owner told her she couldn't sleep there—he had his insurance to worry about, he said. She had hoped the police officer would take her to a warm house or, at the very least, the local jail, but instead, he dropped her off at a public garage. Annie tried the door of an empty big-rig truck parked there, found it unlocked, and climbed inside to keep warm. She must have fallen asleep, because the next thing she knew it was morning, and another police officer was banging on the window, telling her to wake up. Fortunately, he'd come to get her and didn't seem to think she'd done any trespassing in the truck. When the officer saw how Annie was limping, he insisted on taking her to see a doctor. And the doctor insisted on keeping her in the hospital while he X-rayed her leg.

Two days passed before the doctor cleared her to leave. Back at the stable where she'd left her animals, she was relieved to find Tarzan looking healthy, his cut all but healed. Before long, they were back on the road. As the crow flies, Annie was not more than thirty-five miles from Manhattan, and while the stretch of land between the Bear Mountain Bridge and northern New Jersey was hilly and rural, with the suburban towns surrounded by open countryside, she still noticed that the drivers were more apt to speed by without thinking to slow down and give the animals some space, and strangers were no longer so friendly when she knocked on their doors.

The coming of television and mass media to America had an unexpected effect: it was bringing stories of crime from all over America right to people's doorsteps.

Annie wasn't following the news, but a high-profile murder trial, the Sheppard murder, was the hottest story of December 1954. On the night of July 3, 1954, a handsome Ohio neurosurgeon, Sam Sheppard, and his wife, Marilyn, had entertained neighbors at their shorefront home on Lake Erie, near Cleveland. Early the next morning, Marilyn Sheppard had been found bludgeoned to death in her bed. Sheppard claimed that he'd been sleeping soundly on a daybed when he'd heard the cries from his wife. He'd run upstairs to the bedroom, seen a shadowy form, and been knocked out from a blow. Sheppard, who had pleaded innocent, claimed that his memory was fuzzy, as he'd been hit over the head, but he blamed his wife's death on a "bushy-haired intruder," a stranger. Now the entire country was focused on the trial's verdict, which would come on December 21.

As Annie and Tarzan traveled south toward the New Jersey border, she was not thinking of bushy-haired strangers or murder most foul. But she was worried. The roads here seemed much more crowded than back home. Plus, it wasn't just people and cars that had her concerned. She'd been on the road for more than a month, heading south the whole time—or more or less south—and it was not much warmer here than it would have been in Maine. That surprised her. She had been keeping track of the days by looking at newspapers, and she knew she was going to turn sixty-three somewhere along this desolate road. It seemed a lonely stretch to Annie, and she knew she'd have to cross much of New Jersey and some of Pennsylvania before she felt like she was getting anywhere remotely close to the South.

Now Annie and her companions were still traveling along Route 202, which hugged the Hudson River as far as Haverstraw before cutting west. The road was surprisingly rural for its location, running along the eastern edge of Bear Mountain State Park. She'd be crossing into the Garden State before long.

New Jersey has been called the birthplace of motor trucking. The New Jersey Turnpike had opened to great fanfare in 1951. Situated as the southern portal to the great city of New York, the state had made the jump into motor transport early, working to improve roads, reduce tariffs, and even advocate for building the Holland Tunnel to better connect it to the metropolis. In Annie's Maine, the nineteenth century still felt close. By contrast, New Jersey had raced into the twentieth century with motors roaring. Annie had worked out a route that would allow her to skirt New York City, but crossing New Jersey on horseback would not be easy. She had planned to stay on Route 202 across the entire state, unaware that this road was known as the chief east-west truck route.

Fortunately, unbeknownst to her, she had had a stroke of luck. The truck drivers along the route were spreading word of the zany trio crossing their state on foot. The truckers began to keep tabs on her, stopping to give her advice on road hazards or the best places to find a decent cup of coffee or bowl of soup. She had never seen so many giant trucks in her life. Tarzan didn't like them, but Annie began to look forward to the sight of them—especially after she passed along word that they should definitely *not* honk as they passed. And it wasn't just the truckers who'd adopted Annie. She soon learned that each police department across New Jersey would provide her with an escort as she passed through its jurisdiction, and the officers would make sure that she and her animals had places to stay.

On December 13, Annie was not even a quarter of the way across the state. The weather was gray and cold. Earlier in the day, two young patrolmen had met up with her to tell her that she should plan to stop when she reached the town of Wayne, where they'd arranged a cot for her in the town's jail and found a stable for Tarzan. Annie had joked that it would be fitting, since today was her birthday and she had been born in a jail. About an hour later, when she reached the edge of town, she found the same two patrolmen waiting for her. After they escorted her to the station, one officer led Tarzan away, assuring Annie that he'd found comfortable lodgings and that the horse would be well cared for, while the other showed her and Depeche Toi the small jail cell and told her to freshen up. He was taking her to his home to meet his wife for dinner.

The home of Irene and Joseph Mikalczyk was a spacious Dutch Colonial set back from a wooded residential road. The officer's young wife was a lively brunette with a flash of mischief in her eyes. She greeted Annie warmly, with an air of barely suppressed glee. Instead of inviting

Annie inside, she beckoned her toward the garage. With a flourish, Joseph lifted the garage door and out came a giant cheer: "Surprise!" The garage was filled with smiling people, balloons, and signs reading "Happy Birthday!" From the crowd, Annie heard a familiar whicker, and Depeche Toi, tail thumping, squirmed out of her arms and disappeared underfoot. As people parted, there stood Tarzan, eyes bright, as if to say, *Got here first!* At his feet was a rubber bucket filled with steaming oats. Around his neck was a rope of flowers.

"We couldn't let you pass through Wayne without celebrating your birthday," Irene said. The rest of the evening raced by in a blur as Annie's kind hosts filled her plate with Polish delicacies—and Tarzan was not forgotten. He had a special dish of hot wine over oats, which the hosts explained was a Polish tradition. For Annie and Depeche Toi, there were gifts wrapped in ribbons and bright paper. When Annie unwrapped the presents, she found two pairs of fur-lined gloves, and for Depeche Toi, there was a packet of dried beef liver.

At the end of the evening, a horse trailer came and picked up Tarzan to truck him to a nearby stable, and a patrolman drove Annie back to the Wayne police department's building, where the officers had made up a comfortable bed. That night, before she went to sleep, she filled up pages and pages of her diary, describing the people she'd met and the food she'd eaten, and the many kindnesses she'd been shown.

To remember a birthday as special as this one, she had to go all the way back to her fourth, when Grandfather Libby had given her a dark red Durham milking heifer, along with a note of transfer that read, "Delivered to my granddaughter, Annie, in care of her mother. Signed, George Libby."

The next morning Annie was heading toward Philadelphia, but she wasn't destined to make it very far that day. She had just reached the outskirts of Wayne when a truck towing a horse trailer pulled up alongside her and a dark-haired young woman burst out and introduced herself.

"My name is Millie Rose," she announced, and she explained firmly that she'd come to pick up Annie and her animals. They needed a rest, and she aimed to give it to them. She had a big house and lots of room in Trenton. Annie and her animals were spending Christmas with Millie and her husband. Annie tried to protest. She'd been planning to spend Christmas in Philadelphia, but Millie insisted.

Annie could see that Millie Rose was adept with animals. She swiftly loaded up Tarzan and invited Annie and Depeche Toi to climb into the cab. It was almost midnight when they arrived at Rose's Riding Academy in the White Horse neighborhood of Trenton, seventy miles south of Wayne. Millie's property, forty acres that she and her husband had purchased cheap in the 1930s, dated back to the Revolutionary War. Their home had been built in 1773. The spacious two-story brick Georgian structure was faded but stately, its eight front windows gracefully topped with limestone lintels. The acreage that spread out behind it was incongruous in what was now an urban neighborhood; in subsequent years, the Roses would fight a mostly losing battle with the county, which wanted to annex their land to build roads. When the back part of their farm was seized by eminent domain to make a highway, the Roses' daughter, a teenager at the time, sneaked out in the middle of the night and galloped a giant Percheron over the just-graded dirt surface—so furious was she to see her horses' pastures paved over. But all of that was still in the future when Annie arrived at the Rose academy—and the house and its lands still looked much as they had looked during the Revolutionary era.

Annie couldn't help noticing right away that the Rose house was full of pets: twelve monkeys, ten cats, a rabbit, a black bird that could cuss, and even a llama. As if that weren't enough, they had some two dozen dalmatians. All of their animals had been rescued, Millie explained. "We don't like people who abuse animals," she said. "People can call the police, but animals can't." The house's cellar still had a dirt floor, and that was where the Roses raised baby lambs and goats.

Millie introduced Annie to her husband, Carney, a wiry cowboy and trick rider with bright eyes and a warm smile. They had a big stable with plenty of room for Tarzan. Their own horses ranged from a giant twenty-one-and-a-half-hand Percheron, to the tiny miniature ponies Millie trained to perform with monkeys riding on their backs, to Carney's trick horse, Fox, who performed widely at horse shows and state fairs. In his most remarkable trick, Fox would lie down at the command "Play dead" and remain so utterly still that he appeared not to breathe. The way the horses whinnied when the Roses entered the barn, and the way Carney and his wife took time to greet each of them by name, as if they were all old friends, signaled to Annie that these were people for whom animals were members of the family.

They had prepared a comfortable stall for Tarzan, knee-deep in fresh straw, with a hay net bursting with fragrant timothy and a bucket of rolled oats. A large bag of carrots leaned up against the wall outside his stall, and Carney fished an apple out of his pocket and offered it to Tarzan when he said hello. As Annie settled her horse in, Carney unpacked all her stuff, clucking about the fact that she really ought to be distributing the weight of the gear better, while Millie explained that she'd been following the trio's journey in the papers and thought it was high time that Annie's horse and her dog had a decent rest. Annie chuckled at the way this woman put it—no mention of Annie herself needing a rest. She could tell she was going to get along with the Roses. They thought about animals just the way she did.

Millie Rose wasn't kidding. She simply wouldn't hear of Annie going back out on the road until the first of the year. The Rose household was a crazy menagerie, with critters wandering freely around the premises. It reminded Annie of the times back in Maine when she'd bottle-fed her piglets and they'd grown up so tame that they'd stroll into her little house whenever they pleased, which she never minded, even though she knew it made the neighbors gossip. Life was lively around the Rose household, and not just because of all the pets. Carney was a great raconteur—full of old stories about his days on the rodeo circuit and his stint training animals for Ringling Bros.

Rose's Riding Academy was more than a haven for animals. Neighborhood children with nowhere else to go could get off the school bus at the stop in front of the stables and spend their afternoons there while their parents worked double shifts. Carney believed that horses could keep children off the streets. He never had to say a stern word. His philosophy of how to treat kids was the same as the way he treated horses: give them something to do and they'd stay out of trouble. If a child wanted to ride and the family had no money, Carney would loan a pony, because at Rose's Riding Academy, there was always a spare one around.

Carney had grown up with horses. He and Millie had married young—love at first sight. In 1954, they had not yet started a family. Their animals were their only children. Carney had taught Millie everything he knew. He was ahead of his time in believing that a woman could do anything a man could do. "Never wait for a man to help you—you can help yourself," he liked to say. And Millie had been an eager learner; there was no task too difficult for her. She could even shoe a horse. Part Native American and part Irish and all no-nonsense, Millie was a true animal whisperer, born with a seemingly innate ability to communicate with all kinds of creatures. But woe unto any person who didn't meet her high standards for their humane treatment.

Annie had met so many kind people along her way, but with the Roses, she felt a deep connection. When Christmas came, the day was a delightful hodgepodge celebration of animals and people, and most of the morning was spent out at the barn, mixing up hot bran mashes for the horses and serving up meaty bones for the dogs. It was the biggest four-footed-and-two-footed celebration anyone could possibly imagine. Annie, Tarzan, and Depeche Toi felt right at home, and, unexpectedly, Depeche Toi even got along beautifully with the monkeys.

The Roses made their credo clear: they adopted anyone, four-footed or two-footed, who seemed as though they needed friendship, kindness, and shelter. Annie did not have to leave. Carney and Millie both thought that Annie should stay all winter. What was the hurry? They could put her to work around the barn.

Annie did consider their kind offer, but in the end, she decided she just couldn't stay. She didn't want to take advantage of their hospitality, no matter how freely given, and she needed to keep moving south if she was to have any hope of getting past the worst of the winter weather.

Finally, Carney and Millie agreed to let her go. Carney helped Annie completely rearrange her packing system, both to make it more efficient and to lighten Tarzan's load. The Roses wished her all good fortune and gave her a ride to the outskirts of Philadelphia, where they'd arranged to have an officer from the Fairmount Park Mounted Guard meet her. It was a new year and she was on her way.

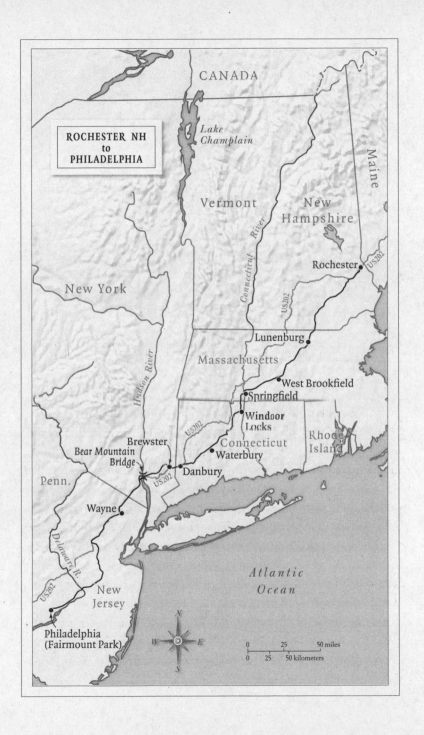

CANADA

ROCHESTER NH
to
PHILADELPHIA

Lake Champlain

Connecticut River

Vermont

New Hampshire

Maine

New York

Rochester

US202

US202

Lunenburg

Massachusetts

Hudson River

West Brookfield

Springfield

Windsor Locks

US202

Brewster

Connecticut

Rhode Island

Bear Mountain Bridge

Waterbury

US202

Danbury

Penn.

Wayne

Delaware R.

US202

New Jersey

Atlantic Ocean

Philadelphia
(Fairmount Park)

N
W   E
S

| 0 | 25 | 50 miles |

| 0 | 25 | 50 kilometers |

How dreary—to be—Somebody!
How public—like a Frog—
To tell one's name—the livelong June—
To an admiring Bog!

—Emily Dickinson

———

1955

———

CHAPTER

15

The Clover Leaf Inn

THROUGHOUT MOST OF THE eighteenth and nineteenth centuries, Philadelphia was America's second-largest city, before falling to third place (behind Chicago) in 1890. Still, the city that Annie motored across in 1955 was many times bigger than any place she had yet seen along her way. The City of Brotherly Love reached its peak population in 1950—it would decline by almost half a million citizens in the following years. One of the city's most redoubtable institutions, the Philadelphia Police Mounted Patrol Unit, had once had sixteen stables in the city and more than 160 horses. But in 1952, twelve of the remaining forty-four horses were transferred to the Fairmount Park Association, and the rest were sold off at auction. A local paper mourned the loss: "Familiar facets of Philadelphia join the old lamplighter in limbo today. . . . Authorities no longer believe that horses have a place on the crowded city streets." The last twelve horses were retained only for parades and other ceremonies.

Annie Wilkins had announced to the press that she intended to ride Tarzan straight through the city. But it turned out that the police did not want Annie riding on Philadelphia's busy thoroughfares. Instead, they arranged for the mounted patrol to truck Annie across town, stopping just long enough for the trio to pose for a press photo along Roosevelt Boulevard, and for Annie to drop in to the central post office so that she could retrieve her mail. Tarzan spent a couple of nights at the mounted patrol stables in Fairmount Park, where the patrolmen had gotten together a collection to buy him a new set of shoes, a welcome gift as he'd not been shod since Brewster and the shoes took a beating with his long days on pavement. Bright and early the next morning, two mounted patrol officers rode with Annie, Tarzan, and Depeche Toi along the beautiful bridle trails of the twenty-four-hundred-acre Fairmount Park.

Leaving the leafy remoteness of Fairmount Park, Annie, Tarzan, and Depeche Toi headed west on City Avenue. Since the 1890s, City Avenue had been a thoroughfare for streetcars, first horse-drawn, then eventually electric. Philadelphia's western suburbs were some of the oldest suburban towns in America. First platted in the seventeenth century, this expanse was one of the first urban areas in America to push its populace outside the city limits, creating a pattern where people lived away from where they worked. Philadelphia added train lines in the 1850s and streetcars in the 1890s, making the small surrounding towns accessible for commuters. The western suburbs, in particular the Main Line, which stretched northwest along Route 30, had some of the country's most concentrated wealth.

The patrolmen escorted her as far as Cobbs Creek before bidding her safe travels. Their parting directions were clear: just keep heading down the Baltimore Pike, they told her. She hoped to make it as far as Media, thirteen miles away, a leisurely amble, especially after several days of rest. The weather was holding up—crisp and cold but with no rain or snow in the forecast.

Annie's saddlebags were stuffed with all of her mail. Tarzan was in good spirits, full of pep as he zigged and zagged along the side of the road, taking small hops whenever a truck rumbled by. Here at the city's edge, there was still a constant flow of traffic. Depeche Toi was riding in front of her. There was still too much traffic for her to let him trot alongside. Sometimes, when she was riding along a quiet stretch, she would read letters, but here, with Tarzan acting jumpy, she felt that she needed to give the road her full attention.

At some level, Annie was surprised to find herself on the far side of Philadelphia in the new year of 1955. Sure, she'd had faith when she'd started out—and plenty of gumption. Still, she had given the folks back home only two places to send her mail: Springfield and Philadelphia. She'd always heard that it was much warmer once you got to Pennsylvania. The way she'd figured it, she'd be out of money by then and out of New England, and maybe she could find some work down there. Seemed like a good enough plan before she left, but she'd learned two big things along the way. One: people in Maine overestimated how warm it was in Pennsylvania in January. And two: most strangers are a lot more generous than you'd think they would be.

She'd never have guessed how little money she'd have to spend along the way. Annie had paid for so few meals and so few beds, and she had been turning a tidy profit in nickels and dimes as she'd sold her autographed notecards. So far, almost nothing had been as she'd expected.

So now here she was clopping past her modest expectations—Philadelphia at her back and still moving along with her health holding up and money in her pocket. As she headed toward the town of Media, she wasn't sure what would come next. Maybe she'd find a place to sleep. The rest of what might unfold remained a mystery.

Annie didn't know it at the time, but the road she was traveling along—labeled as Route 1 but known locally as the Baltimore Pike—was one of America's celebrated "auto trails"; it connected Philadelphia to Baltimore. Before roads had state numbers, they were marked by colored paint on utility poles or trees along the routes, helping early car tourists to navigate. This western route out of Philadelphia had historic significance: Union troops marched west along it during the Civil War, and it was an important avenue along the Underground Railroad. Here was a road that had once been well suited for travel by horseback, its inns and taverns strategically spaced a day's ride apart, each with a stable for horses and an ample supply of food and ale, as well as a bed, for travelers.

But in the mid-1950s, the western suburbs of Philadelphia were expanding exponentially, and along the Baltimore Pike the road was changing rapidly, flanked by new car dealerships and modern businesses. Automobile travelers could stop for quick meals at modern restaurants like the Fernwood Diner, in East Landsdowne, with its iconic 1950s architectural style of rounded angles and gleaming chrome.

But even in this modern landscape, there were ample reminders of the past. As Annie neared Media, she was approaching the site of the former Black Horse Inn. For two hundred years, the eighteenth-century stone structure had been a familiar landmark along the Baltimore Pike, a way station for weary travelers heading to and from Philadelphia. By the 1930s, there were so many automobiles traveling along this road that a brand-new cloverleaf intersection was slated to be constructed at the corner of Route 1 and Route 352, a bypass that led into the borough of Media. The cloverleaf would be located right at the spot where the Black Horse Inn had welcomed travelers since before the Revolution.

Locals were angry and fought hard to prevent the destruction of the historic structure that had housed Continental Army soldiers on their way to the Battle of Brandywine, but when the county's first cloverleaf intersection was unveiled, the inn was gone. Progress. Cloverleaf intersections were considered the state of the art in highway design when they were first introduced. Most automobile accidents occurred at intersections, so the cloverleaf was deemed an engineering marvel, allowing traffic to flow freely through intersections with no stops—thus cutting down on accidents as well as traffic jams. They were plunked down outside towns, gobbling up empty land, as well as any structures in their way. Outside Media, not far from the location of the old Black Horse, there was a new inn and restaurant, called what else but the Clover Leaf Inn, built near the highway to encourage business from motorists. But by 1955, the novelty of the intersection had already faded, and locals assumed that the Clover Leaf Inn was named for good luck, not for the once marvelous but now commonplace highway interchange.

As Annie approached the outskirts of Media, she wasn't thinking about highway engineering—she was looking for a likely place to spend the night. Since she'd left Philadelphia, she'd not been approached by anyone offering her an escort or a place to sleep. She was back to figuring it out on her own. She'd had a good day of riding, though. Tarzan had settled down as they'd gotten away from the city congestion, and Depeche Toi seemed delighted to be out in the countryside again. When she spotted the sign for the Clover Leaf Inn, it did indeed seem like an intimation of good luck. Here was a cozy-looking spot, with a pasture full of equines out back. Tarzan whinnied a greeting, and the three inhabitants of the pasture, two horses and a donkey, trotted over to the fence to greet him.

Bonnie D'Ignazio, ten years old, was upstairs in her family's apartment above the restaurant when she looked out the window and saw Annie and Tarzan clopping down the road toward them. She could scarcely believe her eyes. This woman, her horse, and her little dog seemed to come out of nowhere. A moment later, Bonnie heard a knock on their door. She ran downstairs, following her mother, and sure enough, there was the same woman, now on foot but holding her horse's reins, standing on their doorstep.

Ida D'Ignazio was born to be an innkeeper's wife. A pretty black-haired woman, she was always neatly attired in starched dresses and shiny pumps, even when going about her daily chores. When she did housework, she simply tied an apron around her waist. She exuded a quiet warmth that made her guests feel welcome. Annie looked more like a tramp than a potential guest at the inn, but Ida listened as Annie asked if she might leave her horse in the pasture overnight. Bonnie, hiding behind her mother, full of wonder at this out-of-the-ordinary turn of events, listened raptly as the woman recounted her story. Her horse's name was Tarzan. The two of them had ridden all the way from Maine, and most astonishing of all, she planned to ride all the way to California. Bonnie held her breath, hoping that her mother would not turn this fascinating stranger away—but she needn't have worried. Ida was always collecting strays—adopting animals that wandered onto their property, inviting

lonely people over for meals when she thought they had nowhere else
to go.

She called her son, Leonard, to help get Tarzan settled in the pasture.
And then, to Bonnie's delight, she invited Annie to spend the night in
the inn as their guest. The local Lions Club was meeting that evening for
dinner at the Clover Leaf, and Ida supposed that they'd be interested if
Annie would join them for dinner and tell them all about her unusual
journey.

In Media, the local newspaper had recently declared that "Reds"
were not welcome in Delaware County, but apparently no such restric-
tions applied to horseback hoboes. Annie, who had to just get over some
of her qualms about her clothing, was seated as the guest of honor at the
table and invited to give a speech to the assembled Lions. A newspaper
article later described the evening: "The Lions stayed up until 1:30 A.M.,
roaring with laughter."

The D'Ignazios insisted that Annie stay with them long enough for
Ida to have time to do all of her laundry. As Annie packed up, she had
fresh-smelling clothing, a week's worth of sandwiches, and, for Tarzan, a
sack of carrots and a sack of apples.

Tarzan stood patiently as she loaded him up piece by piece, following the packing system Carney Rose had invented for her. Now, with the
efficiency of practice, she went through her routine: first halter, then
bridle, her wool saddle pad, and her McClellan saddle, worn as soft as
butter from her long daily rides. Next came the blanket rolls, efficiently
secured with leather straps, and the saddlebags, stuffed with postcards
and letters on one side and her notecards, her source for money, on the
other side. She pulled on her two wool union suits, fresh from the laundry, her dungarees, and two shirts. She affixed her bonnet over her hair,
and her wool buffalo plaid coat, and got ready to hit the road. She was
headed toward the next sizable town along the Baltimore Pike: Kennett
Square. She'd heard that the police were friendly there, and that they'd
most likely help her find a place to stay.

The countryside along the pike was mainly wooded and, past Media,
quiet and rural. The weather was cold, and maybe she'd gone a bit soft,

staying in the warmth of the D'Ignazios' inn, because the biting chill seemed to cut through her clothing.

People had told her that when she reached the corner where the Baltimore Pike crossed the Wilmington–West Chester Pike, she'd head downhill a ways, and, before long, see George Washington's headquarters. Annie was traveling along a road once known as "Ye Great Road to Nottingham," along the same route once traveled by Lafayette and George Washington himself. She knew that her ancestors on both sides, Stuarts and Libbys, had fought in the Revolution. She wondered if any of them had ridden this route just as she was doing now.

A while past noon, she passed the small town of Concordville, with its white frame Methodist church, which reminded her of the churches back in Maine. She paused to look in the window of the drugstore's soda fountain. She was so cold that it seemed appealing to stop for a hot cup of coffee, but she decided to keep going. Tarzan was stepping along calmly, taking an interest in everything around him, not too jumpy today on this quiet road, and Depeche Toi was poking his nose into whatever he could. His tail was plumed up, making a half-wag with each of his rapid strides. She'd be better off getting where she was going than stopping now.

Past the Wilmington–West Chester Pike, she rode through an area of woodlands interspersed with fields. Tucked behind high hedges here and there were grand estates—elegant houses of wealthy country people, with barns and garages and lawns and, she guessed, plenty of servants. Annie was starting to think she might need to begin looking for a place to stay. The roadway had been hillier than she'd expected, and she hadn't seen anything that looked like a town since Concordville. But she didn't have the guts to approach any of these estates—their giant wrought-iron gates were not welcoming, and the houses that, she figured, must lay beyond some of them couldn't even be seen from the road.

It was already past three when she spotted a small cluster of buildings, down in a valley with a broad creek with a bridge across it, just beyond. The water was rushing by, brown and choppy, with ice caught up on the reeds and brambles that grew along its edges.

At first she wondered if this was Kennett Square, but it didn't look like a town proper. From where she sat aboard Tarzan, all she could see beyond the bridge was the road heading up a long series of hills—it was a bit daunting to confront such terrain so late in the day. But then she spotted a diner with a sign that said "George's Place," and again she was tempted at the thought of a hot cup of coffee. Tarzan was still moving along energetically, though, and Depeche Toi was chipper as always, and if she was planning to make it to her destination, she knew she had better press on while she still had light.

As it happened, Annie didn't get far. A group of neighborhood kids seemed to come out of nowhere, clustering around Annie and Tarzan and stooping down to pet Depeche Toi, who reveled in the attention.

Then Annie heard a voice calling out to her. She looked up to see a woman wiping her hands on her apron as she stepped out onto the wide wooden porch of a building with a sign out front that read "Chadds Ford Inn."

She asked where Annie was headed, and when Annie pointed west—in the direction of the river and the railroad tracks—the woman shook her head. "All hills between here and there, and it's late in the day. You better get off that horse. We'll put him back in the stables. You can spend the night, and we'll give you a hot meal." The woman added kindly, "We're not full up, so I'll charge half price and kick in dinner. How does that sound?"

Annie looked up at the hills in the distance and realized she'd better stop after all. The woman introduced herself as Eleanor Flaherty. She showed Annie to a room in the inn and told her to come down for supper when she was ready.

Later that evening, Annie came down to the tavern. There was a big fire roaring in the high fireplace, and wooden tables scattered around the interior. A couple seated in the corner called Annie over, asking if she was the woman on horseback from Maine. They'd spent some time in Maine themselves, they said, and invited her to join them for dinner.

The man, who introduced himself as Andy, had the ruddy, lined skin of an outdoorsman and was dressed in simple farm clothes, but he still had the look of a city boy about him. His wife was sturdy and handsome. Her name was Betsy.

Annie soon learned that Andy had spent a good bit of time in Mid-Coast Maine, about eighty miles east of Minot. He was a painter, he said, but he mostly seemed interested in hearing from Annie. He bought drinks and asked her lots of questions. Annie kept them in stitches telling them about Uncle Waldo and the farm in Maine, and the pigs that used to get loose and run around the neighborhood. Andy continued to call for rounds of drinks, while Annie regaled them with stories. The rest of the patrons in the inn, used to the eccentricities of their most famous citizen, watched the unusual dinner party with amusement.

The following morning, when Annie went out to the barn to get Tarzan, she found this same fellow sketching her horse, with Depeche Toi settled companionably at his feet. She thought it was a good likeness and told him so. By the time she left, the Flahertys had explained to Annie that the man she'd charmed was Andrew Wyeth. In 1963, the celebrated painter would grace the cover of *Time* magazine. But even if Annie had understood just how famous Wyeth was, she wouldn't have acted any differently. She didn't look down on the down-and-out; nor did she look up to the high-and-mighty. She was imbued with an innate sense that we were all created equal—people, animals, rich, poor, everyone. Had she asked him for the sketch of Tarzan, she would have had something much more valuable to sell than her dime-apiece notecards; but instead she told him he'd better hurry up and finish, because she needed to get on the road.

Eleanor Flaherty came out onto the porch to wave goodbye as Tarzan, Annie, and Depeche Toi departed, heading the short distance to the bridge and the railroad tracks beyond. She could see ice trapped on the Brandywine, which was a dark brown color on this gray January day; luckily, there was none on the road. It had rained overnight, but no rain was falling now—though it was cold. The Flahertys had assured her that she could ride to Kennett Square in less than a day—and the weather report was not predicting rain or snow. So Annie headed toward the bridge across the Brandywine feeling confident.

The bridge itself was narrower than the road, and along its sides were iron cables. As they stepped onto the concrete span, Annie thought she felt Tarzan's front foot slide a little, but she assumed that he was adjusting to the unaccustomed surface. She didn't realize that the bridge was covered with a thin sheet of ice. As Tarzan picked his way carefully along, Annie heard the susurration of the water rushing underneath them, the crisp *clang clang* of Tarzan's metal shoes, and the creaking of the saddle. She didn't at first hear the *rat-a-tat,* like a series of small explosions, of a rattling truck, moving fast, belching out backfires like small bursts of gunshot.

Tarzan's ears flicked forward and back, and his head flew up. He spooked rapidly sideways. Annie grabbed hold of his neck with both hands, trying to stay on. His front hooves landed over the cable that served as a guardrail along the side of the bridge—and her 170 pounds of weight went one way while the saddle went the other way. With one foot still in the stirrup, Annie crashed to the ground as the truck sped by. Tarzan's hind legs slipped out from under him, but he managed to right himself and stay on the bridge; Annie, however, felt her leg twist and catch in the stirrup as her body slammed against the icy road. She was dangling half off the bridge, the roaring of the brown river underneath her. She kicked, trying to free her foot from the stirrup, and Tarzan stepped sideways, closer to the abyss . . .

Both horse and dangling rider were about to go over and plunge into the icy stream when Depeche Toi, always alert to danger, ran in front of Tarzan, barking at him, and the horse took a half step back. At the same moment, Annie was able to kick her foot out of her boot. That was the last thing she remembered until she looked up and saw John Flaherty, from the inn, peering down at her with a worried expression on his face. When Depeche Toi saw Annie's eyes open, he wriggled forward and licked her on the face. But where was Tarzan? She tried to sit up, and realized that she was dizzy and her head ached. Tarzan stood a few feet away, his brown eyes looking straight at her. When she said his name weakly, he nickered.

Flaherty and some other men helped Annie to her feet. He explained that they'd been able to extricate her horse from the bridge's cables without much trouble and that he didn't seem hurt. But Annie was clearly unsteady on her feet.

"You're coming back with us," Flaherty said.

Annie wanted to protest, only she realized that there was no way she could move ahead in this condition. So back to the inn they went, the trio having traveled no more than a few hundred yards. The Flahertys put Tarzan back in the stables, with Depeche Toi to keep him company, and Annie rested.

When she felt mostly herself again, she told the Flahertys she couldn't accept their hospitality a minute longer. Annie packed up Tarzan and, because she wasn't taking any chances, led him and Depeche Toi across the bridge, this time without mishap.

Annie kept walking, across Ring Road, where Andrew Wyeth's father, the illustrator N. C. Wyeth, had been killed in 1945 when a train collided with his car, and up the long stretch of winding hills that rose like blue clouds in the distance. By midafternoon, she'd reached the Old Kennett Meetinghouse and passed the grand estate of Pierre S. du Pont, who had died in April of the year before and whose estate would open to the public in 1956 as Longwood Gardens.

As they plodded along, Annie could understood why Eleanor Flaherty had told her that she would never make it to Kennett Square that first day. The nine miles between Chadds Ford and Kennett Square seemed interminable. To make matters worse, as they went along, Annie noticed that Tarzan was favoring his right hind leg, and from the way Depeche Toi kept close, she could tell that he was worried, too. Tarzan seemed agreeable enough, and Annie kept muttering different kinds of encouragement to him—though she wasn't sure if it was more for him or for herself. When she realized her horse was straining, she climbed off and began to lead him.

The long uphill climb finally settled back into more of a downhill slope, and at last she saw the brick buildings of the borough of Kennett Square. As soon as she reached the outskirts of town, Annie looked for someone to tell her where to find a veterinarian. But the first person she ran into was a reporter from the *Wilmington Morning News*. He was staked out on the highway where it led into town; he'd been waiting to interview her.

"Aren't you scared to travel alone?" the man asked.

Normally, Annie didn't mind speaking to the reporters, but right now, she was worried about Tarzan and in no mood. "I'm trying to find a veterinarian to take a look at my horse," she said, hoping her curt tone would discourage him.

Luckily, when it came to veterinarians, she had happened upon the right place. Just a bit farther up the road, she would run smack-dab into more horse veterinarians than she knew what to do with. The equine veterinary center for the University of Pennsylvania, the Bolton Center, was just up the road. The *New* Bolton Center, a bystander insisted. The vet school had moved into a brand-new location that year.

Annie was made to understand that the New Bolton Center usually took care of a much higher class of horses than Tarzan; its personnel were famed for their ability to get a racehorse, or a steeplechaser, or a show horse back on its feet. But Annie was determined to find a doc to look at Tarzan's leg. She figured her horse was as good as any—and better than most.

It was late in the afternoon when they ambled into the stables of the New Bolton Center. Just over two months had passed since their departure from Minot.

At the veterinary outpost, Annie managed to find a vet who was willing to take a look at Tarzan. She watched anxiously as he made an overall survey of the horse, then spent extra time examining the sore right hind leg. If her horse wasn't fit to go on, she knew she'd have to stop now. She was just far enough away from home to make it hard to get back, and not far enough south to have beaten the winter. Depeche Toi, as was his habit, ran off to explore the stables, but sensing Annie's worries, he came back and jumped into her arms. She petted him absentmindedly as she watched the vet carefully probing Tarzan's bruised leg.

When she got nervous, Annie tended to ramble on, and so she prattled about how she was heading for Roanoke and from there was planning to travel toward Memphis, how she'd started out from Minot and hoped to make it to California, and on and on. The veterinarian didn't say much, just slowly slid his fingers along each nook and cranny in Tarzan's leg. When he gave the horse's fetlock a little squeeze, Tarzan flinched and stepped a bit to the side.

"I figure I weigh about two hundred pounds all told, by the time you add everything I'm carrying. It's a lot of weight for a horse. People have told me I should get a pack horse . . ."

The vet continued to ignore her, but at last he turned and spoke. His manner was matter-of-fact, but Annie could see that he was not thinking that anything Annie had told him made the slightest bit of sense. It was January. She wouldn't find warmer weather until she got significantly farther south. Did she have any idea just how far it was to Memphis, Tennessee? Her horse was not badly injured, but he needed a rest. The vet didn't say much else, then walked away.

Annie was left to contemplate her future there in the drafty barn. She leaned in close, letting Tarzan's nose rub against her cheek, as she settled into the idea that she'd just run into a major flaw in her plans. She hadn't gotten as far as figuring out what she should do about it when the vet came back.

"You're going to stay here the night," he said. "That horse needs a rest. Between here and warmer places there are bridges and mountains and tunnels, and your horse is not going to make it all the way. I've arranged a ride for you. A fellow by the name of Vernon Mercer is going down to Kentucky to pick up some Thoroughbreds. He'll give you a ride in his empty van." A ride in a van as far as Kentucky? How much could that possibly cost? And why would anyone even want to do her such a big favor? Annie didn't know what to say.

She could see that the veterinarian wasn't going to budge. She was not going to ride out of there, and that was final. And she could understand his point. Snow was falling outside, she was still stiff and sore from the hard fall on the bridge, and Tarzan definitely needed a break. Maybe when they got down south she could take a pause to figure things out, but right now, the offer of a ride sounded too good to pass up.

"I don't have much money," Annie said.

"He's driving down there anyway. I don't think he's going to ask you for much."

BY 1957, IT WOULD be possible to get on a highway and drive from New York City to Chicago without hitting a single traffic sign. In January 1955, when Annie climbed into the cab of Vernon Mercer's horse van, where Tarzan had been comfortably settled, the easternmost part of the Pennsylvania Turnpike, one of the early marvels of highway engineering in the United States, was not yet complete. The pike had been designed to make it easier for motorcars to cross the mountains in the western part of the state, and was intended to be almost completely flat. Seven tunnels had been specially constructed to pass through rather than over the higher elevations, and because much of the road was rural, modern rest stops had been built alongside the highway, with easy on and off access in both directions. The Pennsylvania Turnpike also marked a departure from all of the rural routes and highways Annie had followed so far. Horses were specifically barred from it, and from all of its roadways and tunnels.

As they sped along the highway and through its tunnels, Annie started to sense for the first time just how vast the expanses were that she was trying to travel on horseback. She realized that she could have slogged along all through January and never made it across Pennsylvania. At least, with this ride, she had a fighting chance to make it through the winter. If providence hadn't brought her to that place, she didn't know what she would have done. For the first time since leaving Minot, Annie, Tarzan, and Depeche Toi were actually headed toward California, or at least in a significantly westward direction. Aboard the horse van, they crossed through Pennsylvania, headed south through West Virginia, and into Kentucky.

The horse van's destination was the heart of Thoroughbred country, just thirteen miles east of Lexington.

*Adhere to your purpose and you will soon feel as well as
you ever did. . . . If you falter, and give up,
you will lose the power of keeping any resolution,
and will regret it all your life.*

—**Abraham Lincoln**

—

Log Cabins

ON JANUARY 10, 1955, after spinning along the highways for forty-eight hours, Annie, Tarzan, and Depeche Toi arrived in Kentucky, stopping for a break just a few miles east of Paris. They'd been driven more than six hundred miles. Annie was excited to have come so far—the distance she'd traveled in just two days by truck was more than a hundred miles greater than she'd managed in two months on horseback. "At last," she thought, "I'll be into warmer weather."

Clearly, Annie was not well acquainted with Kentucky winters. The ride to Kentucky had been a piece of good fortune, but the weather that awaited her was not. She and Mercer were greeted by a bleak day with below-average temperatures and snow, slush, and ice all over the state, with a forecast for more of the same. Annie was so excited to have escaped south that even though she saw the leaden skies and felt the bite in the air, she didn't pay them much attention.

Her driver's final destination was a Thoroughbred farm in Bourbon County, outside Lexington, where he was picking up some bloodstock before returning to Pennsylvania.

A few miles past the small town of Paris, Mercer pulled into a large gravel parking lot alongside a roadhouse called Terry's Corner, a white frame house with a couple of gas pumps out front and a café inside. Its sign featured a picture of a horse van.

Terry's Corner was close to a railroad loading site where Thoroughbreds used to be shipped in and out by train, but since the war it had become more customary to transport horses in specially fitted-out trucks. Mercer unloaded Tarzan while Annie set to work gathering up all her gear. Mercer assured her that if she headed toward Lexington, she'd shortly come to a rental stable where she could put up her horse for the night.

Tarzan was chipper and eager to hit the road, all signs of stiffness in his leg having cleared during his rest in the trailer, and Depeche Toi darted everywhere, nose fluting, taking in the scents of this brand-new place. Annie, too, looked around with interest at this new environment she found herself in. At her previous pace of three or four miles an hour, changes to the landscape had come so gradually that she'd had time to get used to them. Now Annie and her companions might as well have landed with a bump in the Land of Oz. The highway between Paris and Lexington was one of Kentucky's most beautiful, lined on both sides with some of the country's most prestigious and well-kept Thoroughbred farms. As they rode along this quiet two-lane road, they passed stone antebellum mansions set well back from the road. Stone fences that reminded her of the ones back in Maine lined the roadway, and ornate wrought-iron gates set off well-manicured pastures and long driveways. Rolling out in front of each mansion were large green pastures, with horses in every one.

On the very day Annie arrived in Kentucky, a photo of herself with Depeche Toi and Tarzan was featured on the front page of the *Lexington Leader,* and so for the next few days, as she traveled through Lexington, then west toward Versailles, she found warm welcomes and plenty of places to stay. There were so many horses around that she felt hopeful about finding the pack horse she now knew she needed to lighten Tarzan's load. But having paid a good chunk of money to the van driver to help out with gas, she didn't come across a single horse she could afford.

Mercer had been kind enough to leave her with a folded paper map of Kentucky highways, and when she'd told some locals that she wanted to head toward Tennessee and stick to back roads, they'd traced her a route that cut south and west across Kentucky and would take her to the state line north of Nashville. But there was a lot of Kentucky to get through first, and the weather was cold, with no promise of better conditions in sight. In 1965, Kentucky would open a seventy-one-mile toll road between Woodford County, west of Lexington, and Elizabethtown, to the south and west, but in 1955, the narrow road from Versailles wound through rural, hilly country. Annie's route would take her southwest along Highway 62 to north of Elizabethtown, then due south toward the Kentucky-Tennessee border along Route 31E, a segment of the Chicago-to-Miami route known as the Dixie Highway. Miami Beach developer Carl Fisher had cobbled together this route to make it easier for people to escape the frozen Midwest and travel to the sunnier climes in Florida.

ANNIE WAS PASSING NEAR Lawrenceburg, Kentucky, in the midst of a snowstorm, when a woman emerged from a roadside diner and told her she needed to get herself, her dog, and her horse off the road. Cars were skidding all over, and Annie would be likely to get into an accident or be the cause of one. The woman and her husband owned the diner, as well as the gas station adjacent to it. They found a stable down the road for Tarzan, and once he was settled, they gave Annie the keys to an apartment over the gas station and told her to stay as long as she wanted. Stay through the winter, they insisted. They could put her to work in the diner—she'd be doing them a favor, and January was no time to be out on a horse in these parts. The weather was bad enough that Annie realized she had little choice but to take their offer—at least for a while.

The apartment was warm and cozy, and Annie and Depeche Toi had the place all to themselves. It was more than she could have imagined for herself when she'd left Minot. Depeche Toi curled up at her feet, contented, and licked her hand as if to encourage her to maybe think of finding a home here, a place where she could work to earn her keep and wouldn't be a burden to anyone.

Annie felt it, the tug, the easy way, this charmed possibility to start a new life in this little town where she had no roots and that she had never even heard of until today, but she just couldn't do it. The siren song of the road was stronger, and since when had a Maine woman let herself be put off by snow?

She was up in the morning early, out by the road, fumbling with stiff fingers as she went through her familiar routine, saddle blanket and saddle, breastplate and blanket roll, burlap sacks of hay and grain, and leather saddlebags stuffed full of mail. In spite of yesterday's contentment, Depeche Toi seemed excited to go, circling around, then squatting on his haunches expectantly, his tail thumping the dirty slush by the side of the road.

Annie was almost all ready to set out. She had grabbed the cinch to tighten it up an extra notch before mounting when she lost her balance. Her feet slipped out from under her on the icy road and—slam!—she fell hard on her shoulder. A biting pain signaled to her immediately that something was terribly wrong. Her arm felt as if it was broken.

Her hosts had come out to say goodbye. The wife helped Annie up and escorted her back into the apartment she had just left, while the husband led Tarzan back up the road to the barn. Depeche Toi followed closely behind Annie, his ears tucked down, his tail still. When the doctor arrived, he pronounced the arm "not broken" and wrote a prescription for some pain pills. But broken or not, Annie's left arm wouldn't budge; nor could she use the hand properly. Mortified, she had no choice but to stay put.

By the third day, Annie did not feel she could burden these kind strangers any longer. She insisted that she needed to get on her way, and even though she couldn't pack up Tarzan by herself or mount without help, she was soon in her saddle and on the road. In the words of Henry Ward Beecher, "The difference between perseverance and obstinacy is that one often comes from a strong will, and the other from a strong won't." Whether Annie was persevering or being obstinate was a matter of perception; either way, she left. Favoring her arm, coughing, and still with only one horse, Annie headed down the road again, with an awful lot of winter stretching out in front of her.

Highway 62 meandered through Anderson County along back ways that seemed even more isolated than her home in Minot. There were plenty of ragged-looking farmhouses; some were just log cabins—the sort that still had privies and no electricity. Places not so much unlike the place she'd left. People were friendly to her—curious, but kind. There was the family with a girl with cerebral palsy who told Annie about the help she'd received from the March of Dimes. Farther down the road, on a Sunday, Annie stayed with an elderly brother and sister who encountered her as they were walking to church. They skipped church in order to host this stranger who had crossed their path—but all they wanted to do was discuss the Bible with her. Since her own religion was more seat-of-the-pants than chapter-and-verse, she felt like she barely escaped with her soul intact. For days she'd been heading toward the town of Glasgow. People had been telling her about shortcuts, and assuring her that the town was just down the road a piece.

By the first of February, Annie, Tarzan, and Depeche Toi were heading more or less due southwest toward Route 31E, more than a hundred miles from where the truck had dropped them off—good progress given the hilly terrain, winding roads, and bitter weather. They were heading in the direction of Elizabethtown, where Thomas and Nancy Lincoln, Abraham's parents, had lived in 1806–07. In the 1950s, E-town, as it was familiarly known, had a population of about five thousand people.

When Annie turned southward on 31E, she was roughly following the Lincoln family's path. In 1963, metal road markers would inform travelers along this route that they were following the Lincoln Heritage Trail, a route that guided motorists to visit Lincoln-related sites in Illinois, Indiana, and Kentucky. The trail was the brainchild of the American Petroleum Institute, which aimed—for obvious reasons—to encourage people to undertake tourist excursions by car. In 1809, the Lincolns decided to relocate from Elizabethtown to the acreage they had purchased on the North Fork of Nolin Creek near Hodgen's Mill (present-day Hodgenville). When the Lincolns had traveled there by horse and wagon, the twelve-mile trip would have taken all day. In 1955, an automobile could cover this stretch of highway in about half an hour.

Annie, Tarzan, and Depeche Toi were traveling at pioneer pace— a speed that allowed them to see the beauty of the natural landscape just as the pioneers might have seen it. Before reaching Lincoln's birthplace, the threesome passed Knob Creek Farm, where the Lincoln family lived from the time Abe was two years old until he was eight—the location he described as the first place he remembered. The Knob Creek valley was framed on both sides by steep, heavily wooded limestone bluffs. The Lincoln farm was located not far from the bank of Knob Creek, and just next to what was then the main road that led from Louisville to Nashville.

The modern highway passed alongside the creek, but earlier travelers, pioneers with their wagons loaded up with possessions, had to ford the creek near the Lincoln farm. The paved road Annie rode her horse along, a road designed for automobiles, was less than thirty years old, but still in this valley, there were faint echoes of travelers on foot and travelers on horseback, of Native Americans coming and going from their hunting grounds, of missionaries of every sect hoping to spread their version of the truth, of peddlers and pioneers, soldiers marching home from the War of 1812, and men, women, and children being driven toward the slave markets of Nashville, accompanied by the heartless clanking of their shackles and chains. This parade of humanity passed right by young Abraham Lincoln's front door; when Annie, Tarzan, and Depeche Toi walked by, however, they were alone but for the occasional swish of rubber tires sweeping past.

The trio rode straight through the center of Hodgenville, where the courthouse square was graced with a cast-bronze statue of its most famous citizen, placed there in 1909 at the centenary of Lincoln's birth, and then along toward Sinking Spring Farm, about three miles out of town.

The farm where Abraham Lincoln was born had been named Sinking Spring, after a spring whose source emerged from a rocky ledge and then cascaded into a deep sinkhole located on the property. The Lincolns lived on the farm for just two and a half years before a title dispute forced them to move farther up the road to the Knob Creek Farm. In 1894, a New York entrepreneur bought Sinking Spring, hoping to make it into a tourist attraction. Believing that the original Lincoln log cabin had been moved to a neighboring farm, the new owner then bought the cabin and returned it to its original site. But lacking money to develop the site for tourism, he decided to capitalize on the cabin itself, removing it from the farm and taking it on the road, where it was exhibited, oddly enough, alongside Jefferson Davis's birthplace log cabin, until it was eventually dismantled.

The logs from Lincoln's cabin ended up being stored in a basement on Long Island, New York, and were largely forgotten until 1905 when Robert J. Collier, the editor of *Collier's* magazine, purchased Sinking Spring and formed a group to raise money with the goal of returning the dismantled cabin to its original home and building a monument around it. The board of trustees was made up of luminaries including Mark Twain, who wrote, in a 1906 appeal, "There is a natural human instinct that is gratified by the sight of anything hallowed by association with a great man or with great deeds." Money was raised from schoolchildren and ordinary citizens, with no individual contribution allowed to be greater than twenty-five dollars, so that the monument would be seen as "of the people."

On February 12, 1909, the first step was completed when Theodore Roosevelt laid the cornerstone for a vast granite monument that would be built to house the original Lincoln cabin. A crowd of ten thousand people gathered in the muddy fields of Sinking Spring to watch Roosevelt's symbolic act. But before its new home was completed, the authenticity of the cabin stored on Long Island fell into dispute. Were these the *real* logs of Lincoln's cabin? Could Lincoln's logs have been mixed up with Jefferson Davis's along the way?

The matter was not settled until a panel of experts was assembled to debate the log cabin's authenticity. At last, after the panel ruled in favor of its origins, the dismantled cabin was removed from the Long Island basement; loaded onto a flatcar; adorned with red, white, and blue bunting and pictures of Lincoln; and sent across the country to Kentucky, where it was reassembled. Around this small rustic cabin, the architect John Russell Pope erected a neoclassical temple of granite and marble, with fifty-six steps, each one symbolizing a year of Lincoln's life, leading to a massive ornate door. Inscribed over the door are the words "Here over the log cabin where Abraham Lincoln was born, destined to preserve the Union and free the slave, a grateful people have dedicated this memorial to unity, peace, and brotherhood among the states."

Ninety years after Lincoln's death, Americans embraced the simple log cabin as a symbol of a heartiness, purity, and pioneer spirit that had supposedly gotten lost. Back in 1916, when the completed Lincoln birthplace monument was officially dedicated by the U.S. government, Frank Lloyd Wright's son was inventing a toy—Lincoln Logs—that would end up perpetuating this log cabin obsession for future generations. By the 1950s, Lincoln Logs were a staple of suburban children's toy chests—"The Original Lincoln Logs: America's National Toy" were packaged with a picture of a boy and a girl and a fort flying an American flag.

In the early part of the twentieth century, there was an upsurge in nostalgia about America's pioneer past. This reverence for the log cabin and the frontier days reflected a longing for connection to the nation's origin story that people feared, with industrialization and urbanization, was getting lost. And so it was with Annie. In 1955, her story ratcheted deep into the American psyche: her life alone on a small farm, her horse, her dog, her fearlessness and determination. Yet she rode right past the giant Lincoln shrine on the hill, and if it made an impression on her, she never mentioned it. Not surprising. She was closer to the Lincoln log-cabin life than most people in the mid-twentieth century—she'd lived without electricity, running water, indoor plumbing, without modern communications, without a car. She'd traveled on horseback, carrying what little she needed along with her, and, most important, had the courage to take her destiny into her own hands. She connected mid-century Americans to a past they revered, one from which they felt increasingly disconnected. To her, the rustic log cabin was life itself; and as for giant granite monuments, she'd never shown a tendency to be impressed.

The trio arrived in Glasgow, in Barren County, Kentucky, on February 17, 1955, five and a half weeks after being left by the side of the road near Lexington. On that day, the local paper reported that the temperature had dropped to fourteen degrees. The locals had noticed "cold clouds" coming in, and were thus alerted to the inclement weather. When Annie arrived in town, she was escorted to city hall, where she was greeted by the mayor and the head of the chamber of commerce. She spent the evening at the city jail, just up the street from the main courthouse square, as the guest of the police dispatcher. A reporter for the local paper caught up with her in her jail cell.

Meanwhile, a city council member in the next big town, Scottsville, announced to the council meeting that he'd seen Annie and her four-footed fellow travelers along the road north of town on several occasions and that she'd been treated as a guest of honor up in Glasgow. Determined not to be outdone by their rival town, the Scottsville City Council quickly moved to arrange accommodations for their celebrated guest, and so when the triumvirate arrived there, the police escorted her not to the city jail but to the town's finest establishment, the Jacksonian Hotel. The three-story brick structure ornamented the southwest corner of Scottsville's traditional downtown square. Annie was escorted into a lobby hung with crystal chandeliers, ornate mirrors, and elaborate draperies, and then up one of the twin wooden staircases that led to the second floor. She was treated to a robust country-style dinner of fried chicken, country-style ham, cornbread, biscuits, and a never-ending supply of vegetables, slaw, and desserts. Meanwhile, Tarzan and Depeche Toi were staying just outside town at the farm of another city council member.

The citizens of Scottsville were generous in their attentions: a beauty parlor donated a haircut and permanent wave, and Annie was given a new pair of boots. She enjoyed their hospitality from Friday to Monday, and stopped to pose for a picture on the way out of town. According to the newspaper, she was "very appreciative of the fine treatment she re-

ceived in Scottsville." There was a problem, though. She'd been coughing incessantly for about a week now, and even with the rest in the hotel
room, she was feeling worse. She was afraid she'd better hit the road
again. If she got sick, she'd wear out her welcome at the Jacksonian very
fast.

The next southern Kentucky town she was heading to was Franklin,
and she thought she'd make it by the end of the day if she got an early
start. The weather was bitter. It was snowing on and off, and she kept
coughing all the way there. As she rode into town, she was feeling weary,
so she stopped at the first house she saw that had a barn. The woman
who answered the door said she'd be happy for Annie to put her horse
in the barn; then come back up to the house, she added, for a hot meal.

By the time Annie got back around front, the man of the house was
home. He introduced himself as Dr. Carter Moore. By chance, she'd
stopped at the home of the town's chief physician. As soon as he heard
her coughing, he told her that she didn't sound very good and he'd need
to take her down to the hospital for a checkup. Turned out, it wasn't just
a hospital, it was *his* hospital. The Carter Moore Community Hospital.
He listened to her lungs and told her she was brewing bronchitis and
that she'd be spending the night right there. He gave her a shot of a
brand-new formulation, a sulfa drug, and by the next morning, she was
feeling considerably better. Nevertheless, Dr. Moore wouldn't hear of
her leaving, as the weather had turned to freezing rain. He kept her in the
hospital for three days, checking on her every day. Finally, Dr. Moore
gave her the all-clear, and she hit the road again.

Many times on her journey through Kentucky, she had spoken to
reporters and given her opinion on a variety of topics: religion (people
seemed more religious these days), strictness toward children (thankfully less, and it was an especially good idea that young people were allowed to dance; Annie was in favor), Eisenhower (people seemed to like
him), and the Cold War (not much to say about that). But the most important thing, Annie told a reporter of the Scottsville *Citizen-Times,* just
before the Lincoln's Birthday holiday, was that the "American people

still welcome travelers as much as they did in pioneer days. I've had some trouble being taken in by people, but generally I've been welcomed by strangers."

Tarzan walked along the side of the Jackson Highway with a hearty resistance to all of it—the cold, the hills, the burden he carried. Although he still jumped and skittered, Annie took it as a sign of his spirit. She sat aboard "looking like an eskimo," she later wrote, in her layers of clothing, with her bundled blankets and feed sacks. In Kentucky, she had borne long stretches of loneliness. She had banged up her arm; she had fought, on and off, that cough that always seemed to want to bring her low but never quite did; and Depeche Toi had learned to compromise—more often riding up with Annie, where they kept each other warm.

And they continued to make friends along the way—because people instinctively recognized them as the kind of restless, authentic pioneers that had passed this way many times before.

If you want to go fast, go alone.
If you want to go far, go together.

—African proverb

CHAPTER

17

A New Friend

ANNIE CROSSED THE BORDER into Tennessee just south of
Franklin, Kentucky, heading toward Springfield. But the
weather, which had seemed okay in the morning, had turned foul again.
She was still about ten miles north of Springfield, near the tiny farm
town of Orlinda, when a farmer came out to the road and flagged her
down. Melvin Dixon told her to put her horse in the barn—but the family had a sick child at home, so he didn't think she should come into the
house. Instead, he offered to call the sheriff in Springfield, who said
they'd put her up in the women's wing of the jail.

The jail turned out to look more like a hospital or a school than a
prison, with expansive porches along two sides. The women's wing was
on the second floor. Annie was surprised to see that it had accommodations for twenty-four female prisoners—what kind of town *was* this? Re-
assuringly, while she was there, all of the beds were empty except for
hers. The weather was so inclement that Sheriff Alley forbade Annie
from traveling along the roadway until the snow cleared up, because she
might cause an accident. For almost two weeks, she stayed in the Springfield jail, holding court as civic groups came to visit; she spoke to schoolchildren and the women's club, the Rotarians and the Lions Club. She

had so much free time that she got busy answering letters she'd been carrying with her since Philadelphia. Meanwhile, newspapers across the country reported that the Maine horsewoman had been delayed by snow. A couple of times, the sheriff had given her a ride up to the Dixon farm to check on Tarzan and Depeche Toi, and each time, it was hard to say goodbye—although they seemed contented together in the stables. But at least the jailhouse was warm and dry, and the jailer's wife served her delicious meals three times a day. Even so, Annie was relieved to retrieve Tarzan and Depeche Toi and head on her way.

The one thing that had truly hit home for her while she'd been traveling across Kentucky was that she really had to think about getting another horse. The six weeks she had spent there had been by far the most difficult of her journey—but people kept telling her that the Kentucky hills were nothing compared to the mountains out west. The closest she'd come to affording another horse had been outside Lexington, when she'd been offered a sturdy mule for fifteen dollars. At that point, though, she'd been so low on cash after paying the truck driver that she didn't think she could spare it. So Kentucky horse country had been a disappointment in that sense—she'd gotten all the way across the state and still had only one horse.

South of Springfield, Annie and her friends were headed into Cheatham County. She'd been told she'd be hitting more hills and that it would most likely be cold. They were walking along Route 49, passing through Sycamore on the way to Ashland City, when she spotted some people who, in spite of the temperature, were sitting out on the front porch of their big white house high up on a hill overlooking the road. Word of Annie's impending visit had preceded her, and the Jacksons were waiting for her, hoping to hail her as she passed with an offer of a spot for Tarzan in their stable. As she settled herself on the porch among these new folks, one of them called ahead to Ashland City to alert the local sheriff, Sheriff Bradley, that Annie would soon be on her way.

Before long, Sheriff Bradley arrived with a reporter from *The Ashland City Times*. Having moved to a warmer seat inside the Jackson farmhouse, Annie repeated her story, explaining the reason for her departure and adding the other details she knew they'd want to hear. The reporter asked if Annie could reload the horse and get on board so he could take a picture. Even though it was late and cold, and she was tired from a day in the saddle, she didn't want to repay the local hospitality with rudeness, so with the help of Jackson and Bradley, she did as he asked. Wyatt Jackson remarked to the reporter that the horse was remarkably sturdy.

The farmer was impressed with the horse's hardiness, and Annie bragged that this was a New England horse—most likely a Morgan, which was one of the hardiest breeds in the entire country. They didn't grow them like that anywhere else, she said proudly. But the men warned her that she better not go saying that all over Tennessee, because they were pretty proud of their own horseflesh.

The sheriff's family had invited Annie to stay with them overnight. Bradley's daughter Bonnie, nine years old at the time, was struck by the big brown horse, and proud that her father was such an important person that he was in charge of helping her. Ashland City was the county seat, a small town prettily situated on the banks of the Cumberland River. There was something about it that reminded Annie of her hometown of Minot.

Although Sheriff Bradley warned her that the road ahead of her was difficult and the weather forecast was for freezing rain or snow, the next morning was clear and cold, and since he wasn't giving her an order to stay put, she decided to press on. She passed the bridge over the Cumberland River. Beyond it, the roads were narrow, and sure enough, by late morning it was raining on and off, and a lot of cars kept whizzing by them. She was continually having to pull off the narrow road, and the wet clay balled up under Tarzan's feet, making him slip and slide when they went back onto the asphalt.

Annie had made only five miles when she found a barn where Tarzan could lodge. The owner didn't want her sleeping in the barn, though, so in the end she called up Sheriff Bradley, who came and picked her up and took her back to his house. In such a manner she passed almost a week, riding a few miles forward each day but returning to Ashland City by car to sleep overnight. While Bradley was kind and considerate, never telling her "I told you so" or ordering her off the road, Annie was near her wit's end. How was she going to make it across the country when she couldn't seem to make it to the next town? Finally, she assured the sheriff that she'd soon manage to get all the way to Charlotte and on to Dickson, and he couldn't spend his time driving through the hills to fetch her every day. She wished the kindly fellow a hearty thank-you—and he told her not to worry; he was just doing his job. Annie wasn't sure it was his job to keep a foolish old woman safe, but she was grateful just the same.

She wasn't so far from the next sizable town, but the narrow, mountainous roads, made more treacherous with frequent switchbacks, felt endless. Plus, the roads meandered, heading her back north as often as south, and all the while she was being pelted with cold rain. Her shoulder was aching; worse, that persistent cough was back. Each time she thought she had it licked—the sulfa drugs in Franklin, the rest in the jail in Springfield—the cough sneaked up on her, and here it was again. She felt the old fear deep inside her well up. What would she do if she got sick again, sick enough that she couldn't travel? She thought back to the kindly doctor in Maine, and about him telling her that her health wasn't good enough for her to ride. And because of that injured shoulder, her left arm was not much use—her hand would fumble and she would drop things. Tarzan seemed to be holding up okay—no return to the limping—but she knew that on this treacherous terrain, a truck skidding by could spell ruin for all of them.

As the rain fell, and she felt Tarzan carefully picking his way over the icy black spots, and the steep drop-offs swung into and out of view, there was nothing she could do but keep going. Annie would not have been familiar with Plutarch's saying "Many things which cannot be overcome when they are together yield themselves up when taken little by little," but she did understand its spirit. Out on this desperately dangerous, cold road, where the three were strangers except to one another, the only way to tackle this situation was one step at a time. The road kept taking them higher into the hills, and the rain just kept pouring down, harder and harder. At long last, she found a stable; its owner persuaded her that she should stay put until the rain cleared. Gratefully, Annie unloaded Tarzan, cleaned the mud off his legs, and accepted a ride from yet another local sheriff, who brought her into the small town of Charlotte. He didn't want to put her in a cell, so he piled up some mattresses in a storeroom and told her she could stay as long as she liked.

The townspeople were friendly, and some of the men dropped by to shoot the breeze and hear about her trip. Eventually one showed up and introduced himself as Mr. Richards. He invited her to come out to lunch at his house.

When they were finished with their meal, the Richardses said they wanted to show her the prettiest sight in the world. The rain hadn't eased up at all, so Annie didn't think she was going to see much, but they insisted on driving her about five miles out of town, to a farm. Looking unnaturally excited, Richards pointed to a weathered old pole barn. "There it is!" he said.

"It's beautiful!" Annie was trying to be polite, although she didn't see anything about the old barn that seemed special.

"Just wait until you see the inside," Mrs. Richards said.

They ducked through the rain and entered the barn, where Annie was shocked to see a crowd of people—at least ten or twenty men and women were gathered there.

"All right, Harry, bring him out," Richards called out. Turning to Annie, he said, "We read in the papers that you needed a second horse and couldn't find a good one at the right price. Now let's find out what you think of this one. His name is Rex."

The man named Harry led out a horse. A solid bay with four white feet, he stood at least two hands taller than Tarzan, but what struck Annie more than anything was the sensible look in his eye. Whereas Tarzan had always been a bit of a scamp, Rex looked like a solid citizen, an elder statesman. His neck was set nobly upon his withers, his face was big and square, and his expression was patient but wise.

Rex's four white stockings were dramatic—white hair up to his knees on all four legs. In Maine there was an old saying: "A horse with four white feet is only good for the crows." But Annie had always thought that the white markings made a horse look all dressed up for a night on the town. Some people called those white markings chrome—like the shiny stuff on a brand-new Ford. Annie had seen some horses of his breed with their tails doctored to set up high, but this one's tail was glossy and hung naturally.

"He's a genuine Tennessee walking horse," Richards said proudly. "The best our state has to offer. The best riding horse you'll find anywhere."

They went over his particulars: he was about fifteen, still sound as a dollar, well behaved, and perfect as a saddle horse.

Still, Annie looked up at him. She already had trouble hoisting her five feet and 170 pounds onto Tarzan's smaller frame.

"I'm afraid I'd have trouble climbing aboard that one," she said, not wanting to be discouraging but still needing to be sensible.

Richards smiled broadly. He looked affably at Rex, who seemed to know what he was about to say. "Stretch," he commanded.

Rex spread his forelegs and hind legs—bringing his back low enough to the ground that Annie could mount.

With everyone watching her expectantly, Annie picked up the reins and rode Rex around the barn. She was amazed by the smoothness of his rocking gait—this was the most comfortable horse she'd ever been on, and he was so obedient, too. Just a touch of the reins and he'd whoa. A nudge of the heels and he walked forward again, nice as you please.

After a few circles, she halted, and when she said, "Stretch," Rex obligingly rocked down again, standing stock-still so that she could dismount. Annie slid heavily to the barn floor, shook herself, straightened her dungarees, and smiled. Rex reached out his nose to her, and she stroked the soft white spot between his nostrils. Clearly, he already thought they were the best of friends. The Richardses, along with the gathered crowd, were looking at her expectantly. These people were so kind, and so eager, and she didn't want to repay their kindness with a rebuff—but she guessed they didn't understand how little money she had. Annie wasn't ashamed of being poor, and she had a habit of speaking her mind—even so, she felt bad about disappointing this couple who'd obviously gone out of their way to help her find a horse, and who'd planned her meeting with Rex as a kind of celebration.

Before she spoke, she did some figuring in her head. The amount she could spare, ten dollars, seemed like an insult to offer for such a fine saddle horse.

Richards raised his eyebrows, still smiling.

Annie looked at her feet. "I like him," she assured the assembled citizens. But she felt obligated to continue: "I'm not even going to ask the price. I'm sure I can't afford him." She looked up at Mr. Richards, who was still smiling as if he hadn't heard her.

He chuckled. "Oh, I think you'll like the price," he said. "As a matter of fact, we were so sure you were going to like him, we've already taken care of it."

As if on cue, Rex reached out and nudged Annie's arm, looking for another pat, or maybe hoping she had a carrot somewhere about. He flicked his ears forward, lowering his head.

She was thinking about saying no—she really was. She didn't want to be beholden to anyone, and she didn't want to feel like a charity case. She had been planning to find a horse cheap enough that she could pay for him fair and square, and she figured that there must be one somewhere—she just hadn't found him yet.

But Rex had already stolen his way a little bit into her heart.

Mr. Richards could see her hesitation. He quickly assured her that he expected her to pay him back. When she asked how she could do that, since she'd soon be on her way, he told her that it would be as easy as could be. All she had to do was tell people, when they asked her where she'd gotten such a fine horse, that he was a prime example of the horse-flesh of the great state of Tennessee.

By now, the rest of the people were laughing and applauding. She reached out her hand toward Rex, and he repaid her with a soft nicker. At last, Annie admitted to herself that she'd gotten herself a new horse—and they'd thrown in a bridle and saddle for good measure. To make it official, they handed her a legitimate bill of sale, and her mouth gaped open in surprise before exploding into a smile. They had valued Rex at eight hundred dollars.

Now her only worry was how her two gentlemen friends would respond to having a new man in the family. Richards had arranged to have Rex trucked over to where Tarzan and Depeche Toi were staying. When Rex backed off the truck, he took in his surroundings in a nonchalant manner, and he was unperturbed when Depeche Toi scurried out and ran right up to him, tail aloft, eager as ever to explore anything new. Annie watched to see if Rex would spook or shy away from the dog, but the big horse seemed inclined to like all creatures. He reached his nose down low and greeted Depeche Toi. If she didn't know better, she would have sworn they were already friends. Tarzan, meanwhile, was looking over his half door at the goings-on. If he was jealous seeing Annie with another man, he didn't let on. Annie led Rex up to the stall door and explained to Tarzan that Rex was now a member of the family and they had better get along.

Tarzan, with his rakish good looks, had always appeared a bit like a scallywag. If he were a fellow, Annie had decided, he'd curse like a sailor, drink a bit too much hooch, be frisky in the afternoons and sleep late in the mornings. Now here was Rex, tall and cool, his gait as swank as Fred Astaire's. The white markings on his legs and face made him look as dressed up as a movie star in a fancy tuxedo. What a pair! Her Yankee Morgan horse and her southern Tennessee walker. They'd better get along. They'd better work as a team. They still had an awful lot of country to cross before they ever got to California.

Annie was eager to set off the next morning. She figured she'd keep riding and packing up Tarzan until she had a better sense of how this two-horse deal was going to work. She'd love to ride that smooth-as-silk bay, but Richards had warned her that the horse had not been out much for the last few months and would have to work up to Tarzan's level of endurance.

The foursome set off, still a few miles shy of Dickson. Even though Annie had been dreaming of adding a second horse since all the way back in Connecticut, she hadn't realized how seasoned in their grooves the three companions had become until she tried inserting a new member into the mix. There wasn't any biting, or kicking, or squabbling between the horses—Tarzan had taken to Rex immediately, and Rex was such an amiable soul that he could have made friends with anyone. So harmony among her animal companions wasn't the problem, but Annie herself suddenly felt as if she didn't have enough hands. Rex's stride was so much longer than Tarzan's that her little Morgan had to jog to keep up. She couldn't figure out whether she should keep the lead long and let Rex move ahead or keep it short and be dragged along. It felt as if she were back in the early days when Depeche Toi used to wrap his lead around bushes and telephone poles and she'd have to ride around in circles to unwind him. Keeping three eager gents going along the roadside was more complicated than she'd realized, and getting them off the narrow roads when cars came speeding by took some maneuvering that she'd have to get used to.

One big difference Annie did notice right away. Tarzan had never liked trucks—not the rumble of their motors, not the slapping of the tires, and certainly not the deep blast of the air horn the truckers sometimes tapped out as they passed. Thanks to them, Tarzan had bunnyhopped and skittered his way across five states. Annie's memory of the ditches they'd landed in was still fresh. But here was Rex, first day on the road, and she noticed that if he paid attention to trucks at all, it was just to flick a lazy ear in their direction. Nothing seemed to faze him—not the horns, not the tires, not cars zipping past so close that she could feel their fiery motor breath. Rex, it seemed, was unflappable.

So Annie put him on the outside and kept Tarzan on the inside. She wasn't sure what kind of roguish gossip her stalwart friend might be whispering into Rex's ear in horse language, but Tarzan was behaving himself so well that Annie wondered if suave Rex had given Tarzan a lecture about good manners.

However, poor Rex got lathered up climbing hills. He did not have the stamina that Tarzan, the little Yank from the rocky hills of Maine, seemed to have been born with. Annie traveled only three miles the first day, and didn't want to press him farther. Worse, when they took off the next morning, she noticed that he'd developed a cough, as well as saddle sores from the free saddle she'd been given. It didn't seem to fit him properly, and it didn't fit Tarzan, either.

When she arrived in Dickson, she pulled into the first stable she saw. The stable owner called a vet to check on Rex, and Annie watched anxiously as the man looked him over, putting a stethoscope onto the horse's chest and listening to him breathe. She wasn't sure what she was going to do if Rex turned out to be sick—and if, with all those friendly kisses her boys had exchanged, he might have passed it along to Tarzan, too. But the vet reassured her that her horse was well taken care of and not seriously ill. They'd be okay to resume their journey after a couple days of rest.

Annie used the time in Dickson to hunt up a different saddle. She traded in the ill-fitting saddle for an old military one that was comfortable to ride in, but this time there was no gift involved—she paid almost half of her cash on hand to cover the cost.

The most interesting part of the stop in Dickson was that the local feed store owner offered to weigh her gear. She was trying to figure out how to distribute the load now that she had two horses—and it was then that she discovered what a remarkably strong horse Tarzan was. He had been carrying a much heavier load than she'd realized—a total weight appropriate for a twelve-hundred-pound pack horse, yet he weighed only nine hundred pounds.

Annie redistributed the weight so that Rex carried fifty pounds plus her as a rider and Tarzan took the rest. When they started out again, heading toward Camden, Annie took turns, riding Rex for a while, then Tarzan. The horses had a tendency to egg each other on, each trying to keep his nose a bit in the lead, as if attempting to prove he was in charge, but as they went along, they learned to pace themselves—Tarzan speeding up and Rex shortening his stride a bit—so that they were walking closer to the same speed. Their system worked fine except in times of heavy traffic, when they had to pull off the road into the Tennessee mud.

The mud was hard on the horses. It balled up in their shoes and got caught up in their feathers—in Rex's case, smearing his pretty white stockings—but the mud was worst of all for poor Depeche Toi. The dachshund in him meant he was built low to the ground, like those sleek sports cars she used to see up in Connecticut. With the mud so thick, his belly barely cleared the ground, and it clumped up in his long coat. Depeche Toi had trooped obligingly through rain, sleet, and snow, but the mud was clearly bothering him. He was constantly stopping to lick his paws and try to clean himself up.

Although Annie tried not to push Rex too hard, a spell of rain started up before she reached Jackson. She was headed to the home of Mrs. Casey Jones, the widow of the famous train engineer. Jonathan Luther Jones, nicknamed Casey after his hometown of Cayce, Kentucky, had been a train engineer for the Illinois Central Railroad. On April 30, 1900, when his engine was barreling toward a collision with the caboose of a stalled train, Jones stayed aboard to pull the train's brake, sacrificing himself to save his passengers. His story was popularized in a song called "The Ballad of Casey Jones," and he became a folk hero, his exploits on "Ole 382" a triumphant story of man over machine during the industrial age. He was Jackson's most famous citizen, and in 1956, his widow's home would be opened as a museum. Mary Jones was in her nineties; a recent fall and a broken hip had put her in a nursing home, so she passed her time writing letters, and she'd sent one to Annie, inviting her to stop by for a visit. Annie couldn't resist meeting the real-life Mrs. Casey Jones.

Annie's visit with the Widow Jones was a success. Over tea and cookies, they swapped stories about life in Tennessee versus life in Maine. Annie didn't linger, however. She was worried about Rex again. He seemed listless, and when she poured out fresh grain, he only picked at it. She called a vet, who came over and said he was just worn out; he wasn't as fit as his traveling companion Tarzan. Annie hadn't been planning on staying on in Jackson, but she felt that Rex needed to rest. Her visit with Jackson's most famous citizen had inspired local interest, so as she passed the time hovering around the stable, a steady stream of visitors stopped by to say hello and take a look at her horses. After five days, she'd sold enough notecards to refill the coffers she'd emptied to buy the saddle. Rex was looked over and pronounced healthy. And now, in the last week in March, at last the weather had warmed up—no rain and sunny skies, as the four companions left Jackson behind and headed down the road toward Memphis.

Four days later, night was coming on when Annie realized that both of her horses needed new shoes. She'd dismounted to spare them and was walking along the edge of the highway when a police officer from Memphis pulled up alongside her and told her that they'd been looking for her—they'd expected her to arrive in Memphis earlier, and they wanted her off the streets before dark. He told her that they had a stable waiting for her and that the most direct route was walking down a one-way parkway against the traffic. "Stay to one side," he advised, "go through the underpass, and we'll meet you at the other end."

The parkway was mostly deserted as they walked along. They had covered about two miles, with just a few cars passing by, when suddenly two cars roared up alongside her, squealed to a stop, and about ten young men piled out.

"Where do you think you're going?" one of them said.

Annie explained that she was heading for a stable.

"Oh, you're a woman," the same person said, his tone unfriendly. "A woman bum! This is a one-way parkway and you're going the wrong way."

"I know it," Annie explained equably. "But the police told me to come this way. It's the shortest route to the stable, and they want me off the streets before dark."

The gang of young men crowded around her in a menacing way, and they all started shouting and jeering at once, hollering at her to turn around and go back.

Annie tried to stay calm, but Depeche Toi started barking at them, circling at Annie's feet, aware that something was wrong. She held tight to the horses' two lead ropes—she could see their eyes flashing and their nostrils flaring. If the horses took off on her—especially here, of all places—she'd be in real trouble.

She repeated what the police officer had told her, not knowing what else she could say. Annie could recognize a riled-up group when she saw one. There on that dusky highway outside Memphis, she was vividly brought back to the street outside the shoe factory where she'd worked in Lewiston, when she'd mount up on her donkey to ride back to Minot and the boys would taunt her and call her names, including the one that stung the most: Jackass Annie.

Well, she'd fought back then, and she was going to hold her ground now. She was scared, but what else could she do? That was when the youngest-looking guy in the gang cried out, "What are we waiting for? If she won't do it, we will! Grab the horses! Let's show this crazy old lady how things are done in Memphis!"

He shoved Annie and yanked the lead ropes from her hands. Depeche Toi lunged forward, biting the assailant's pant leg and refusing to let go. But there were too many of them—the others surrounded the dog, kicking him and laughing; even so, Depeche Toi hung fast. Annie felt hot breath on her neck, and her arms were yanked behind her. "Take the horses!" the young guy shouted.

At that moment, flashing lights appeared, and whoever had grabbed her arms hastily let go. The same police officer who'd sent her this way pulled up and jumped out of the car.

"What's going on here?" he asked.

"Nothing. We were just talking to the sweet old lady," the young guy said.

"Who owns these cars? It's illegal to stop on the parkway."

The young guy immediately dropped his bravado—he was tall and skinny, and now looked like a cowed schoolboy.

Annie straightened herself up and glared at the crowd of young men, as if to say, *You messed with the wrong woman!* But when the policeman asked if she wanted to press charges against the boys, Annie said no. She hoped they'd gotten a scare, and that was good enough for her.

When she arrived at the stable, she realized it was a fancy place—full of beautiful show horses. Nobody asked if she needed a place to stay, and she was too shy to request permission to bed down in one of the fancy-looking empty stalls. She made up her mind to walk the short distance to downtown and try to find a cheap hotel.

Annie had grown used to being recognized by people and treated with kindness, but in Memphis, no one realized who she was. Walking down the city streets, she soon discovered that people saw her as nothing more than a bum. When she tried approaching passersby to ask where she might find a hotel with reasonable rates, most people wouldn't even give her a decent answer; they just scurried away without replying. Finally someone suggested the Salvation Army, but when she got there, she realized that they only had rooms for men. The clerk recommended a rooming house nearby, and by the time she arrived, she was so tired and discouraged that she went ahead and booked a room, even though it was a sorry-looking joint. The room was dismal, the mattress lumpy, and it was so cold that she had to sleep in her coat.

Although she wasn't enjoying Memphis, she couldn't leave until the horses were shod, and the blacksmith wasn't going to get to it right away. When he finally showed up, he shod Tarzan but said that he didn't want to shoe Rex until he'd had some rest. He was footsore—most likely not used to walking on pavement. The smith promised to come back in a couple of days.

Forty-eight hours after arriving in Memphis, the horses were shod and sound, but she had spent so much money that she was almost down to her last dollar as she headed for the bridge across the Mississippi. The only blessing was that the newspaper coverage had finally caught up with her, and as they rode out of town, she did a hot business signing autographs and selling notecards.

Even getting out of Memphis proved tough, as the first steps over the bridge required crossing a metal plate. Tarzan—bridge hater that he was—walked right onto it, ignoring the clatter of steel on steel, but Rex, the prince of calm, got spooked and wouldn't take a single step onto the plate. After several tries with Rex approaching, then swirling around, a crowd gathered—everyone seemed to have a piece of advice. Finally a man offered to lead Rex across—that had worked way back in Maine, when Tarzan had refused to cross that first little bridge outside Minot. This attempt, unfortunately, led to disaster. Rex got halfway across, then balked and skidded, doing a half spin, losing his balance, and slamming into Tarzan.

That was when Tarzan decided to weigh in; he was a veteran of bridges by then, after all. He laid his ears back, bit Rex on the neck, and yanked. And that was all it took. Right then and there, it was decided who was in charge. Rex didn't like that bridge—he kept trying to turn around all the way across, as if he didn't want to leave his native Tennessee—but from that moment on, between the two boys, the big one and the small one, the dandified gentleman and the country rough-neck, Tarzan was the boss.

*There is something about riding down the street
on a prancing horse that makes you feel
like something, even if you ain't a thing.*

—**Will Rogers**

—

CHAPTER
18

Lost

THERE IS A TIME in every journey when a person is hit, with the heavy brick of certainty, by the knowledge that life isn't a game. That there is no swooping, logical, Milton Bradley–esque path to follow. That your choices, or destiny, or whatever other power you attribute life's turns to, may lead you to a spot that has inescapable consequences— consequences you may not like or think you deserve. Annie Wilkins hit that place about fifteen miles east of Forrest City, Arkansas.

The state of Arkansas had always held sway over Annie's imagination. Some places become more than just locations to us; they begin to embody possibility, glittering at the edges of consciousness like some incandescent Xanadu. Annie had been born with a foot in two equally powerful American traditions. One foot was as firmly planted in Maine as those stubborn rocks that littered the fields, symbols of a family that after one giant lurch across the ocean had stayed put for hundreds of years. But the other foot itched with wanderlust, with a belief that some- where out there was a locale that just might be better. For Annie, that place, unlikely as it might seem, had always been Arkansas. It had shim- mered on the edges of her imagination, not just a state but a state of mind.

After Annie's father had lost one of the many jobs he'd cycled through during her childhood, he'd done what so many other down-on-their-luck Americans had done before him: he'd taken off for points west, certain that he would find a place where his family could prosper. He was gone for months, and when he came back, he was full of stories—about crossing the Mississippi River in Memphis, about walking through Arkansas until he arrived in the city of Little Rock. His favorite story was about a hotel he'd seen for sale. A good hotel with a nice location, right near downtown, at a price that, by Maine standards, seemed like a song. He could make his fortune as a hotel proprietor, Annie's mother could cook up homestyle meals, and Annie could be the chambermaid, the laundress. The way he told it, that Arkansas hotel was the Stuart family's surefire ticket into the prosperous class. For Annie, the word "Arkansas" had always conjured up images of a better life.

Of course, no matter how cheap that hotel was, it was out of the price range of her tramping father. He'd left Little Rock fired up to return to Maine and find investors, but somehow that project had fizzled, leaving only the glowing trail of missed opportunity in its wake.

After Rex's seeming unwillingness to leave Tennessee, the quartet had managed to get across the Memphis & Arkansas Bridge and take their first footsteps in that thwarted promised land.

Rex's cough was long gone, and his stamina had improved so much that Annie had taken to riding only him, letting Tarzan carry more of the heavy load. It was April now, and finally, after all this time, the weather had warmed up. They sauntered along, feeling pretty fabulous.

By now, the friendship among the three animals had developed, and Annie amused herself as they rode, watching them converse in their own silent language. After so many hours and days and weeks in the saddle, Annie knew their every move. If Tarzan's left ear flicked back twice, that meant he heard a truck approaching. Rex ambled along without a care in the world, his eyes sometimes drooping so that he seemed half-asleep, but he perked up at every crossroad, and he glanced up hopefully each time they passed a house with a long driveway. He wasn't out-and-out lazy, but he was always eager to stop for a rest. He'd shed his winter coat, put on muscle, and looked glossy, and he seemed every bit aware of his handsome appearance.

Tarzan, on the other hand, always seemed more interested in getting there—as if all the stories about California that Annie had whispered to him to give herself confidence when they were first setting out had inspired him to see the Pacific Ocean as quickly as possible. Tarzan reminded her of her fellow troupers during the time she'd spent in vaudeville: happy to say hello to new folks, yet just as happy to pack up and move along.

Depeche Toi, by this point, was a seasoned traveler. Mornings, he'd trot with his tail held aloft, sniffing and chasing after every little thing. Afternoons, he'd do three complete circles, a full ballerina-style pirouette, on Tarzan's back and fall sound asleep, where'd he'd snooze like a portly gentleman in a Pullman sleeper car.

Annie was east of Forrest City when she learned that she was going to meet up with a fellow traveler, a man by the name of Walter Devine who had set off on his bicycle with the goal of visiting the capitals of all forty-eight states—the same fellow she'd heard about from that TV producer back near Windsor Locks. A lean, bearded, bespectacled man of about thirty-five, Devine always cycled in a shirt that bore the slogan "Visiting all 48 States" embroidered above his name. He told the press that he was from Portland, Oregon (true), a former logger (possible), and unmarried (false). In fact, Devine had served as a private in World War II, married a woman from his hometown, and, for reasons known only to himself, decided back in 1952 to hit the road on his bicycle. Devine would continue his voyage for nearly two decades, expanding his original mission from visiting all forty-eight states to visiting the world. He died back home in Portland in 1973, his exploits apparently forgotten.

Whereas Annie's approach to her journey had been somewhat haphazard, Devine, who had already been on the road for a few years, was highly systematic. Each time he'd arrive in a town, he would call every single media outlet, saying that he would "consent" to an interview. Then he'd make a beeline to the town hall, where he'd ask to meet the mayor. In this way, he'd mastered the art of getting press for himself wherever he went.

When reporters for the AP wire service realized that these two travelers were going to cross paths, one eastbound, one westbound, somewhere along Route 70 in Arkansas, they arranged for them to meet. Annie rode along the shoulder, waiting for Devine to cross her path, a line of cars following her to watch the event. The terrain was pancake flat along that part of the highway, and the bicyclist first appeared as a tiny speck, then gradually grew larger. He, too, was trailed by a line of cars; they had followed him out from Little Rock.

When at last the two got within a few hundred yards, two police cars blocked traffic in both directions so that the reporters would have plenty of time for their interviews and photographs. Walter Devine shook Annie's hand and demanded an autograph. Annie gave him a notecard, gratis. Mostly, they were curious about each other. Devine was interested in the business aspects of her journey. He wanted to know who was sponsoring her, and when she said no one was, he seemed skeptical. He claimed to be sponsored by a major television show, which he did not name, and said that if he could get the signatures of the governors of all forty-eight states by 1956 he'd be appearing on that show. He also told her that she'd be sick to death of horses by the time she got to California. At this, Annie laughed.

"A bicycle isn't a friend and doesn't have a personality," she said. "These horses are my family."

The whole scene was a bit silly, in Annie's view. She was mounted upon Rex, and each photographer wanted the same shot, of the cyclist shaking her hand. Devine, determined to show his face for the photograph, turned his back toward her as he grinned for the cameras. By the following day, the photo of their meeting had been seen in newspapers from Puyallup to Bangor, and in contrast to Devine's camera-ready smile, Annie and her critters seemed nonchalant, as if it were all in a day's work. Tarzan's eyes were half-closed, handsome Rex was upstaged by Devine, and Depeche Toi was lying at Rex's feet, sound asleep.

The meeting with the cyclist delayed Annie. Not long after she got under way again, the sky turned a greenish color and darkened, and she realized she'd better start looking for a place to spend the night. Few houses appeared along this stretch of the highway, but with her replenished funds from the brisk sale of notecards in Memphis, she thought she could spring for a motel. When she came upon an attractive set of cabins called Carl's Court, she decided she'd better pack it in early. A fellow with a corral full of horses just adjacent to the motel told her that she could keep hers there overnight. There were seven horses in the field. She wasn't crazy about the idea of turning Tarzan and Rex loose with horses they didn't know, but the owner assured her that they'd be perfectly safe there, and she could see that she didn't have a lot of options.

About midnight, she was awakened by the loud rattle of rain on the tin roof of her cabin. She thought of poor Rex and Tarzan out in the middle of it, but the horses wouldn't mind the occasional drenching as much as she herself would have. The rain pelting the roof was so loud that at first she didn't hear the pounding on her motel room's door. When she opened it, the motel manager was standing outside. He'd gotten a phone call from the corral owner: the horses had busted down a fence and broken loose. He'd looked everywhere, and unable to find them, he'd phoned the police.

It was pitch-black outside, and the rain was falling in thick sheets, but Annie asked the man to just give her a moment so she could get her coat and boots on and she'd come have a look.

"There's nothing you can do in this rain," he said. "I'll keep you posted if there's any news. Go back to sleep."

Going back to sleep was out of the question. Instead, she pulled on her daytime clothing, and after going out and seeing for herself that a section of fence was down and there were no horses left in the corral, she headed over to the motel office. There she sat, bleakly counting the minutes until there would be at least a glimmer of dawn. But by six in the morning, the sky had hardly brightened, the rain had not relented, and when breakfast was served in the motel's little dining room, Annie had no appetite. She sipped some black coffee and looked miserably out the plate-glass windows at the sheets of rain that obscured her view.

Depeche Toi seemed to sense that something was wrong. Normally, he'd give Annie's hand small comforting licks whenever she petted him, but today, he couldn't seem to muster the energy. He lay curled at her feet, plunged into the same bleak mood she was in.

The motel's day clerk seemed to enjoy her company as she sat there morosely, but he was the sort who relished sharing bad news. He talked about how the rain might not let up for days, how no one would spot the horses if they strayed from the road—and that was before he got on the subject of the cypress swamps. "If they get as far as the cypress swamps . . . ," he kept repeating at intervals. The potential upshot was dire: "It may be weeks before they're found." He'd fall into silence, then bring it up again: "Those cottonmouths in the swamps have killed many a horse and cow."

Annie didn't even respond. At no point along her way had she ever felt this down. She was stuck in the motel with no means of transport, no way to go out into the rain and find the boys. She could imagine rakish Tarzan leading placid Rex on a merry chase, the two of them up to no good. It would have made her smile, if it weren't so worrisome to contemplate. Those highways were not made for horses—she'd learned that herself plenty of times—but if they strayed off the roads, there were holes to trip in, and barbed wire to get tangled in, and the fearful cottonmouths in those swamps that everyone who'd been in and out of the office that day kept talking about.

She kept going back in her mind to the day she'd set off from Minot, thinking she'd make it to California or die trying. Turns out, she realized, it's a lot easier to think something like that while you're sitting on your own front stoop than when you wake up one morning in the rain thousands of miles from a single person you know and you find out that two of your only three companions are gone.

Finally, late in the afternoon, the phone rang, and the motel clerk picked up. He began nodding and saying, "Yep, yep," not looking over at Annie, clearly relishing that the news was coming to him first. He slowly set the heavy receiver down in its cradle, drawing out the suspense before he finally focused on Annie and got ready to share the news: A motorist had spotted a herd of horses going single file along the road. A black horse (must be Tarzan, Annie figured, that son of a gun) was in the lead, the mares were following, and a handsome big bay was bringing up the rear (it would be just like Rex, Annie thought, to let ladies go first). They were headed in the direction of a village about ten miles east.

Annie spent the next few hours on pins and needles. She finally accepted a fresh cup of coffee and a slice of pie, but she was so nervous that both grew cold in front of her. Three hours passed before the police called back with news: they'd caught the mares, but the two geldings had run off, and it was too dark to go after them. The officers were not going to look any more until the following morning. Up until that moment, Annie had been nervous, yet with an underlying certainty that surely no harm would come to her companions. That evening, as the sun set a second time without her seeing them, it hit her hard. Life came with no guarantees. She might never see her horses again.

At last, Annie reluctantly agreed to go back to her cabin and try to get some sleep. The rain continued to ricochet off the roof, and she lay wide awake, staring at the ceiling. Her only comfort was the warmth of Depeche Toi, who had curled up right against her chest. Once in a while, she'd think she heard knocking on the door and get up to answer, but each time no one was there—just the wan lights illuminating a small circle of the sopping parking lot, the flickering neon Carl's Court sign, and the empty road.

Annie knew what it was like to be run off on. She'd had two husbands, and neither one had stuck around. She'd never heard a word from Robinson after he got locked up, and Wilkins had run off when he'd gotten tired of pestering her to deed him the farm. But men—now, they were a good bit different from horses. She'd never met a man as faithful as Tarzan, nor as good-spirited. Furthermore, a man tended to be jealous and wanted to keep a woman to himself, whereas her three four-footed companions had never seemed to mind sharing Annie's attention.

Rex and Tarzan had told her more secrets with the whispers of their warm breath, brought her more comfort with the tickle of their whiskers, and kept more promises with their chocolate-brown eyes than any man she'd ever met. They'd run off, but not because they wanted to abandon her—she was certain of that. If something happened to them, she'd be alone, she'd be stranded, and she'd have let those two fine fellows down.

Oh, people had asked her what she'd do if something happened to her, if she got sick out here or died somewhere between her hometown and the sparkling shores of California, and she'd always just laughed them off and said, "Bury me wherever I drop." Now, however, lying on the lumpy motel mattress, listening to the rain rattle the roof, not knowing where her boys were, she realized it wasn't as simple as all that. She wasn't a woman alone. She was part of a team made up of three tails, fourteen legs, and, most important, four hearts.

Annie had never been a churchgoing woman, but her family had always said their prayers. Her father had taught her that it was wrong to say "asking prayers," instructing her never to directly request help from the Lord. "If you're deserving, you don't need to say anything. He will help you. If you're undeserving, then He has every right not to help, and you're wasting His time and yours."

This time, however, Annie decided that she had no other choice. She prayed, offering thanks for her health, for her little dog, who was pressed up against her heart, and for the eighteen dollars she currently had in her pocket, which had allowed her to stay here in this motel with a roof over her head on a rainy night. "I thank Thee for giving me permission to go to California," Annie said. "And I know I can't walk there, so I'd appreciate some advice."

With the problem thus out of her hands, Annie managed to fall asleep.

The next morning, the horses were found, twelve miles back down the road, when they walked straight up to a roadside ice cream stand,

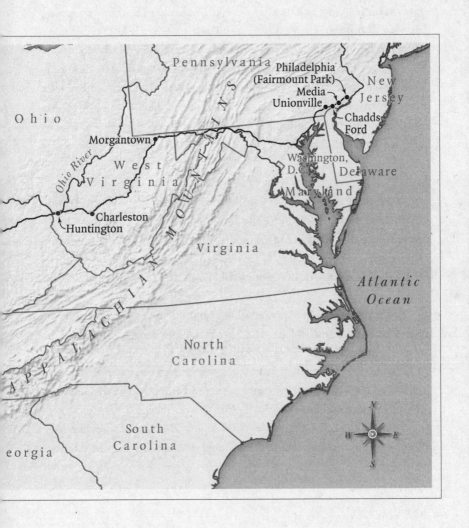

nonchalantly, acting as if they'd both like a banana split. Annie hitched a ride back with the police. If she was expecting to see a little contrition from her buddies, she was sorely mistaken. They were both chomping on roadside grass when she arrived, and they looked up and nickered softly when they saw her, as if it were just another day. Yet Annie could have sworn she saw a little Huck Finn twinkle in their eyes: How could she blame them for wanting a little freedom? Wasn't that what she herself had set out in search of?

IT WAS ALMOST MAY by the time Annie reached Little Rock. When she picked up her mail there, she found an invitation from the Cheyenne, Wyoming, chamber of commerce. If she could make it to Cheyenne by the end of July, she was invited to ride in the parade for Frontier Days, the biggest rodeo in America. But could she possibly get there on time?

Annie spread out her latest road map and counted up the number of states between where she was and Wyoming. She traced her finger due north from Little Rock into Missouri, then west to Kansas City. The way it looked on the map, she could zigzag north and west across Kansas, and if she cut across the northeast corner of Colorado, she'd be almost to Cheyenne, which lay just past Colorado's northern border.

Somehow, the Arkansas traveler's hope had returned, just like her horses. Annie and the boys were heading for Wyoming's capital city.

Map out your future—but do it in pencil.
The road ahead is as long as you make it.
Make it worth the trip.

—Jon Bon Jovi

—

CHAPTER

19

Maps

A MODERN MOTORIST LOOKING TO travel from Little Rock to Cheyenne would be efficiently routed along highways and interstates, guided seamlessly through Tulsa and Wichita, zipped past Denver and Fort Collins, Colorado, to cover a distance of about a thousand miles in fifteen hours of driving time. Google Maps would helpfully also suggest that a traveler could fly from Little Rock to Cheyenne, even adding the flight times of under two hours and an array of booking options.

Thanks to twenty-first-century mapping systems, drivers can move from one destination to another without ever quite figuring out where they have been or just how they got there, as long as they follow the directions given by an electronically generated voice. But in the 1950s, people chose their routes based on maps, maps that were created with the auto traveler in mind.

The first road map for drivers, a map of Vermont, was issued in 1911 by the American Automobile Association. The Gulf Oil Corporation began issuing free maps of New York, Pennsylvania, New Jersey, and New England in 1914. By 1923, Standard Oil (later known as Esso, now

ExxonMobil) was putting out maps of the mid-Atlantic region. By 1930, the practice of distributing free road maps at gas stations had firmly taken hold—every major oil company printed its own maps. Conveniently, they showed the location of their own chain of gas stations (often called filling stations in the 1950s).

Maps were not just images of roads. They were also compendiums of useful information.

On a typical 1950s paper map, you were informed of town populations and locations of county seats. You might find a table showing each state's land area, or when it was admitted to the Union. Maps offered helpful tips, like accepted hand signals (for those without directional lights) and instructions for how to pass another car safely on a two-lane road. Many had indexes showing mileage between major towns. But what they *didn't* do was tell you which road to take.

The major distinction on a 1955 gas station map was between red routes and blue routes. Red routes were principal routes, and blue routes were back roads. Red routes promised to take you from point A to point B. Blue routes promised to take you from point B into the nearest town. Red routes were paved, though almost exclusively two-lane except near major cities. Blue routes were often linked by the blue dashed lines that indicated unpaved roads—best to be avoided by motorists, especially during mud and snow seasons.

While Annie had once quipped to a reporter that she was able to find her way because she had "studied geography once," in fact, she increasingly often relied on these gas station maps. But there was something misleadingly democratic about a 1955 road. In the pre-interstate world, a map of rural Arkansas appeared to show a tight web of interconnected towns, linked by roads that—at least on the map—all seemed as if they were probably good enough. With its web of red roads connecting the state's cities and towns, a casual observer would see a state full of big towns and small towns of roughly equal importance, and a wealth of possible routes to choose from, both red and solid blue. One could imagine traveling northwest or southeast with equivalent ease. On a pre-interstate map, if you found yourself in Little Rock, Arkansas, and wanted to get to Cheyenne, Wyoming, you might feel that there were lots of different equally sensible ways to go.

So when Annie decided to cut due north toward Missouri, hoping to cross the Ozarks, then zigzag her way west across Kansas, the map wasn't going to tell her that this might not be the best idea. It wasn't going to keep rerouting her or suggest that she try a faster way. There was only one main road across Arkansas: Route 70, which ran from Memphis southwest to Oklahoma. But since Annie was planning on heading north, she ignored it. The main problem with the route she chose was that she wouldn't hit a town of any size until Springfield, Missouri, about 215 miles away as the crow flies. All the same, according to her gas station map, there were plenty of little flyspeck towns along the way.

As she headed north from Little Rock with Rex, Tarzan, and Depeche Toi, she was headed for the Ozarks, one of the United States' more isolated and insular regions. Crisscrossed by rivers, heavily wooded, riven by narrow hollows, and peaked by twisting ridges, it was beautiful, and inaccessible enough to be mostly unaffected by modern progress. The area had low population density and low per capita car ownership compared to other places. So it is surprising how closely the region's development was tied to the rise of the automobile. Between 1880 and 1920, the populations in Missouri's two biggest cities, Kansas City and St. Louis, grew exponentially, increasing more than tenfold. The Ozark region, which prior to the 1880s had a very small population, experienced a population explosion as well. Timber was the reason. The voracious demand for wood—both to build the cities of St. Louis and Kansas City and for ties to lay railroads across the West—led to boom times.

But the region was logged out by the early 1920s, and the environmental results of stripping the hills of their trees was devastating. The deforested hills were prone to mudslides, and the soil, already poor for farming, was further eroded. By the time of the Great Depression, much of the population had left, and the region was plunged into poverty. The remaining inhabitants—at first mostly Scotch-Irish migrants from the Tennessee highlands, and later German and Irish immigrants—

preserved the area's regional culture: its music, folktales, and a distinctive dialect. In the 1940s, noted ethnomusicologist Alan Lomax traveled to the Ozark region to collect and record the distinctive forms of music and storytelling that lingered there as the population dwindled. But as the deforested areas filled in with second-growth forest, and as Missouri invested more resources in roads, the Ozarks found a new life—as a tourist destination. And because the railroads had never deeply penetrated the area, this scenic region became an automobile destination.

The developing tourism, furthered by a push to designate the area's rivers as the Ozark National Scenic Riverways, a protected national park, led to a clash between the locals, with their distinctive high-country culture, and those hoping to market the area to automobile-driving tourists from St. Louis and Kansas City. Residents were given instructions about how to be polite to tourists, and town centers were told to close down their blacksmith shops and keep children and animals off roadways. By the 1950s, electrification had reached the Ozarks, but only as far as the larger towns, causing rural areas that had once had a family living in every holler to empty out.

Along Highway 65, Annie passed through the towns of Greenbrier and Damascus, Dennard and Lexington, Campbell and Marshall, each just a tiny hamlet, but folks were friendly and happy to offer her a place to sleep, to find a stable for Tarzan and Rex, and to give her an idea of how long it would take her to ride to the next town. Just past Omaha, Arkansas, the road ran along the Arkansas-Missouri border for a few hundred feet, so that by varying which side of the road she was riding on, she could choose which state she was in. Annie and the boys were fifty-eight miles south of Springfield when she crossed into Missouri, the eleventh state on her journey. Not long afterward, some people in a big yellow car pulled over—they were from the Marshfield, Missouri, chamber of commerce, a few miles east of Springfield, and they wanted Annie to make a stop in their town. Not realizing that it was a bit out of her way, Annie said she'd be happy to oblige. When you get to Marshfield, ask for Dot Murphy, they said.

Four days later, Annie, Tarzan, Rex, and Depeche Toi sauntered into

Marshfield. By the time the fourteen legs, three tails, and one broad-brimmed sunshade hat arrived in Webster County, Missouri, they were looking rather spry. Rex and Tarzan were both sleek and shiny, well muscled from their trek through the hills, and well fed by the Ozark farmers. Annie looked taller in the saddle. Shorn of her several layers of winter clothing, she was less roly-poly, and her more than six months on the road had actually slimmed her down. She had always been a sturdy woman, but now she looked like the kind of person who might lead a parade: her face was suntanned, her posture erect, and her expression was confident and forthright. She hadn't made it to California yet, but she had come a long way.

The town of Marshfield, at 1,490 feet above sea level, claimed the quirky honor of being Missouri's highest county seat. It was a town made prosperous by its relative proximity to the city of Springfield, and by the rich farmland surrounding it. Marshfield was lucky for another reason. Route 66 passed right through its downtown. Dubbed America's "mother road" by John Steinbeck in the 1939 classic *The Grapes of Wrath,* it cut a diagonal path through hundreds of small towns in Illinois, Missouri, and Kansas, connecting them to the giant metropolis of Chicago and facilitating the movement of truck-borne goods, particularly grain. With its construction entrusted to WPA road crews, the building of Route 66 gave work to unemployed men during the Great Depression, until it was declared "fully paved" in 1938. During the Dust Bowl years, hundreds of thousands of people migrated along the completed sections of Route 66 on their way to California.

Marshfield was a compact town of about two thousand citizens, laid out on a nineteenth-century scale, similar in scope and aspirations to thousands of other towns that dotted America's vast interior. The court-house held the place of honor in the town center, and typical businesses flanked out along Main Street: a Woolworth's five-and-dime, a drugstore with a soda fountain, a hardware store and a furniture store, a bank, a lawyer's office or two. Before automobile travel became the norm, farmers rode into town in horses and buggies, which they hitched along Main Street. They'd crowd up the streets on Saturdays, but the rest of the time, most traffic was on foot. The inhabitants of Marshfield all lived within walking distance of the town center and did their business locally—banking at the local bank, getting a trim at the barbershop, mailing letters at the downtown post office, and sitting on a jury at the local courthouse among people they knew. Annie had ridden her horse right down the Main Streets of countless similar towns by the time she arrived.

So today, as Annie and her companions rode into Marshfield at a leisurely clip, she had a good idea about what to expect. As usual, she had no particular plan as to where she would stay—or, in this case, how she would reconnect with the woman in the yellow car, Dot Murphy. But she figured that herself, her horses, and her dog were enough of a spectacle that in a small town, all she had to do was show up and she'd be "found."

In 1880, Marshfield was the site of a catastrophic tornado that flattened the entire town, killing ninety-nine people in less than a minute. The Marshfield Cyclone, as it came to be known, was covered from coast to coast in the press. The number of deaths in such a short time span was staggering, and the condition of those who did survive inspired widespread fascination. Their injuries were often minor, but many survivors appeared extremely apathetic, evincing little interest in the disaster itself—or anything else, for that matter. These symptoms were duly noted and puzzled over. The term "shell-shocked," coined in 1915, had so far been used only to describe soldiers affected in battle, but the citizens of Marshfield were suffering from the post-traumatic disorder later known as PTSD. One medical curiosity inspired a second. The devastation of the town's buildings was so complete that many small springs were uncovered, and when one injured victim claimed that the waters of a particular spring had brought back his vision, Marshfield became, for some years after, a center for pilgrimages, as people sought its healing waters.

By the middle part of the twentieth century, the town had been mostly rebuilt. But the miraculous waters had been forgotten, and the place might have fallen into decline had not another kind of miracle shown up, when Route 66 was slated to go straight through the middle of Marshfield's downtown. Business began to boom as a raft of new hotels and restaurants that catered to east-west car travelers sprung up along the main thoroughfares. But as the number of cars on the road continued to expand exponentially in the 1950s, the Main Streets of towns like Marshfield grew so clogged with through traffic, and with travelers stopping for food and services, that the streetscapes, designed on a human scale, became impassable traffic jams.

A film produced by the American Road Builders' Association in 1955 laid out the solution clearly. The coming interstate highways, by being routed outside town centers, would help farmers bring their crops to market more efficiently and would help small-town businesspeople by providing travelers who wanted to stop in town with an off-ramp to a less crowded Main Street. Clearly, when planners imagined these highways bypassing the small towns, they never foresaw people on broad highways zipping past with never a thought of stopping in town, as chain motels, gas stations, and restaurants gravitated out to highway exits and "business routes" that passed through these small towns were ignored.

Marshfield, evidently, was a forward-thinking town, because by 1955 a plan was already in place to create a bypass so that Route 66 would go around it instead of bisecting it. To the townspeople, the bypass seemed like progress. In 1948, President Harry Truman had visited Marshfield while campaigning. The citizens of Marshfield, in the middle of the twentieth century, might reasonably have thought that they were a town that mattered.

WHILE MARSHFIELD, MISSOURI, was busily planning to detour traffic away from its Main Street, some sixteen hundred miles to the west, in Anaheim, California, Walt Disney was putting the finishing touches on a new kind of Main Street: Main Street U.S.A. Disney had modeled Disneyland's Main Street on the town of Marceline, Missouri, where he spent part of his boyhood, starting in 1906. Even though the family moved on in 1910, he always considered it his hometown. Marceline, about two hundred miles due north of Marshfield, was similar to it, and to hundreds of other small midwestern towns.

Disneyland's Main Street captured a moment in time—a world designed to the scale of a human on foot, a scale that was about to be obliterated by the coming car-centric world. Architectural historian Vincent Scully wrote of the demise of the traditional Main Street and Disney's re-creation of it: "In the period of the 1950s and 1960s when Disney came up with Main Street, it and indeed all traditional urbanism was despised by modern architects and planners alike. Disney, with whatever hokum, revived it, and in doing so brought into being a public awareness of architecture's fundamental dimension, which has to be that of the town, the city, the human settlement entire." In 1920, the future Pulitzer Prize–winning American author Sinclair Lewis had portrayed Main Street as the apotheosis of provincial narrow-mindedness. To reject the small town was the essence of being modern. But in 1960, five years after Disney opened his fantasy Main Street in California, *The Andy Griffith Show* would create a more loving view of Main Street, wrapping the town of Mayberry in a gauze of sentimental goodwill. America's fading Main Street towns would soon become stand-ins for something people thought of as "the real America."

In 1955, as Annie was crossing the continent on horseback, America's historic Main Streets had never looked better—but had a Doomsday Clock been set for their demise, it would have read one minute to midnight.

None of that was apparent as two horses, a dog, and a rider clopped into town. Annie, arriving in Marshfield, asked the first person she saw where to find Dot Murphy, and Dot, once located, swiftly arranged for Annie and her animal friends to spend a few pleasant days in Marshfield, as guests of the chamber of commerce. Annie did plenty to earn her keep: she spoke about her travels at a luncheon and at an assembly, she was interviewed by the local newspaper and radio stations, she took a garden club tour and umpired the first inning of a Little League game. The chamber of commerce sent Annie's clothes out to be laundered, and Dot Murphy embroidered her name across the back of a brand-new moleskin shirt. Rex and Tarzan were put up in luxury at the local stable.

There was a treat in store for them, as well. The horses were taken to the feed store, and the citizens of Marshfield looked on with delight as Tarzan and Rex were about to be turned loose in front of a giant wall of burlap bags stuffed with grain and urged to choose whichever sack they liked.

Annie let Rex go first. She tossed the lead rope over his withers, and when he turned to look questioningly at her, she clucked a bit, smiled, and gave his butt a little shove. The big walking horse, forever nonchalant, took a few steps forward and then stopped agreeably. He pricked his ears forward, as if to pose for the popping photographic flashes, then ambled over to a nearby stack of feed bags. His pink-and-white nostrils fluted as he nuzzled the top of one, all the while looking over at Annie as if waiting for a signal. The master of ceremonies for this bit of journalistic stagecraft raised his hand to signal that Rex had chosen, and the big sack, heavy with grain, was placed beside Rex for another round of pictures.

Now it was Tarzan's turn. The little Morgan had a look of mischief in his eyes, and when Annie tossed the lead rope over his neck, she didn't need to give him any encouragement. He beelined straight over to a large stack of feed sacks and grabbed hold of one with his teeth—making the assembled crowd roar with laughter. A great show was made of extricating the exact bag Tarzan had chosen from the tall stack of bags, and the crowd burst into applause. Next, more photographs, Tarzan and his bag of oats, the horses and their prizes together, and more photos with Annie and Depeche Toi, all looking very pleased to be there.

From Marshfield, the quartet headed west, following Route 66 through Springfield before traveling northwest toward the small town of Ash Grove. But unbeknownst to Annie, once again the national newspapers considered her "lost." The AP wire service didn't know where she had gotten to. In spite of Dot Murphy's best efforts to put their town on the map, the story of Annie's well-staged visit to Marshfield had not been picked up by the national news.

The other Main Street, Disney's Main Street U.S.A., had no such problem. In May 1955, as Annie was riding out of town, an AP wire service reporter walked around the unfinished Disneyland with Walt himself as his tour guide. Disney declared that Main Street U.S.A. would "represent a small American town of a gentler era" and explained how all of the buildings and houses would be created at just a bit shy of full scale.

But as Annie left town with her brand-new embroidered shirt and the full-to-bursting sacks of grain slung over Tarzan's shoulders, she might have been surprised that Americans felt the need to remember a gentler era. She was quite satisfied with the present.

Free as the air, that's me. Earth and sky and horse under you.
What more could a man want? . . .
Folks are just too grabby, wanting land, wanting houses,
wanting money in the bank.
Give me a quiet horse and a peaceful stretch of country.

—from *Saddle Tramp* (Universal Pictures, 1950)

—

CHAPTER
20

Last of the Saddle Tramps

ANNIE, TARZAN, REX, AND DEPECHE TOI arrived in Jackson County, Missouri, on the outskirts of Kansas City, right before Memorial Day weekend. In 1955, the southern outskirts of Kansas City were still a speckling of small towns, with the newer suburban housing marching outward, so that rows of boxlike postwar homes often ended at a ditch, with nothing but waving grass beyond. Maybe Annie didn't have a good idea of just how big Kansas City was. The traffic was getting heavy, the sky was threatening rain, and she was hoping she'd find a stable before it got too late, or that a police car would pull up and offer to help. But so far, not even a friendly passerby had rolled down a window to ask where they were headed. She'd heard that there was a stable where she might be able to board her horses if she just continued up Highway 71, but she didn't have a reliable idea of how long it might take her to get there, and right now, the sky looked as if it was about to unleash its fury.

Depeche Toi, always alert to the weather, was standing up on Rex's back, sniffing the air with his sharp, pointed nose angled skyward, nostrils quivering. Annie, too, smelled the tang of rain, as well as grass, damp asphalt, and the familiar scent of salty, sweaty horse, combined with the leathery aroma of her well-worn saddle. But Depeche Toi would have added multiple additional aromas: rabbits hidden in the field, the trails of porcupines that might have waddled by, the two dogs out in the yard a mile or so down the road. Annie had learned by now that when Depeche Toi acted like this, something was about to happen. Tarzan had clipped on ahead and taken a slight lead, but he kept flicking a single ear, occasionally turning his head to look back at Annie. More than once, he'd stopped dead in his tracks, and Rex had given him an affectionate nudge on his haunch—the walking horse's way of saying, *Let's get a move on now.* Only Rex seemed unagitated by the brewing weather. He strolled along with his head low and his ears hanging lazily. Annie held the reins slack, wondering what this afternoon would bring.

They were just outside Raytown, a working-class suburb on the southern edge of Kansas City, when the rain started pelting down in earnest. When Annie spotted a gas station, she rode up to speak to the attendant, hoping to get some advice about where to find a nearby stable.

"You'll drown before you find a stable," the man said, then directed her to a church up the road that had a shed out back where the preacher used to keep his mule. He said there was a dry creek out behind the shed that might start running some, given the rain, so that she could water the horses.

Having found the church, Annie waded through the shoulder-high wet grass until she located the shed. Tarzan took one look at the flimsy structure and snorted a loud trumpet of breath, one eye flaring white, then backed up so hard that he almost yanked the rope out of Annie's hand. Rex, always inclined to take Tarzan's lead, also balked. Depeche Toi ran inside, sniffed around, and ran back out, as if to say, *Don't worry, fellows, all clear in there,* but even when Annie tried to coax the horses into the dusty, low-roofed shed by holding sugar lumps in her hand, they refused. So she decided to let the horses stay outside, and started quickly unloading her gear under the shed's cobwebby roof.

She was already soaked through, but at least her bedroll was still dry.

She spread it out on the shed floor. By then, the rain was easing up a bit. She hitched the horses to a wire fence near the shed, got them some grain, and pulled her big anorak over her head. Cold and wet, she set off back the way she'd come in hope of finding a place to get a hot meal somewhere along the road.

About half a mile along, she reached a diner, and sat down for a meal of beef stew, pie, and coffee. The restaurant owner recognized Annie from the papers and offered her a bag of meat bones to take back to Depeche Toi. She was passing the gas station where she'd gotten the tip about the shed when the sky let loose with such a heavy torrent that she could hardly see. The attendant spotted her and yelled out, "Get in here, quick!"

Annie gratefully ducked inside. The attendant told her she could stay inside his office all night, but she didn't feel comfortable leaving the boys out in this weather. She wanted to get them hitched under some trees to give them some shelter, so she took off again as soon as the rain slackened a little.

She hadn't made it halfway through the field next to the church when she recognized Rex's high-pitched call of distress. She found him unhurt but with his rope tangled up: the buckle of his halter was caught on the wire, and he couldn't work himself loose or reach the ground to graze. Depeche Toi was circling anxiously at the horse's head, and Tarzan had his haunches crowded up against Rex's to calm him. Annie fumbled with the wire and halter, her fingers wet and slippery, and managed to free him. As soon as she'd released his buckle, he nuzzled Tarzan, stretched a friendly nose down to Depeche Toi, and then set to munching the wet grass as if nothing had happened.

But Annie was rattled. She was always so careful with the way she hitched the horses. Every farm girl knows how quickly a horse can get himself into a pickle without even trying. Had it been Tarzan who'd gotten caught up in the wire, he might well have panicked and injured himself. Chiding herself for wanting that hot meal, she waded through the wet grass until she found a stand of trees that would provide some shelter from the rain, then circled round and round, making sure there were no hidden hazards that could make it unsafe to tie up the horses there. Once they were safely secured in the trees' shelter, Annie finally trudged back to the shed, soaking wet and shivering, truly looking forward to that dry bedroll, which might have seemed hard and uninviting on another day. But as she neared the flimsy structure, she heard a roaring sound, and she saw the bad news: the dry creek had overrun its banks. Her gear was completely soaked. Her bedroll was wet through, the grain bags were sodden, and every stitch of her clothing as well. Annie shivered, coughed a few times, and hoped that she was just chilled and not coming down with a fever.

Depeche Toi was curled up in the only dry spot in the shed, and the boys were settled and comfortable under the trees, and so Annie, feeling defeated, trudged back to the gas station and asked if she couldn't, after all, spend the night in the office. Since there was no place to sit, she squatted, leaning up against the office's plate-glass window, dripping rainwater on the dirty linoleum floor, waiting for this horrible night to pass.

The gas station attendant was friendly, but like the motel clerk back in Arkansas, he seemed to delight a bit in the macabre. He pointed to a big sign in the window that said, THE GAS STATION ATTENDANT DOES NOT HAVE ANY CASH and showed her how he dropped the bills he received through a slot in the floor where the safe was located. He told her that the gas stations on the outskirts of the city had become targets and that stickups were frequent during the late-night hours. Annie looked out the window, through the rivulets of rain that ran down the glass. Right now, the two gas pumps were empty, and the yellow lamp that hung between them cast a small circle of light, which only obscured the rest of the surrounding area. Occasionally headlights would flash by, followed by red taillights—it was too dark and rainy to see the cars themselves.

The attendant explained the thieves' method: two men would show up in a car to pump gas, and one would use the washroom while the other attended to the car, but then the first man would emerge from the washroom and the two would overpower the night attendant. He told this story with mordant glee, as if relating a ghost story at midnight during a sleepover.

As the night went on, Annie gradually slid down from her crouched position and managed to fall asleep in a half squat, leaning up against the wall. Sometime later, maybe about three A.M., she was awakened by the flash of headlights and the tinkle of the bells on the gas station's office door. The rain had let up a bit. She saw a man get out of the passenger side and walk toward the washroom, then disappear behind the building. When the gas station attendant returned inside the office to work the cash register, the driver followed him inside. Annie was still cold and half-asleep, but through the window, she saw the first fellow come back from around the side of the building. Looking at the attendant at the register, she could see that he hadn't noticed that anything was amiss. Where Annie was crouched, behind the door, she wasn't particularly visible, and obviously the customer hadn't spotted her—and then just as she was thinking this, the man who'd gone to the washroom pushed the door open.

Annie stood up and burst forward, toward the two of them. She wasn't tall, but in her giant anorak, she seemed taller and certainly looked like a man. Startled, the fellow who'd just entered backed up, right out of the office, and retreated back to the car. The driver hastily pulled a couple of bills from his pocket, paid for the gas, and left.

That was when Annie realized that the friendly attendant was shaking like a leaf.

"You deserve a medal," he told her. "They ran off because they thought you had a gun in your pocket."

"I'm so tired, all I deserve is sleep," Annie said. She resumed her squat-sit, up against the window, and thankfully, the next time she opened her eyes, it was morning and the station owner was there, telling the night man that a station just five miles down the road had been hit in the middle of the night by a pair of thieves and the attendant had been badly beaten.

By now, Annie had been on the road for more than two thousand miles and seven months. She'd passed through big cities and small towns, and aside from the juveniles in Memphis, who'd seemed more interested in stirring up trouble than in doing any real harm, Annie had never had a brush with any kind of serious danger. Oh, she'd been afraid—of the cottonmouths down in Arkansas, of the twisting, turning roads in Tennessee, where a single wrong step could plunge you off a cliff, and, of course, of traffic, the single biggest killer, as everyone knew. But people? Strangers? Nope. They were all Americans; they all shared a sense of responsibility and an expectation that you should treat people, even those you don't know, with neighborly kindness.

Annie must have known that in the 1950s, Black travelers would not have been nearly so welcome everywhere. Traveling through Jim Crow America as a Black person would have meant careful planning to find places where Black guests were welcome—even in states north of the Mason-Dixon Line. So the freedom of the open road was not equally available to all citizens in the mid-1950s. And many women didn't feel comfortable traveling alone much in the mid-1950s either, but perhaps because she was older, and dressed in men's clothing, she'd not had any trouble of that kind. Mostly, Annie just wasn't a fearful person. She was imbued with a trusting nature and an unshakable belief that, in general, people were good. And yet, the neighborliness of mid-century America was predicated in part on the fact that people mostly interacted with people they already knew; whether in close-knit urban neighborhoods, such as Hungry Hill in Springfield, or in the tiny towns she'd passed through, like Brinkley, Arkansas, and Waverly, Tennessee, Americans pretty much knew their neighbors. They hadn't yet developed a wide-spread sense of mistrust.

But there was something anonymous about gas stations along high-ways between big cities, pit stops where everyone was just passing through. Where the sixty-mile-an-hour pace of cars would ensure that each person who stopped would have come from somewhere far away and be headed off to somewhere else. Here, everyone you met would be a stranger.

Annie was a hobo, a tramp, a wanderer, but she couldn't remain anonymous, held back as she was by living creatures' needs—her own and her companions'. She needed a place to lay her head at night, food, and directions to the next town. Her horses needed to be fed and watered, and given a safe place to spend each night. When Annie had been a young woman in Grafton, New Hampshire, the town had supported a tramp house, a place where transients could find shelter and some company as they passed through. By 1955, however, people moving along at their own pace had become a rare sight, and a new kind of tramp had taken their place—the stranger in a car who was going to bypass downtown and stay only long enough to gas up before heading off, never to be seen again. In 1955, the murder rate was at an all-time ebb, substantially reduced from its height in the 1930s, when tramps and vagabonds had been abundant during the Great Depression, and not yet spiking upward, as it would starting in 1960. Annie's experience in the gas station was a portent of the new anonymity of interstate America that was very soon to be the future.

She spent the entire next day trying to dry out her gear with the help of her little Sterno burner, and finally, still pretty much damp through, she headed north, hoping to find a stable that would take in her horses. Having made it as far as Swope Park, she was wandering around, lost, trying to locate the park's stable, when the Smith family of Raytown stopped to see if she needed any help. They kindly offered to put up her horses in their pasture and take her to their house to rest. Annie stayed with them for three days, while they helped her dry out her gear, and they offered to truck her horses across the city when she was ready to go.

In the meantime they took Annie to the central post office to pick up her mail, where she found almost a hundred letters containing invitations and encouragement from all over the country. One of the letters she received was a plea from a chamber of commerce; she'd been invited to visit Dodge City, Kansas, which was trying to cement its claim as the true city of cowboys. The city's boosters thought that America's best-known saddle tramp might bring some much-needed publicity to their town. In a note she wrote to a friend back east, Annie declared that she had taken on a role as an informal spokesperson for Dodge City, after Oklahoma City had tried to "steal the title of Cowboy City" with its oil money. So Annie officially rechristened herself "The Last of the Saddle Tramps" and would tell anyone who asked that in the rivalry for the Cowboy Capital of America, she stood with Dodge City.

So it was June by the time the Smith family set off with Annie, pulling Tarzan and Rex in a horse trailer, and trucked them across Kansas City, Missouri, and then Kansas City, Kansas. The four travelers were dropped off on the far western outskirts of the city, headed toward Topeka.

For the first few days out of Kansas City, Annie *felt* like a real saddle tramp. For a week, the quartet simply pulled off and camped by the side of the road. The truckers passing along Route 24 West had unofficially adopted her, as their colleagues had in New Jersey. They told her not to camp too far from the road so that they'd see her as they rumbled by. She spent a comfortable night in a roadside motel in Topeka, but she'd been warned that the route she was planning to take across Kansas, up toward Cheyenne, was going to be desolate, without a lot of places to stop, and that it might be hard to find food and water. (At least she didn't need gasoline.)

Annie had spread out a map of Kansas that said, TRAVEL WEST WITH CONOCO, and traced her finger along the route that would get her north and west, sticking more or less on main roads, taking her across Route 24 to Manhattan, then northwest across the Republican River at Clay Center. On from there, she would head toward Phillipsburg and Norton, cutting across on 36 West. She'd leave Kansas, crossing the border into Colorado just beyond St. Francis. But that was a distance of more than four hundred miles, and she now had less than sixty days to make it that far. Between Topeka and Manhattan, the days were getting hot, though the nights were still cold, with a heavy dose of dew in the morning. Annie had been told that she'd be able to find a blacksmith in Manhattan—she was worried about the boys' shoes. Worse yet, she'd started coughing again. The same cough that had dogged her all the way through Kentucky and Tennessee was back, only this time, if possible, she felt even worse—with fever and chills, and sometimes that cough wouldn't let up.

Fortunately, when she rode into Manhattan, she was able to locate a stable without too much difficulty. But by the time she got there, she was feeling so dizzy, she didn't have the strength to unload the horses. The stable owner realized she was in rough shape and led her to a seat on a bale of straw while he unloaded Tarzan, and told her to ride along on Rex—she'd find a doctor about two miles up the road.

Those two miles felt like ten, but Rex made a point of taking care of her, staying carefully to the side of the road and flicking an ear back now and again, as if listening to make sure she was still aboard.

Although she found the doctor's office easily enough, when she tied Rex up outside and went in, the receptionist told her the doctor wasn't there. Annie asked where she might find another doctor in town, then broke down in a coughing fit. Instead of expressing sympathy, the receptionist yelled at her for not taking care of herself and told her that there were plenty of other doctors in town—only she wouldn't be able to see any of them without an appointment.

Annie staggered back out to Rex and had to stand on a car bumper to heave herself into the saddle. By the time she arrived back at the stable, she could barely keep herself upright. The stable owner had placed her bedroll on a bale of straw near Tarzan's stall, and Depeche Toi was waiting for her there—thumping his tail with relief when he saw her and jumping into her lap and licking her hand as soon as Annie lay on the straw bed.

When the stableman noticed her, he came over and asked what the doctor had said, and Annie confessed that she hadn't been able to see him. A woman overheard them and came over to ask what was wrong. When Annie explained what the doctor's receptionist had said, she was incredulous.

"Can you believe this?" the woman said. "This is the United States of America, and she can't find a doctor to see her? How do you like that?" She offered to phone her husband, who was a state trooper, and he promised he would take care of it.

In the 1950s, medical breakthroughs were coming along quickly: penicillin and sulfa drugs were working miracles on previously fatal infections, Jonas Salk had developed the polio vaccine, hospital care was rapidly advancing, and improvements in the safety of anesthesia were creating better surgical outcomes. The cost of health care was rising, however, and the government was trying to come up with ways to grapple with it. Traditionally, doctor's fees had been relatively modest and patients had paid out of pocket to cover their medical expenses, but the kinds of treatments dispensed by these GPs were often ineffectual—or, in the case of seriously ill people, tended to concentrate mostly on recommendations for rest and nursing care.

During World War II, some large companies had come up with the idea of offering "fringe benefits" like health insurance as a way to compete for scarce workers. The number of Americans with health insurance increased dramatically, from just 20 million Americans insured in 1950 to more than 140 million in 1960, or about 75 percent of the population. That 75 percent was mostly made up of working-age Americans. Older people, retirees, or those, like Annie, who worked for themselves had no way to pay for health care except from their own savings, and when that wasn't sufficient, they had to rely on charity. It was Annie's refusal to accept that charity—her Maine doctor's offer of a spot in the county home—that had driven her away from her hometown in the first place.

In 1955, the typical general practitioner who treated all kinds of maladies, from birth through death, and charged fees that were within his patients' budgets (or, not infrequently, accepted payment in kind, especially in rural communities), was still a staple of every American town. The idea that it might be difficult to see a doctor was unthinkable. Annie had been sick on and off since before she'd left Minot, and she'd had several hospital stays since her departure; in each case, the doctor had either waived his fee or accepted a nominal one. But American health care was at a crossroads. Soon the system would have much more to offer, but it would be harder and harder for the average person to pay for it.

Annie was sixty-three, and after Medicare was put into effect in 1966, she'd have health-care coverage, just like all Americans over the age of sixty-five. But this was 1955, and she planned to pay the doctor, if she could find one, with the rolled-up bills in her pocket—money mostly earned one dime at a time from her notecard sales—which, fortunately, had been brisk in Topeka. It was reasonable for her to expect that her dollars would be enough.

And they were. When the state trooper arrived, he offered to give Annie a ride to the hospital, where she was promptly seen by a doctor, who gave her a shot and some pills and told her not to travel for ten days.

The next morning, Annie woke up on the straw bale, with Depeche Toi curled up beside her and Tarzan and Rex staring over their Dutch doors, as if wondering what she had to say for herself.

She felt so much better that she decided to wait the one day it would take for the horses to be shod. She would have loved to rest, but she was determined to make it to Cheyenne in time for the parade. So a day later, Annie set out, headed toward Clay Center—ignoring the stableman's warning that the road up there was pretty desolate. She started out well enough. The boys' new shoes rang on the pavement, and both horses were frisky and full of energy. But Depeche Toi seemed worried, hovering near Annie and licking her hand, the way he did when he wanted to comfort her.

And sure enough, not half the day had gone by before she realized she should have listened to the doctor. She was getting dizzy again, and feeling so weak that she decided to loop a leather strap around her waist to keep herself in the saddle. She kept slumping forward, which concerned Rex. He would halt whenever she slumped. The jolt would wake her up again. When she passed a roadside diner, a fellow came out and asked her if she was lost. She said no, as long as this was the road to Clay Center. He said, "It's the right road but you're heading the wrong way." Annie realized that she must have actually blacked out and the horses had turned around. He brought her a bowl of soup and told her she looked sick and shouldn't be on the road—he had a trailer out back she could rest up in. He warned her that between where she was and Clay Center, there wasn't much there.

But Annie was determined to press on. "I'm feeling much better," she insisted. "And I can't waste another minute feeling sorry for myself."

Still lashed to the saddle, Annie rode until dusk; then she found a grassy spot by the side of the road and slowly, painfully began her routine to set up camp. A car pulled over and people started taking pictures of her. But when they asked her to pose next to the horses, she was too tired to even be polite. "Lady, these are union horses," she said. "They only work eight hours a day."

Annie continued on like this for the next few days, still having dizzy spells, still securing herself to Rex. With each passing day, the weather got hotter, and she was having trouble finding water. Even worse, it turned out that Tarzan was afraid of the big wheat combines working in the fields they passed. Every time he saw one, he snorted and whirled around, tangling himself up with Rex. Rex was such a solid fellow that he'd face the monstrous arms of the noisy machines without flinching, but Annie, feeling so weak, worried that Tarzan was going to jerk the rope out of her hands and take off running. Although there wasn't very much traffic out here, what there was tended to go fast.

Then a miracle seemed to happen. She started to feel better. The dizzy spells eased up. Once she got her strength back, a few short jerks of the lead rope settled Tarzan down and showed him that she meant business. Depeche Toi stopped riding right on the pommel in front of her and resumed his more spacious perch on the blanket roll across Tarzan's haunches.

The weather continued hot—over a hundred degrees for several days running—but she had never felt better since setting off from Maine. It seemed as if the heat had just baked the illness right out of her. Though her cough had waxed and waned since the fall, she'd never shaken that troubling sensation—like needles in her lungs when she breathed. But now, somehow, amazingly, as she passed across the wide-open expanses of northwest Kansas, surrounded on all sides by seemingly endless wheat fields and giant sunflowers that smiled like happy growing children turning their faces up to the sun, her breath grew easy.

Maybe it was the fresh air of camping that made the difference. Since entering Kansas, she'd spent more nights out under the limitless glitter of the night stars. Or maybe it was just that the farther west she got, the more she felt like a real saddle tramp, following that mythic American pathway west, alone, on horseback, with no boundaries to hold her back. Sure, there was traffic along Highway 36. Big trucks lumbered by, always sending Tarzan into a sideways hop. Often as not the drivers would roll down a window and call out a friendly greeting, or pull off to share bits of news—how far to the next water or shade tree, where she might find a promising campsite, the best cup of coffee, a friendly motel with a corral alongside. Annie enjoyed these encounters—much more so than when truckers kept rolling but greeted her with the rumbling *awoooga* of a horn. Tarzan would do a pirouette, and half the time she'd have to circle Rex around just to get the whole situation unwound. She'd thought that Tarzan would be used to traffic by now, but ever since that truck had sideswiped him on Bear Mountain in New York, he'd been afraid of large vehicles, and now she realized that he was not going to get over it.

About ten miles beyond Norton, Kansas, she found herself enjoying the big blue bowl of sky and the pink edge across the western horizon. Each breath she took felt marvelously free, as if all of the earth's air could be swept up in her lungs and expelled again, to mix with the sunset, and the waving fields of grain, now taking on a slight purplish cast, and the gravel alongside the road, tinted by the sun, each pebble a nugget of gold, each nodding blue bachelor's button like an audience bowed in awe at the sight of a mighty sun king. Surrounded by so much beauty, she thought it impossible not to feel very much alive.

Annie found a nice clearing not far off the highway, with grass for the boys to graze on and water nearby, and was trying, without much luck, to pound her tent pegs into the ground when a car pulled up. A woman got out and said hello.

From the trunk of her car she pulled out a folding table and two chairs, and then a dish covered by a cloth, which turned out to have a tuna casserole keeping warm inside.

The woman, who looked maybe forty, didn't want to share her name or say where she was from. She simply explained that she had been wanting to meet Annie and had driven out from town hoping she could feed her a home-cooked meal.

As they ate, the woman explained that she was sick. Doctors had told her she didn't have much time left to live. Her expression as she related this was earnest, as if she thought Annie might have some secret piece of wisdom for her.

"Do not give up," Annie said. "Doctors told me the same thing. They don't know everything."

"They know," the woman said, shaking her head.

But Annie insisted. No one could know the future. "With all due respect to doctors, most don't know what's foreordained and what isn't."

Annie delivered this statement of philosophy in a matter-of-fact manner, in her typical Down East lilt, and she wasn't sure if the woman found her words helpful. But she believed it. No one could know what was going to happen. You could mull it over all you wanted, but that didn't make you any better informed about what was coming down the road to meet you. Annie had learned something during her time on the road: in times of trouble, one thing did help. Simple acts of kindness. She could never in a million years have imagined this impromptu picnic by the side of the road. No amount of worrying or planning or imagining would have conjured up this moment. Yet how very much it meant to Annie that this woman had decided to spend one of her numbered days making a tuna casserole, covering it with a cloth, and putting it on the backseat of her car, then sliding two metal folding chairs and a card table into the trunk and driving west along Highway 36, headed toward a stranger who might be hungry, whose day might be eased by someone who was willing to spend a few moments thinking of how to be helpful to someone she didn't know.

And what could Annie give in return? She wasn't sure. But there was another thing she'd learned along the way. When Annie had set off on this improbable journey, when she had ignored the doctor, and her neighbors, and the naysayers and had gotten in the saddle to ride, with that simple act she'd dipped deep into an American truth. That truth had been portrayed countless times in movies and TV shows and Zane Grey dime-store novels. And that truth was this: Maybe your destiny is foreordained, but what is to stop you from riding straight out to meet it?

When she bid goodbye to this lovely woman, Annie reminded her that hope is an endless well that never runs dry—all she needed to do was keep hold of her bucket and keep going down for another draw.

Annie had passed over Beaver Creek and was still shy of St. Francis when she hit a turnoff toward a blocked-off stretch of spanking new roadway. A crew was hard at work, and the road boss approached to tell her that they'd just finished construction of a brand-new segment of four-lane highway. It would save her more than thirty miles on her trip and was set to open in just three days. Of course, it wouldn't have helped her much—pedestrians and equestrians were to be expressly forbidden from riding along that stretch of the road.

"Good thing you've got that letter," the man said, giving her a broad smile and a wink.

"What letter?" Annie asked.

"The one from the governor of Kansas giving you permission to be the first person ever allowed to test-drive this new highway. Didn't you tell me you had a letter like that but you lost it?" The road boss was grinning.

Annie nodded but didn't say yes, since that would have been an outright lie.

He motioned for his crew to move the orange-and-white wooden barrier aside, and Annie and the boys rode forward onto a broad ribbon of highway, gleaming black asphalt wide as a football field with four full lanes, and not a soul on it. She spent the next three days riding along that empty road. One night, she laid her bedroll right in the center of it, just because she could.

And that's how the last of the saddle tramps, as she'd taken to calling herself, rode out of Kansas: on a brand-new superhighway that had been designed for cars and heavy trucks and turned out to be just about perfect for horses, a dog, and the very much alive sixty-three-year-old Annie Wilkins, who was breathing easy.

The dose makes the poison.

—**Paracelsus**

—

Poison

ACOUPLE OF REPRESENTATIVES FROM Cheyenne's chamber of commerce caught up with Annie as she was heading west into Colorado, and they had a message for her: Better hurry! She needed to be in Cheyenne by July 26, just two weeks away and with close to three hundred miles still to cover. Annie told them she was planning to head west as far as Denver and then north to Cheyenne, but they told her not to: she needed to cut diagonally northwest toward Greeley and then north to Cheyenne, which would cut some fifty miles off the route— only then would she have a chance to make it. They offered to send a truck, but Annie declined. With the weather this fine, she didn't want to be cooped up in a car, and besides, whenever possible, a saddle tramp should arrive in the saddle. She promised to try to make it, then waved goodbye.

For the next few days, Annie headed north, then west, across true cattle country—barren and windy, with long steep hills. Flanking the road, wherever there were what looked like long driveways, the entries were blocked by cattle guards, but there were small towns as well along Route 34, spaced so that she never had to go without water and easily found places to put up for the night. Every house had a stable. No one minded if she pitched a tent—and some folks even invited her to sleep inside.

On her third day in Colorado, she pulled up at a stable near Eckley and began unloading the horses in a rich grassy field. She'd planned to ask if she could board the boys in the stable for the night, but the grass field was so appealing that she'd stopped there first, intending to let the horses graze a bit. Once Tarzan was untacked and unloaded, he shook, then pawed the ground, circled a few times, and lay down to roll, rubbing the itchy sweat from his back, a spectacle Annie always enjoyed watching because he always looked so blissfully happy. While she was untacking Rex, Tarzan walked over to the stream at the edge of the field and starting drinking. Seemingly from nowhere, a cowboy leapt out and yanked on Tarzan's ear and forelock, forcing the horse to stop.

"Are you trying to kill this horse?" he hollered at Annie as he swung a rope around Tarzan's neck and dragged him away from the stream. Someone upstream had dumped poison into the water, he told her, attempting to kill the rodents that were getting into his grain. What looked like a crystal-clear stream was filled with a substance that was toxic to horses. Fortunately, her horse hadn't drunk too much. They'd just have to hope he'd be all right.

The stream that trickled through the field sparkled in the summer sunshine. It looked like a thousand other streams Tarzan had sipped from along their travels. He looked cheerful, fresh from his roll, with a few blades of grass stuck to his coat, and the expression on his face was jaunty. Could he really be in danger? Annie insisted that the cowboy call a vet to take a look at him. Meanwhile, she spoke to the stable owner, who agreed to rent her a couple of stalls for the night.

The vet checked Tarzan over and explained to Annie that he was sorry, but there wasn't much he could do. They'd just have to wait and see what happened and hope for the best. The poison had been diluted by the water. Tarzan hadn't drunk too much. The vet didn't have an antidote, but her horse looked strong, and he imagined he'd pull through just fine.

Of all her nights on the trail, this one was by far the worst. She crouched next to Tarzan in his stall, whispering to him, but as the evening wore on, it was clear that he was unwell. The horse wouldn't take a bite to eat, nor even a sip of water. By midnight, he was drenched in sweat and pacing nervously around the stall. Annie stood by his head when he stopped, whispering words of encouragement, but she was deathly afraid.

This old boy had been with her from day one. So many things they'd gone through together. By now, she didn't need words to talk to him. Their conversation, rich as it was, took place through gestures, looks, and silences. She spoke with her hands, with a stroke on the side of his velvety nostril, a palm resting on his withers while he munched on hay. She'd come to love that sidewise look he gave her while they were riding along—always a step or two out in front of Rex, always with his long forelock, the tip tinged a rust color, angled over his forehead like the long mop of a handsome but roguish movie star. Tarzan, who would start to jig a little when they were getting close to a stable where they'd be able to spend the night, as if he could smell the grain that would soon ping into a metal bucket. Tarzan, who always knew where Depeche Toi was, who would dip his head low and stop in his tracks whenever his canine friend wanted to hop off or would wait patiently, refusing to move a step, until the dog got a hand up from Annie, or found a rock or slope from which he could hop back on. Tarzan, who had never complained about carrying both Annie and her entire load before Rex came along, and who had never lost his spunk no matter what the day had presented, and who kept just enough wildness under his skin, just enough fear of predators, that every big truck rumbling down the road might be a mountain lion ready to pounce on his back, so he kept his eye out, to make sure his funny-looking herd was safe.

Now Tarzan was restless, making low, moaning sounds. Rex, distressed by his companion's pain, kept whinnying and stamping, circling in his stall. But the worst was Depeche Toi. He wouldn't leave Tarzan's side. He walked around nervously, his tail droopy, panting, turning in circles, as if he could share the pain with his equine friend. Eventually, in the darkest hours of the night, Annie must have dozed off a little, leaning up against the wall of Tarzan's stall. When she awoke, it was to the sound of Depeche Toi howling.

Back home in Maine, a dog howling at night had a meaning—same as seeing a white horse at a funeral or when tallow built up around a candle: a death was expected. Annie shivered, but she tried not to show her distress to Tarzan, afraid that the horse would sense her uneasiness and only feel worse. She remembered the conversation she'd had with the woman by the side of the road, the one who'd told her she didn't have long to live—Annie had been feeling so top-of-the-world right then. But now she realized she'd been cocky. You don't dodge fate without consequences—had she stepped out of the way of danger only to leave her companion in its path? She was terrified that Tarzan was not going to survive the night. She had already made up her mind: if something happened to Tarzan, she would not continue her journey. There'd be no point in going on without him.

But as the sun turned the sky first purple, then pearly gray, then pink, Tarzan was still standing. He lipped a little bit of his hay. He stuck his nose in his water bucket. His breathing had slowed, and the sweat on his coat had dried. Annie paced until the veterinarian came back, but when he checked Tarzan over, he told Annie that the worst was behind them. The poison had gone through his system, and he was going to be okay. Just give him a day to rest up, he said, and you can feel safe going on your way.

By the time they arrived on the outskirts of Cheyenne, Tarzan looking sleek with his shiny summer coat, it was hard to believe that he'd been so sick such a short time before. Annie and her companions had grown closer than ever since Tarzan's dark night. And all of them were happy to be here for the world's biggest rodeo.

In 1955, Cheyenne was a city of about thirty thousand residents. It was the state capital, yet there was nothing about its location that suggested that it would thrive. Boasting the most extreme climate of any city in the forty-eight states, Cheyenne was notorious for its arid conditions, deep snowfall, high winds, and, in summer, approximately ten days of hail per month. In 1873, the British traveler Isabella Bird described it thus: "The surrounding plains were endless and verdureless. The scanty grasses were long ago turned into sun-cured hay by the fierce summer heats. There is neither tree nor bush, the sky is grey, the earth buff, the air [dry] and windy, and clouds of coarse granitic dust sweep across the prairie and smother the settlement. Cheyenne is described as 'a God-forsaken, God-forgotten place.'"

In short, at first Cheyenne showed no real signs of a future. Like so many nineteenth-century western towns, its fortune depended on the railroads—speculators chased the steel rails as they were being laid, trying to guess the direction to buy up land along the hubs and main trunks. Cheyenne was one of the towns that got lucky. In 1867, the site, then called Crow Creek Crossing, was chosen as the location where the Union Pacific Railroad would cross through. As soon as the plan was announced, the population began to expand rapidly, and the town became known as "the magic city of the plains."

Cheyenne's Frontier Days celebration had been the brainchild of Frederick Angier, an employee of the Union Pacific Railroad, who'd been tasked with finding ways to encourage passengers from Denver to increase their use of the trunk lines that radiated out from their city. His idea was for the adjacent towns to organize agricultural fairs that would attract tourists. Heading north along the Union Pacific line, he stopped in Loveland, which offered up the idea of "Corn Days," and Greeley, which suggested "Potato Days," but when he reached Cheyenne, which was in the middle of an economic bust, the city came up short. Not much grew in Cheyenne. For a brief period after the Civil War, it had enjoyed a cattle boom, which had led to enormous profits—there were eight millionaires in a city of three thousand citizens. But in the 1880s, oversupply and several years of bad weather had decimated the cattle industry. That bubble had long been in the past by the time Angier arrived in town.

Having failed to come up with a plan, Angier was waiting to board the train back to Denver when he happened to witness a group of cowboys spending about twenty minutes wrangling a wild horse onto one of the boxcars. Angier was so fascinated by their expert work that he canceled his return trip, stayed in Cheyenne, and suggested that the town develop a booster day that highlighted its cowboys and western lore.

The chamber of commerce decided on a one-day event, named Frontier Day, that would feature demonstrations of cowboy skills.

The first Frontier Day was held in 1897. A seat on the bleachers to watch the rodeo cost fifteen cents, and the festivities lasted six hours; events included bronc-riding contests, wild horse races, and steer-roping competitions. The rodeo was so successful, drawing more than four thousand spectators that first year, that the godfather of western spectacles, William Cody, the famous Buffalo Bill, took note of the crowds and decided to partner with Cheyenne. He was the one who introduced the parade. His fame was such that he was easily able to attract star performers to Cheyenne, and within a few years, the city's Frontier Days and Rodeo was the best-attended cowboy exhibition in America.

By the 1950s, shows devoted to the mythic West were an important segment of television programming. A proliferation of westerns, such as *The Adventures of Kit Carson, The Cisco Kid, Annie Oakley,* plus many more as the decade progressed, were among the most popular shows on TV. Western tropes weren't new to the American mind—nineteenth-century writers like Mark Twain and Bret Harte had popularized stories about the West—but it was the dime-store novels in the genre that turned western fantasies into staples for urban dwellers. With the birth of radio, these stories transferred to the new medium, and then with California backlots standing in for cattle country, they made the jump to television.

More and more, television was bringing incredible vistas of space into living rooms of two-bedroom, one-bath suburban homes—in particular, the freedom of a man (usually a man—the Annie Oakley series, which debuted in 1954, being the exception that proved the rule) on horseback, doing the proverbial "ride off into the sunset." Populating these new developments were people who in many ways felt constrained—by the demands of a workaday world of cars and mortgages and supermarkets, which, while convenient, were much removed from the small-town or rural life of their parents and grandparents, and where each small backyard, where baby boom children played Cowboys and Indians, represented America's true new frontier.

During this time of tremendous social change, the TV western gave people a vivid image of where a horse could take them—just at a time when it was less and less likely that they'd ever be able to go anywhere on a horse or even, as in the days of small-town life, to go very far on foot.

So it was no surprise that by 1955, Cheyenne's Frontier Days celebration was bigger than ever. Although passenger rail travel had peaked during the first two decades of the twentieth century, dipped in the Great Depression, and started to fall rapidly in the postwar era as trains faced stiff competition from both automobiles and, increasingly, air travel, the Union Pacific still sent a special train up from Denver for Frontier Days, a nostalgic ritual that had become a society event for well-connected Denverites. But otherwise, the days of relying on trains to bring an audience to the rodeo were over. Had Frontier Days been wholly dependent on an audience arriving by rail, the celebration would likely have risen and then faded away. Instead, it was saved by Cheyenne's second major lucky break.

Wyoming's capital was fortunate enough to be located along a grand east-west route, the Lincoln Highway. The Lincoln Highway Association had been founded in 1913 by a group of automobile travel boosters with the goal of improving highway travel from the Atlantic to the Pacific while avoiding tolls. A group of trailblazers set out from Indianapolis that year in seventeen cars to select the best route across the western states. In spite of all manner of mechanical difficulties on very rough roads—broken axles, boiling radiators, and flat tires—after thirty-four days, the group triumphantly arrived in San Francisco, where they paraded down Market Street to much fanfare before returning to Indianapolis (by train).

Much to the chagrin of Kansas and Colorado, the Lincoln Highway Association eventually plotted its route to stretch the shortest possible distance—which led the highway straight through Cheyenne. By 1955, the vast majority of the thousands of spectators traveling to the rodeo arrived by car. Towns and businesses located along the route of the Lincoln Highway had begun catering to these road trippers in earnest—and wise to the appeal of the western iconography, hundreds of small- and medium-sized attractions mushroomed along the route, where city dwellers could experience a rendition of the "Old West."

The result was a kitschy pastiche of roadside tepees and cowboy-themed motels, chuck-wagon restaurants and gas stations with a couple of horses tied up outside, offering pony rides to restless children who'd spent hours cooped up in the backseats of cars.

Annie Wilkins was a New Englander, not a westerner, but that didn't matter in the grand scheme of things. Dressed as she pleased, with all of her possessions tied to her saddle, with her two horses and her dog, the self-named last of the saddle tramps was the living embodiment of the new mid-century adventure, the American road trip. Road trippers couldn't actually ride off into the sunset, but come summertime, have car, will travel. Americans packed sandwiches wrapped in wax paper into squeaky Styrofoam coolers loaded full of ice, which melted and turned into a soupy mess by sundown. Every gas station had an ice machine outside so that travelers could fill up their coolers again. Children made beds of blankets and pillows, and played Cows and Cemeteries (passengers looked out opposite windows of the car and competed to count the most cows, but if you saw a cemetery, all your cows "died" and you had to start over) or the license plate game, where people avidly tried to spot license plates from all forty-eight states.

In spite of the odds, after riding for twelve hours most days, and with no further setbacks after the disastrous poisoned water in Colorado, Annie, Tarzan, Rex, and Depeche Toi accomplished their goal. They arrived in Cheyenne in time for the parade. For once, Annie was far from the most famous person in town. Most important of all was the rodeo queen, Miss Frontier, a nineteen-year-old University of Wyoming undergraduate named Nancy Black. The parade committee had also invited a full slate of celebrities to participate in the festivities. The 59th Annual Frontier Days Parade was scheduled to run twice, Wednesday and Friday mornings at ten o'clock. The rodeo brochure assured prospective visitors that there was an ample supply of "Duncan Hines and AAA–accredited hotels" in Cheyenne—back then, Duncan Hines was known as a former traveling salesman who'd compiled guides to restaurants and lodging for travelers. Annie might have been a special invited guest, but she was far enough down the pecking order that the town had arranged for her to camp out by Sloan Lake. The Boy Scouts were sent over to give her assistance in lighting a fire to cook her food. (Annie didn't want to tell them that she was perfectly capable of doing it herself; besides, she enjoyed their company.) She spent a lot of time getting ready—washing the horses and grooming them. She wanted her boys to look their best.

One year later Arthur Godfrey, a well-known television spokesperson and horseman, would show up in Cheyenne, and for the next several years, he would broadcast the rodeo live. So 1955 was the last year Frontier Days was staged exclusively for the people on the grounds, and there were plenty of them. As Montana's *Billings Gazette* proudly announced, "Cars from 47 states were in the parking lots on Tuesday as more than 14,000 spectators crowded the stands."

The Grand Parade's claim to fame was that it was the largest horse-drawn event of its kind in the world. Others, like the Rose Parade in Pasadena or the Macy's Thanksgiving Day Parade in New York, might have technically been bigger, but they used motorized floats. Every single element of the Frontier Days Grand Parade was propelled by hoof. Floats were pulled by horses; participants rode horseback. The only exceptions were the marching bands, which passed on foot, not hoof.

From her proud place in the Grand Parade, Annie rode Rex and ponied Tarzan alongside, while Depeche Toi took his place of honor on Tarzan's back. As they started out, Tarzan got a little excited and jigged and jostled, bumping up against her leg, so that she had to turn and give him a little poke with her toe just to keep him from squishing her and Rex. He had his ears up, and he was looking all around, but with that long forelock swinging along, he appeared every bit the dapper older gent. Rex, on the other hand, with his fancy white markings, looked born to be a parade horse. She thought about those folks back in Tennessee who'd been hoping their horse would spread their state's reputation: they'd probably never imagined that he'd be here, riding right near the front of this giant parade. Annie hadn't forgotten their request, always telling anyone who asked that Rex was a Tennessee walker. And, indeed, he walked along with a smart step that seemed to naturally fall in sequence with the marching bands' cadence. He glanced from side to side, always with his ears forward and his eyes bright. The way Annie figured it, he was hoping some movie producer in the crowd would spot him and want to cast him as a Wonder Horse. And as for Depeche Toi, well, instead of sleeping his way through the parade, he stood on Tarzan's haunches swishing his tail, as regal as Queen Elizabeth riding in the golden carriage and waving to her subjects on the way to her coronation two years before.

Depeche Toi wasn't the only one greeting the crowd. Annie, with a giant grin on her face, waved at the people lined up three deep. She was wearing her broad-brimmed white sun hat and the pink shirt from Marshfield with her name, *Annie,* embroidered across the back, and she couldn't help but ponder the fact that when she'd left Minot, she'd more or less sneaked out of there without even saying goodbye. She'd felt embarrassed, sheepish, as if the audacity to think that she deserved a big dream for herself was something shameful for a person in her situation. Older, unwell, poor, female. Who did she think she was to imagine that she could grasp hold of the flimsy end of a pipe dream and make it real? Wasn't she the exact kind of person who people would expect just to take whatever came to her and swallow it? This day, in this parade, with the flags and the bands and the horses, was something that she couldn't possibly have imagined would ever be part of her future.

Because that's the thing about the future. You can't get there by imagining. You can only get there one step at a time, and the hardest part is taking that first step.

But the parade couldn't last forever. Annie spent a few days wandering the fairgrounds on horseback, posing for photographs and selling lots of her notecards, until she earned enough money to buy herself a general admission ticket to that night's rodeo show.

Featured that evening were the chuck-wagon races. Unlike most of the events, which were native to Cheyenne and had been featured since the rodeo began, this one was an import from Canada's famous Calgary

Stampede, that city's annual rodeo, where imitations of fully fitted-out chuck wagons pulled by teams of horses raced around the grand rodeo arena while the crowd roared in approval. But it was dangerous—every night, several ambulances were called. Racing teams hauling the clunky wagons sometimes collided or tipped over, throwing men under the trampling hooves and tangling up horses and rigs, sometimes causing grievous equine injuries, like broken legs.

Annie was swept up in the excitement. She was watching the event and roaring along with the crowd when a man next to her turned to her and commented that he didn't like the chuck-wagon races—he thought they were cruel to animals, and too dangerous. The men have a choice whether or not to be stupid, he said, but the animals are given no such option. The fellow had the weathered face of a man who spent his life out-of-doors, and Annie noticed that unlike the locals, who wore Stetsons and bolo ties, he was hatless and wore a regular men's tie. She guessed he was at least eighty, but he was lean and upright, and looked strong. Annie was abashed. She'd been enjoying the show, but now her appetite for the event had been taken away. She hadn't been thinking about the horses' welfare, and immediately she agreed with this man. It was humans' responsibility to watch out for their animal companions and not put them in harm's way.

The gentleman introduced himself. Name was Harvey Kelsey. He was in town for the rodeo, but home was a sheep ranch in Uinta County, west of Green River. He inquired about Annie's route and assured her that she'd be passing not far from his ranch. When she made it out that way, she could ask anyone and they'd tell her how to get there. She'd be more than welcome to come and stay as long as she liked. A bit more conversation revealed that there was no husband on Annie's side and no wife on his, but with his polite assurance that he'd "sleep in the barn," he told Annie he hoped he'd see her later that summer.

Annie had taken an instant liking to the fellow. There was something about his dry wit and matter-of-fact delivery that reminded her of Mainers; even more so, she immediately sensed his deep connection to animals. She hadn't met anyone so attuned to their welfare since she'd left

Rose's Riding Academy, in New Jersey. It seemed there was a wife some-where in his distant past who wasn't around anymore, and he had no children, but the fond way he spoke of his dogs—a pair of whip-smart border collies—told Annie that he thought of his dogs as kin.

In 1955, a single man could not, according to society's morals, invite a single woman to his home, not if she was "a good woman." It didn't matter that they were both divorced, that he lived, according to his de-scription, miles from the nearest neighbor, or that she'd been alone on the road for close to a year and was clearly capable of looking out for herself. No. So officially, his invitation didn't happen, and officially, she didn't accept it or promise to look him up when she was headed out that way; nonetheless, they both were aware that his invitation had been noted.

Late July in Cheyenne was glorious—the weather was in the high seventies, with Wyoming's epic blue sky seeming to promise an endless stretch of continuing ease. But the locals had already been telling her not to be fooled. Winter came early in these parts, and she still had to make her way across the mountains. Her next stop was Laramie, and she needed to get a move on. She'd been warned that the cold would come on fast.

Annie had left behind most of her winter gear down south when the weather got hot, hoping to lighten the horses' load. She'd figured she wouldn't need that stuff once she got to California. Luckily, she'd kept a single woolen union suit.

So around the first of August she set off, climbing gradually out of Cheyenne, as she followed the Lincoln Highway westbound. Folks had told her that in Wyoming things are much farther away than they appear, and sure enough she was only one day out of Cheyenne when she caught sight of the town of Laramie way off on the horizon, its grid clearly visi-ble in contrast to the flat brown plain that stretched out around it until the land rolled up to the snowcapped mountains of the Snowy Range, farther on. But they were right: the distance was deceptive. She rode for hours and days, and the silhouette of Laramie against a mountain back-drop disappeared and reappeared but never seemed to get any closer.

About halfway between Cheyenne and Laramie, Annie and her companions passed through the tiny town of Buford and stopped to visit a local roadside attraction known as Tree in the Rock that marked a spot where the workers building the Union Pacific had detoured the tracks around a limber pine that appeared to be growing directly out of a crack in a boulder. There was something about the way that stubborn tree jutted right out of the rock that struck Annie's fancy. Like any Maine farmer, she knew that it wasn't easy to grow from rock. To survive out here, that tree needed to be tough and strong. She took inspiration as she looked at it, and vowed to be as tough and strong herself as she headed toward those mountains that loomed off in the distance—the biggest obstacle she'd yet faced.

There is nothing so wretched and foolish as
to anticipate misfortunes. What madness to
expect evil before it arrives.

—Seneca

CHAPTER

22

Molehills and Mountains

ANNIE, TARZAN, REX, AND DEPECHE TOI reached Laramie after a week of travel—they'd camped out several times, stayed overnight in a motel, and slept in a couple of barns. When she arrived on the outskirts of town, the first person Annie met invited her to come and stay as a guest for a few days. The woman had a corral out back, and she was friendly, and it seemed as though she could use the company. She pointed west toward where the Snowy Range was visible from anywhere in the flat landscape around them, and she told Annie in no uncertain terms that if she wanted to get across those mountains, she'd better hurry, because the snow would fall before she knew it, the roads would be closed, and, in any case, Annie was not properly equipped to cross the mountains. She didn't have the clothes. She didn't have the gear.

Being a New Englander, Annie was at first taken aback by the way these westerners talked about snow. What could somebody from Wyoming tell a born-and-bred Mainer about snow that she didn't already know? After all, she'd braved November, December, and January on the road. She'd ridden through snow in Kentucky, and more snow in Tennessee. But she'd already gotten a taste of the dry Wyoming cold, and she was starting to believe that her summer clothes and her single union suit were not going to get her across, even in August.

Annie's host took her shopping in the city's old-fashioned downtown district and helped her pick out a winter-weight sleeping bag with a zipper and a hood, as well as a hat, a parka, and a new pair of wool gloves. The sleeping bag seemed extravagant to her. She'd gotten along fine with her bedroll of blankets so far, but in truth, until it had gotten warm, she'd spent most nights in beds, on a jail's cot, or at least in the straw of a stable. She'd not been forced to spend a single night sleeping outside in the cold.

Out of Laramie, Annie had two choices for her route. The Lincoln Highway, engineered to avoid the mountains, detoured almost 150 miles out of the way. Highway 130 took a more direct route, straight through the Snowy Range, where it passed breathtaking scenery of granite cliffs and crystal-clear mountain lakes until it reached a summit of 10,800 feet. From there, the road descended through the small town of Saratoga before rejoining the Lincoln Highway in Rawlins.

It might seem logical that a woman riding two aging horses, with no specialized equipment except for her brand-new sleeping bag, with her bags of grain still hung over Tarzan's shoulders and her saddlebags still rattling with cans and a few army rations, would choose the detour around the mountains, instead of plotting the direct route. It seems that the chorus of locals giving her advice would have suggested that she ride north to avoid the mountains, instead of saying, "Get yourself a sleeping bag and you should be fine." But in 1955, Wyoming was truly a land unto itself. Certainly, cars and roads had entered the state pretty much as quickly as everywhere else. The difference was that Wyoming had experienced no real postwar construction boom, no suburbanization, and, for the time being at least, no great proliferation of roads. Its economy was undiversified and very limited, with ranching and mining taking up the lion's share. The railroad that had given the state an economic boost was in decline, thanks to the automobile, and nothing was coming along to take its place. So much of southern Wyoming, with its arid, brittle climate, was not useful for much except cattle and sheep ranching, and the only practical way to manage the animals was on horseback. Dodge City, Kansas, might like to advertise itself as the Cowboy Capital of America, but Wyoming, the Cowboy State, still had a working ranch culture and few paved roads relative to its area. Much of its territory was still best accessed on horseback. So in other words, in Wyoming, riding into the mountains didn't seem like such an unusual thing to do.

In other parts of her journey, stables and blacksmiths, tack shops and feed stores had sometimes been hard for Annie to find, but in Wyoming the number of people who were familiar with and capable of long-distance horseback expeditions remained robust. So whether it was Annie's own stubborn sense of picking her route herself or the encouragement of the Wyomingites who thought trekking into the mountains was well within the bounds of easily accomplished tasks, she chose the direct route from Laramie west to Centennial, then up the winding stretch of Highway 130 and over the summit to Saratoga.

Annie and the boys started out on a sunny August day, heading toward the mountains that loomed large on the horizon, but perhaps even larger in her imagination. She'd been hearing about those mountains since she'd left Maine—the biggest obstacle between herself and California. Now their craggy peaks spread across the landscape in all their majesty, impossible to ignore. Annie had passed through mountains before—she'd been through the hills of Kentucky and had climbed up through the Missouri Ozarks—but she was just now starting to understand the scale of *western* mountains, which, as that long-ago gambler in Connecticut had told her, were completely unlike any she'd seen before. These were the test that marked the divide between possible and impossible. If she and her companions made it to the other side, what else could prevent her from reaching her destination? She set off with her horses, prepared to climb ten thousand feet, and full of a perhaps foolish optimism that they would surely succeed in their quest.

But, as is often the case in life, the size of an obstacle in front of you is a matter of perspective. Just as Annie had sorely underestimated the severity of winter in Kentucky, so she'd overestimated how far she'd need to climb through the Snowy Range. Though she didn't realize it, Annie and her companions had been climbing ever since she'd left Cheyenne. When she reached Laramie, she was already at an elevation of seven thousand feet. From here to the summit would be the most rapid ascent, but she had not given herself credit for all the climbing they'd already done.

At first, the rise in altitude was not particularly noticeable. Tarzan and Rex ambled along peacefully across the wide-open terrain. By midday, it was warm. The views as they ascended a large plateau were sweeping and grand, and sometimes, in the distance, she could see bands of wild horses or the rapidly bobbing white-tipped tails of pronghorn antelope herds. Bald eagles swept overhead. The entire land was suffused with light. During daytime, the sky was an endless bowl of bright blue.

Homesteader Elinore Pruitt Stewart rode across Wyoming on horseback in 1913, and she described the experience of waking up one summer day after camping on the high plains:

> The sun was just gilding the hilltops when we arose. Everything, even the barrenness, was beautiful. We have had frosts, and the quaking aspens were a trembling field of gold as far up the stream as we could see. We were way up above them and could look far across the valley. We could see the silvery gold of the willows, the russet and bronze of the currants, and patches of cheerful green showed where the pines were. The splendor was relieved by a background of sober gray-green hills, but even on them gay streaks and patches of yellow showed where rabbit-brush grew.

As Annie, Tarzan, Rex, and Depeche Toi headed west across the state, their view would have been essentially similar to what that early-twentieth-century traveler had seen on her journey. Wyoming had not changed much in the last forty years.

Late in the day, while the sun sank, its rays shone back on Annie's face as the mountains turned blue and then purple. But as soon as the sun dropped behind the mountains, the temperature plunged. Annie looked for a spot to camp near trees that would shelter the horses. That night, she and Depeche Toi climbed into her new sleeping bag. She pulled the hood up over her head, and, zipped in together, the two of them stayed warm.

By the time they reached the small town of Centennial, they'd climbed another thousand feet in altitude. At that point, Annie could see that those distant mountains were now upon them, and the road began to climb in earnest. The route had been designed to loop back and forth so that the grade was never more than a car could manage, but as they moved into the higher elevations, the air began to thin, making walking more strenuous. This mountain country was good for sheep ranching, so in spite of its lack of settlements, Annie often came across encampments of sheepherders, who always seemed happy to see her. The friendly shepherds were quick to help her untack and find water for the horses, and were always willing to share a hot meal. Instead of tying up their horses, they simply turned them loose, and they advised Annie to do the same.

The horses were incredibly fit after all these months on the road, and they took the increasing altitude in stride. Annie, however, didn't find this part of the journey so easy. With her weak lungs, she was more and more affected by the thinning air. She was okay when she was riding, but just a bit of walking got her winded and starting to feel dizzy. Fortunately, Rex had no trouble carrying her, and when she made camp, she took her time. Depeche Toi, for his part, seemed to thrive in the mountains. There was so little traffic that she let him off the leash, and he darted all over the place, chasing small animals, hopping over streams, exploring rock piles, completely in his element.

First built in the 1870s as a wagon road, Highway 130 had been paved in the 1930s, after which it was dubbed "The Great Skyroad." The thirty-mile passage through the Snowy Range gave travelers access to breathtaking vistas: alpine meadows, glacial lakes, towering granite peaks, and rushing mountain streams. The route was so beautiful that it would later be designated as the nation's second official scenic byway. Impassable due to snow from October to May or June, it was a popular detour for car travelers during the summer months, although even at the height of the tourist season, traffic along the route was light. Therefore, much of the time, as the quartet made their way along the spectacular roadway, it was just the four of them, taking in the birds' songs, the bright-hued wildflowers, and the brilliant butterflies.

Perhaps for the first time since starting off, Annie had a sense of what it really felt like to be alone on horseback in a world free of cars. Each morning she woke up thinking that the hard part was still ahead of them, but up to now, the days had passed without trouble. On the fifth day out of Laramie, Annie realized just how far they had climbed when they reached the snow line. Annie couldn't resist. She and Rex led Tarzan off the road until he had all four feet in the snow. She officially congratulated him—although no one was there to listen or take pictures—on probably being the first Maine horse to stand in snow in the Rockies. Still, she worried about how much farther they would have to climb in the thin air. Around every bend, she expected to come to a place that was too steep for the horses to manage.

So Annie was greatly astonished when, later that day, a crowded parking lot surrounded by picnic tables came into view. With a gasp of delight, she realized they had done it. They'd reached the summit. But she also felt a strange sensation, and it wasn't just the light-headedness that came from the oxygen-poor air. How could it be that she and her companions had somehow climbed the mountains that had loomed so large in her mind without more trouble? Had she become so adept at travel, so accomplished at trekking that even the mighty mountains of the West were no more than molehills in her path? Sometimes life is just like that, Annie thought. You can be so worried about the challenge in front of you that you fail to realize that you've been chipping away at it all along.

The scene there at Libby Flats was breathtaking, with an endless view that spread out toward the even higher peaks of the Colorado Rockies to her south. Families had laid out baskets and blankets and extensive spreads for their mountaintop picnics, and when they departed as the sun was setting, Annie found that many of them had left behind unopened cans of food. There at the summit, at a built-in picnic bench, Annie, Tarzan, Depeche Toi, and Rex had a grand celebration. The abandoned cans were full of fancy and exotic treats, and Annie shared every bite with Depeche Toi, who stood on the table next to her, happily licking the last drops of cling peaches and liverwurst, pink salmon, canned brown bread, and pork and beans, plus a few things that Annie wasn't even sure what they were, while Tarzan and Rex lounged nearby, feasting on well-earned buckets of grain. The four companions celebrated at their own private site on top of the world. Right then, Annie couldn't imagine what could possibly deter her on her way to California—they'd conquered the mountains! Surely it would all be easy going from here on in.

You can't fight the desert . . .
you have to ride with it.

—Louis L'Amour

———

23

The Red Desert

I T WAS THE MIDDLE OF AUGUST by the time Annie, Tarzan, Depeche Toi, and Rex rejoined the Lincoln Highway in Rawlins, Wyoming. With the mountains at their backs, they sauntered along with the confidence befitting a team that had put their biggest obstacle behind them. But the mountains were not Wyoming's only natural barrier. Annie and her companions were headed for a stretch of land that appeared on their Conoco road map like a big empty white box. The foursome was moving toward the Great Divide Basin, one of the more isolated areas in the continental United States. The largest municipality in the area was a small railroad service town called Wamsutter, population 103.

While meager in citizenry, Wamsutter was rich in wildlife. Extensive herds of desert elk and pronghorn antelope roamed the vast open spaces around it. The town billed itself as the gateway to the Red Desert, one of Wyoming's most desolate regions. Annie would not be the first traveler to cross this vast expanse on horseback. Pony Express riders had torn across it in 1860 and 1861, and so many westward pioneers had plodded across this barren stretch of land that the wagon ruts from Conestoga wagons were still visible in places. But there were no Pony Express stops anymore. It was far different for Annie to head off west from Rawlins than it had been to hop from small town to small town, as she'd done through most of New England and across the Great Plains. She and her companions were now traveling into a region where they'd be more alone than ever before.

Annie did, however, have some modern advantages over the Pony Express riders and the pioneers in Conestoga wagons. Her route would run her along the highway, where there were gas stations and motels—although these were few and far between—as well as the railroad, which had station houses along its routes. She had to hope that those stops, along with the food and grain she carried, would be enough. She took off from Rawlins with her usual combination of aplomb and good cheer.

When she first entered the Great Divide Basin, the land looked barren. The soil was sandy, and the sagebrush scrubby and low to the ground. There were few distinguishing markers. Mile after mile looked just the same. But as she rode along, she began to notice the abundant small wildlife: rabbits, desert mice, and kangaroo rats, which scurried so fast across the arid ground that at first she didn't even notice them. Following the path of the Union Pacific Railroad, which ran mostly parallel to the Lincoln Highway, she stopped at the unmanned station crossings, where she was able to find stalls for the horses and water. For long stretches, she rarely spoke to another soul. Day after day passed with nothing to distinguish it. The desert, it seemed, was endless. She kept track of the days by making notations in her diary, and she held on to her sanity by carrying on a constant patter with her animals to keep herself company.

August turned to September before Annie began to hope that they were finally reaching the Red Desert's western edge. She started to see more houses, gas stations, and small motels, as well as, sometimes, ranch houses set far back from the road. Along the way, here and there, she'd come across a tiny general store out in the middle of nowhere, its location seemingly so remote that it was hard to understand how it could stay in business.

She was still about ten miles short of Rock Springs when she stopped in one of those little outposts to ask about a place to camp. The fellow behind the counter gave her directions to a good location: a flat, dry wash with plenty of grass on the hillsides for the horses. When Annie asked about water, the fellow said that although she would find the wash completely dry, it looked like it was going to rain soon, and as soon as it did, the wash would fill with several inches of water for the horses to drink.

Storm clouds were gathering as Annie hurried to follow the man's directions. The sky was darkening as she unloaded Tarzan and Rex and rushed to set up camp, turning them loose and scurrying to get inside the tent with Depeche Toi just as the first raindrops were falling. She had pitched her tent well back from the wash, in a spot where the ground was covered with grass and thistles. It rained for only about five minutes, but as promised, the wash filled just enough to allow the horses to drink. After the rain stopped and the horses were grained and watered, Annie and Depeche Toi headed back to the store on foot to pick up some provisions. The store clerk asked if she'd managed to get her tent pitched before the rain fell, and she said yes, and it hadn't been much of a rain anyway.

"Not here," he replied. "But I hear it came down pretty hard up in the mountains."

Annie returned to camp, shared a dinner of heated-up canned beans with Depeche Toi, crawled into her sleeping bag, and quickly fell asleep. But sometime in the middle of the night, she heard Rex calling out his distress cry, and soon Tarzan joined in. Depeche Toi started barking. Annie was on her feet before she knew it: What could have happened? Were there wild animals? Had one of the horses gotten tangled in the thorny Russian thistles that lined the banks of the wash?

With her flashlight, she looked around, but the reason for the horses' agitation wasn't clear. She didn't see anything amiss. Still, Depeche Toi was barking madly. Something was definitely wrong. She heard a sound like the low rumble of an oncoming train—and the next thing she knew, she'd been knocked flat. Water was everywhere. Her mouth and nose were full, and she was spluttering, trying to catch a breath. Completely disoriented, she couldn't get her bearings or figure out which way to move to safety. Twice she lost her footing and fell back down into the rushing water. She stumbled and thrashed, but the torrent was so powerful, it was hard to fight it. She grasped about blindly, trying to find something to grab on to, only there was nothing.

Just then, she felt something scratch her arm. It took her a moment to recognize that it was Depeche Toi's sharp toenails. Hope surged as she realized he was dog-paddling next to her. But before she could grab hold of him, a surge of water pummeled her, knocking her to her knees. Struggling on all fours, she followed him until she managed to get herself clear. She was soaking wet, coughing up water, and shaking from head to toe. Depeche Toi crowded up to her and started licking her face. The flashlight she'd bought back in Laramie had been knocked out of her hand and was nowhere to be seen. Where were the horses? She called out to Tarzan and Rex, listening for the sound of their hooves or a friendly answering whicker, but she heard nothing. Slowly, her eyes adjusted to the darkness, and she realized they were gone—they must have taken off in terror.

Annie sat on a rock for the rest of the night, with only Depeche Toi to provide a little warmth and comfort. As the hours ticked past, the silence was rent by the high-pitched yips of a band of coyotes, who, she figured, were keeping watch on the two of them with their yellow eyes, although she couldn't actually see them. Depeche Toi, seeming to understand that he was needed, never moved from her lap all night.

As soon as the predawn sky began to lighten, Annie set to work gathering up what was left of her scattered belongings, most of which had been dragged quite a distance down the now almost empty wash. She draped the sodden blankets, her sleeping bag, and her wet clothing over the sagebrush. Her leather saddlebags, it appeared, had protected her letters and notecards, but one of her trip diaries had been swept away, and another was too bloated with water to salvage. Finally, tired, lonely, and soaking wet, she headed back to the little store.

When she told the store man what had happened, he scolded her. She was a "dumb easterner" for not knowing to move her camp away from the wash after he'd told her it had rained hard up in the mountains. Didn't she know anything?

What could Annie say? She knew when Bog Creek was likely to overflow its banks, but she didn't know anything about flash floods in the desert—or at least not until now. She tried to make him focus on her problem: the horses were gone.

Satisfied that he'd gotten his lecture across, the store clerk called the sheriff in Rock Springs, and before long, he showed up in a patrol car. Annie had to repeat the story all over again, while the man busted up with laughter. At least he told her not to worry. They'd find her horses, he said. Annie told him that if she had to guess, she'd bet they had headed back the way they came from, since that's what they'd done the time they got lost in Arkansas.

Later that day, Tarzan and Rex were found healthy and unhurt and, just as she had guessed, more than twenty miles down the road they'd already covered. The sheriff arranged housing along the route for the two overnights it would take her to ride the horses back to this point. The store man's wife promised to get her gear dry in the meantime, so that she could pack it up upon her return.

Drier and wiser now, Annie finally made it to the town of Rock Springs, on the far side of the Red Desert. Happy as she was to have arrived in a bigger town, she felt a growing sense of unease about what lay ahead. It was one thing to travel in winter up in New England, where a farmhouse was never more than a stone's throw away and where lots of people meant lots of policemen watching out for her and lending a helping hand. Her experience of almost drowning in that isolated wash had rattled her. She felt unprepared for all of the lonely territory that lay between here and the West Coast.

The horses could not continue without new shoes, so she had to spend three days in Rock Springs waiting for a blacksmith. When he finally arrived in town, he was glum about her prospects. He kept telling her that there was too much wintry country ahead of her, and not enough time to beat the snows. When she tried to pay him, he refused, saying that it would be bad luck for him to take money from her, since her trip was so surely doomed.

Annie was beginning to wonder why she'd agreed to carry the letter to the governor of Idaho. Way back in Springfield, when Mina Titus Sawyer, the reporter from a small town in Maine, had sent the letter to her, she'd suggested that this would be a good way to get publicity for her trip, and Annie had thought it sounded like a fine idea. Back then, she'd been focused on heading south to beat the winter. She'd figured she'd get to California eventually, but she hadn't yet gone to the lengths of plotting an entire cross-country route, for an entirely practical reason. As it happened, Annie had never managed to get hold of a map of the entire United States, so she'd had to piece her route together one leg at a time, without ever having a good sense of the whole. This method had worked out okay—but it hadn't alerted her to the fact that passing through Idaho was not the easiest way to reach California, nor that it would lead her into desolate country just as the seasons were turning and winter's threat loomed again. Only what could she do? She couldn't reverse course now and ride back across the vast desert she'd just crossed, and she couldn't stay put here in Rock Springs, paying for lodging with no work to do. She really had no choice but to continue on toward Idaho.

Annie set her sights on the last sizable town along Route 30 West, Green River, named for the river it sat next to. From there, she'd continue west until turning onto 30 North, which would direct her toward the mining town of Kemmerer and on to Pocatello, Idaho. It would also route her toward Harvey Kelsey's ranch.

About twenty-five miles west of Green River, Annie passed another one of Wyoming's roadside wonders. Covey's Little America was located along Route 30 North, and it made up almost the entirety of the town of Granger. Surrounded by rangeland used primarily for sheep ranching, Granger owed its life to the fact that it had long been a place that people passed through on the way to somewhere else. Even today, its population numbers only 124. Because Granger was crossed by the routes of both the Oregon Trail and the Mormon Trail, the notorious

Donner Party passed through the town in 1846, Brigham Young in 1847, the gold rush forty-niners two years later, and Mark Twain, on the Overland Stage, in 1861. Finally, in 1868, the Union Pacific Railroad came through. By 1968, Covey's Little America would be Exit 68 on I-80. In 1955, it was a rest stop for weary motorists when Annie, Tarzan, Rex, and Depeche Toi arrived on foot.

Covey's Little America was certainly not the only roadside motel along Route 30, but it was one of the most distinctive. It had been built in 1934 as a combination gas station–motel–café, its remote location chosen by its founder, who later recounted that as a young man, out herding sheep, he had once been lost in a raging blizzard and forced to "lay out" all night "in the exact place where Little America now stands." According to Stephen Mack Covey, the temperature dropped to forty below as the night progressed, and he dreamed that someday he'd return to build a shelter of some kind on "that god-forsaken spot." Later, after becoming a successful rancher with thousands of acres of his own, he fulfilled his promise. He named his rest station Little America after Admiral Richard Byrd's Antarctic exploration base.

The original facility, consisting of twelve cabins, two gas pumps, and a twenty-four-seat restaurant, burned down in 1949, but Covey rebuilt a larger and grander motel, and it became a familiar landmark for travelers along that stretch of highway. Fortunately for Annie and her animals, the weather in early September remained mild, with no blizzards in sight; even so, the view of the gleaming white contemporary buildings of Little America—the neon signs, the motel's rounded art moderne curves, and the brightly lit restaurant—must have looked like a mirage in the desert after her long trek.

Annie didn't stay the night, however—she had other plans. Instead, she headed off the main road, following directions to Kelsey's ranch. She crossed the dry wash gulch, headed downward at a fork, and came across a neat white wooden ranch house about the same size as the home Annie had left behind back in Minot, though this one was in much trimmer condition. And sure enough, the fellow she'd met in Cheyenne came out to greet her. Depeche Toi ran straight to him and jumped up on his leg, treating their host like an old friend.

Kelsey helped Annie untack and unload the horses, then told her to let them loose behind the barn, where they'd find abundant grass and a fresh stream for water. She was hesitant to do so, remembering her run-in with the dry wash that had flooded, but he told her not to worry—Adam and Eve would not let them stray. He gave a whistle toward his house, and to her surprise, two collies jumped out an open window and came straight to Kelsey's feet. They obediently crouched on their hind legs, watching the horses. Kelsey explained that these were his border collies and the best sheepherding dogs he'd ever had. He also made a point of telling her that he had two men out on the range right now working for him, watching a hundred head of sheep. Annie remembered the loving way he'd spoken about his dogs the first time she'd met him; evidently, he was equally proud of his herd of sheep.

Inside, the house was tidy and small—just a single room with a kitchen in the back corner. The table was covered with clean Irish linen, and in the center were a vase of wax flowers and two candles. Kelsey served up a lunch of beef stew with carrots, tomatoes, potatoes, and onions, along with brown rye bread, followed by cheese and ripe pears. When they had finished, he scooped out an ample portion of leftover stew for Depeche Toi, who licked the bowl clean.

Without much preamble he said, "I'll be eighty in December. I'd judge you to be in your early fifties."

"Sixty-four, in December," she admitted.

"Well, you look much younger," he said. "Must be the healthy outdoor life."

They soon discovered that they shared the same birthday, December 13. He told her that he'd been born in Pennsylvania and come to Wyoming by covered wagon in 1890, the year Wyoming became a state.

"We got started here at the same time, the state and I," he said.

He invited her to stay on for at least a few days. "I'll be happy to sleep in the barn," he said.

But Annie demurred. She didn't want to stay on as she was in a hurry to make it to California. As she put it, she was the last of her line, but she'd be the first to see California.

He was smiling. "I ask for personal reasons," he said. "I'm hoping you'll stay here to be my wife."

Annie was so startled she had to put her coffee cup down. "Are you proposing?" she asked.

He nodded.

"You don't know anything about me."

"I know a great deal about you. I've been reading about you for months. And I know that you love animals. What do you think will happen to my sheep when I'm gone, and my dogs?"

Annie realized that he was dead serious. He offered to put half the ranch in her name right then, and deed the rest to her in his will. He explained that he lived all alone out here and he'd never met a woman like Annie—never met a woman who he believed could manage on her own as well as he could.

She told him she'd never been one to rush into things and she'd have to think it over.

Kelsey seemed like he didn't mind a woman who needed to think things over, and he didn't say anything else, just cleared the table and poured her some more coffee and some for himself. After a good long but comfortable silence, he seemed to understand that Annie wasn't planning to say any more about it.

She might well have accepted his offer to stay for a few days, but under the circumstances, it just didn't seem proper. So she set off again, right after lunch. As she prepared to leave, Kelsey told her, "If you decide the answer is no, don't write. So long as I don't know you're not coming back I can keep on hoping."

Kelsey's ranch was about ten miles from the road, and he gave her directions for the fastest way to head back down—she figured she'd find a place to camp along the way. It was all downhill, and she was making good time, but the sun had dropped behind the hills, casting long purple shadows, and it was almost dark when she realized that she was going to have to cross a creek deep down in a gully. She was close enough to the road that she could see headlights in the distance. The boys stomped and snorted when she reined them to a halt. She was trying to figure out how deep the water was from the reflection of the moon on the black surface. It looked passable, so with a cluck and a shake of her reins, she urged Rex forward toward a spot that looked sandy and shallow.

Rex, usually so obliging, trumpeted a warning and took a step back, but Tarzan stepped ahead. Rex started to follow, then suddenly skidded to a stop, and before Annie knew what had happened, she tumbled over his head and was left clinging to the reins. There was no solid ground beneath her feet. Rex dropped his head. Annie held on to the reins for dear life. Depeche Toi jumped off Tarzan and ran to Rex's nose, barking. Rex raised his head and backed up, dragging Annie to safety.

Covered with sand and scraped up, she stood still until she got her wits about her and could figure out what had happened. In the dark, she hadn't noticed that the bank of the creek was hollowed out underneath, causing the ground to collapse beneath Rex's front feet. If Rex hadn't dragged her to safety, she might have fallen into the creek and drowned.

By now it was completely dark, and Annie was spooked, but she felt her way to the more solid part of the trail and led the boys across a narrow part of the creek that she was able to hop across without getting her feet wet. That night, she camped along the roadside, thinking of the small white house in the mountains, and wondering if she shouldn't have stayed put right there.

For her last two weeks in Wyoming, Annie stuck to the highway and managed to find places to stay, though without much human interaction. By the time she crossed the border into Idaho, she'd had a lot of time to do a lot of thinking.

She thought about the second man she'd married, and how he'd run off on her when she wouldn't deed him the farm, and how she'd worked her fingers to the bone until she was so weary she could barely stand up, for years and years, and had finally set off, humbled and nearly beaten, with few options before her.

All that time, she'd been yearning for something—yearning for a time when she didn't owe anybody anything, yearning for a time when the only person who wanted anything from her was her own self. It had been a long journey across America's least populous state, and as she reached Wyoming's western border, her gaze passed across its serene, sweeping beauty one last time. Somewhere, somehow along these long empty highways, accompanied only by the steady hoofbeats of her two equine friends, Tarzan, with his forelock flopping, his ears on alert for scary trucks, and Rex, the pal and companion, her dependable friend in times of need—as handsome as her first husband and as tall as the second one but much, much more loyal than either of them had ever been—and, of course, her fluffy bundle of boundless optimism, her pioneer pup who'd snuggled up next to her heart night after night, somehow, in all the stillness, she'd found her own voice.

There was something in the American spirit, a restlessness that had driven so many immigrants to this country's shores—she'd met so many different people along the way, and the one thing almost all of them had in common was that originally, they were from someplace else. She'd met Bostonians in Maine and Italians in Tennessee. And she'd met a sheepherder who loved animals every bit as much as she did. And his offer was solid, but she knew in her heart that she'd made the right decision, that she didn't want anything that would hold her in place.

What had she learned in Wyoming? That you could still do it. You could still get on a horse and ride off into the sunset. You just had to be willing to let go of everything else—well, almost everything. Annie reached behind her and gave Rex a pat on his haunches, and he flicked an ear back by way of greeting. Depeche Toi, as if on cue, stood up and panted, his tail waving back in his happy slow wag, and Tarzan, who had been lagging behind, gave Rex's behind a nudge with his nose, then jogged a few steps forward to catch up, settling down when he was just a nose in the lead, his old racehorse instincts never completely gone.

That was the other thing she had learned in Wyoming. That cowboy who rides off alone into the sunset? He wasn't alone. He was on horseback. And that is what it is to be a rider. Your best friend is always with you. Annie was gifted in friendship. She had two horses—the rogue and the gentleman, the jogger and the walker, the New Englander and the southerner. And, of course, she had her short-legged furry bosom buddy as well. Annie was part of a team.

So Annie Wilkins, tramp of fate, was not lonely, and after sixty-odd years of running to the commands of others, she was happy to have her own inner voice for company. She was not an educated person, but had she been familiar with the work of the great American poet Walt Whitman, she would have certainly heard the sound of his words in the Wyoming winds: "I celebrate myself, and sing myself. . . . I loaf and invite my soul, I lean and loaf at my ease observing a spear of summer grass."

Annie Wilkins had worked her entire life. And now she could contemplate the world around her at her leisure.

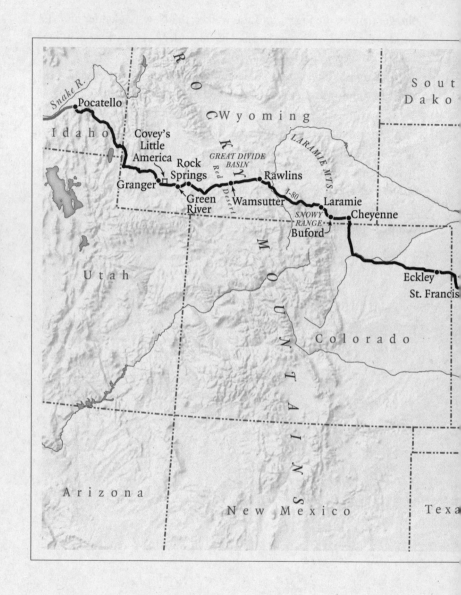

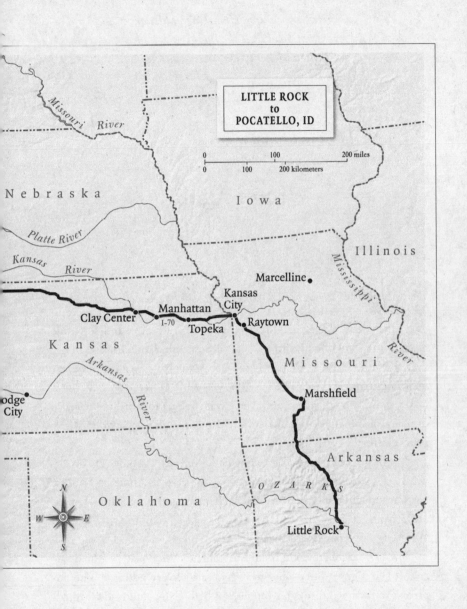

LITTLE ROCK
to
POCATELLO, ID

0   100   200 miles
0   100   200 kilometers

Missouri River

Nebraska

Iowa

Platte River

Illinois

Kansas River

Mississippi River

Marcelline

Kansas City

Clay Center   Manhattan
                     I-70   Topeka   Raytown

Kansas

Arkansas River

Missouri

odge
City

Marshfield

Arkansas

O Z A R K S

N
W   E
S

Oklahoma

Little Rock

Generally speaking, a howling wilderness
does not howl: it is the imagination of
the traveler that does the howling.

—Henry David Thoreau

—

Winter Again

P ASSING THROUGH IDAHO IS in no way the fastest route to Southern California, but a promise is a promise, and so Annie crossed the state line toward the end of September, determined to deliver the letter she'd been carrying in her saddlebag since her very first mail stop in Springfield. The envelope was fairly battered by now, but it was in good enough shape, and Annie was looking forward to the sense of accomplishment she would feel while making her very own Pony Express delivery.

The bright blue skies of Wyoming had given way to some very dreary weather. A steady, cold rain fell every day for a week. Annie had ridden her way straight out of summer and back into impending winter. On the other hand, at least this countryside was not as remote as the part of Wyoming she'd passed through.

The first sizable town in Idaho she came to was Pocatello, the destination she'd given out as her next general delivery address. The approach to town led through a tunnel, but before she could ride through it, a policeman caught up with her and asked where she was going. To the post office, she replied. The officer insisted that she leave the horses with him in a parking lot. She'd snarl up traffic if she tried to ride through the tunnel. The post office was just a short walk away, and he'd watch the horses until she got back.

Annie agreed. She left the young man holding on to Rex and Tarzan and walked the short distance to the post office. When she got there, the clerk found her mail filed under "Horse Traveler. Hold indefinite period." Happy news, until the clerk informed her that only the head postmaster was able to release it, and since he wasn't there, she couldn't have it.

Back at the parking lot, she saw that a crowd had gathered around the horses, who appeared to have escaped from the young policeman. Rex was walking backward in tight circles, his head high with his ears pinned back. Trotting around him, also with his ears laid back, was Tarzan. Surrounding them were six police officers, who all looked scared to death. And Depeche Toi was still perched on Tarzan's haunches, barking and crouching as if he'd lunge at the first cop who tried to step forward.

Annie hustled up, eager to settle the situation. The original young officer, obviously a complete greenhorn when it came to horses, explained that the big horse had tried to bolt and had gotten away from him. No matter that Rex was as gentle as the day is long, clearly something had spooked him, and this had set off Tarzan—always seeking to be the big protector. When Depeche Toi saw Annie, he jumped off Tarzan, trotted over, and leapt up into her arms. Tarzan stopped dead in his tracks and glanced over at Annie for instructions, and Rex whinnied, dropped his head, and went from panicking to looking half-asleep. The police officers, who had been waving their hands in the air, trying to corral the horses, let them fall to their sides, suddenly all feeling pretty sheepish. In a moment, Annie had hold of both horses and was feeding them each a nub of carrot she'd fished out from her pocket. She managed to find a rental stable for the night, got her mail the next morning, and couldn't beat it out of Pocatello fast enough.

IT WAS MID-OCTOBER when Annie and her crew arrived in American Falls, where she planned to camp at Massacre Rocks State Park, famous as a frequent stopping place for pioneers on the Oregon Trail, and known for a configuration of rocks called Devil's Gate whose narrow passage was feared to make pioneers vulnerable to attack. Between the years 1846 and 1869, almost four hundred thousand settlers passed along this two-thousand-mile route, which originated in Independence, Missouri, and ended in Portland, Oregon. Massacre Creek, with its flowing water and abundant grass, marked a popular spot for travelers to rest their horses and themselves. One of its most striking features was the large boulder covered with names and dates, etched there by pioneers as they passed. By the time Annie arrived, travelers typically drove up in cars and wrote their names in a register book with pen and ink. When Annie registered for a camping spot, under "Make and model of car," she wrote: "Lord's Own, horsepower: two."

Even in such a pleasant spot, Annie and her companions stayed only a single night. She was afraid to dawdle longer. As October raced to a close, there was no mistaking the feeling of imminent winter. She passed through American Falls and Twin Falls, heading as fast as the eight legs would carry her to Boise, on the western edge of the state. In 1955, Idaho's capital was a sleepy town of about thirty-five thousand, prettily situated on a plain ringed by mountains. Annie managed to wrangle herself an invitation to sleep in the county jail. From there, she walked to the statehouse, carrying her letter. She'd traveled all this way to deliver it, but when she got there, she felt shy, and not a little bit ridiculous. Nevertheless, she found the governor's office and pushed the door open, telling the secretary that she had come bringing a letter for the governor. The secretary sized Annie up and brushed her off. She could post the letter—but Governor Smylie was a very busy man.

Embarrassed, Annie left, and she was almost out of the building when the woman ran to catch up with her. The governor had been expecting her to show up one of these days, she told Annie. He couldn't wait to meet her! Annie returned to the office, where she was greeted warmly by the governor, Robert Smylie. On his desk sat the largest potato she'd ever seen—a fine specimen that weighed three and half pounds, he told her proudly. He opened the letter of greeting from

Maine's governor and read it with interest, then placed it on the desk next to the gargantuan potato and said with a smile that he was certain that Maine's potatoes were the *second* best in the nation. Annie stoutly defended Maine's own potatoes, saying that his massive specimen reminded her of the ones back home—even if, truth be told, she'd never seen one so big. When he tried to present it to her as a gift, she had to politely decline, explaining that it wouldn't fit in her saddlebag.

Annie spent the night as the city's guest in a local hotel and was invited back the next day to pose on the steps of the capitol with Smylie. After all of these months of relative obscurity, she was rediscovered by the national press. An AP reporter interviewed her on the phone, and soon the news of Annie's meeting with Idaho's governor had spread all across the United States and even, though she did not know it yet, all the way to Hollywood.

On November 7, Annie, Tarzan, and Depeche Toi spent their 368th day on the road just past Ontario, Oregon. Annie's journey had been marked in inches on various maps, miles underfoot, people met, beds slept in, care and companionship with her animals, wrong turns taken, rain, dust, and snowstorms endured, notecards sold and sent, letters received, and, more than anything else, by an astounding number of kindnesses.

But one thing Annie's journey lacked was logic. If you were drawing a route on a map from Minot, Maine, to California, you'd never choose to arrive on the West Coast via Oregon's Highway 20. If Annie had had better tools at her disposal, if she'd been able to sit down with a real road atlas, instead of the regional gas station maps she relied on, she most likely would have understood that getting close to California via its northeast corner was hardly getting close to the "California" she was expecting. If she had been better informed, she might also have realized that Harney County, Oregon, was not just the least populous part of the state but would also be one of the most sparsely settled areas she'd pass through, rivaled only, so far, by Wyoming's Red Desert. In fact, Harney County, at 10,226 square miles, covers an area larger than that of six of the U.S. states, and in 1950 it had a total population of only six thousand people, about half of whom lived in its one midsized town, Burns. On this day, just over one year from her departure from Minot, Burns was still 130 miles down the road.

None of this was apparent to Annie and her furry fellow travelers as they headed west through the arid, sandy landscape of southeastern Oregon. The area around Boise had been relatively well populated, with smaller settlements along the route she'd traveled. And Oregon was more noted for the milder rainy climate of its western, coastal areas, where most of its population was concentrated. So it's understandable that Annie just didn't know what she was heading into. Maybe the explanation is simply that in Annie's mindset, there was something that remained of that pioneer spirit, a determined willingness to confront the unknown. As John Bidwell, a covered-wagon pioneer settler, wrote in 1841, "All the country beyond was to us a veritable *terra incognita,* and we only knew that California lay to the west."

Just over a year on the road, and the group was in fine form. Annie's cough had disappeared as she'd passed through western Kansas, and the horses had never been healthier. Tarzan hadn't lost an ounce of oomph. He still jittered and jumped against Rex whenever he got a notion to, showed a little white in his eyes, and would run the four of them off the road at a moment's notice—and yet Annie knew that if she were a soldier, he was the horse she'd pick to go into battle with. Just like Annie herself, he woke up every morning willing to do a day's honest work without complaint. As for Rex, her Tennessee rambler, it was hard to believe that this was the same horse that had been sick and out of shape when she'd gotten hold of him, this fine blood bay who'd made it through the mountains as if he'd been born to high altitudes. Depeche Toi, admittedly, had become more of a rider as time went along. Now he was almost a trick dog—able to nimbly hop from Tarzan's back onto the saddle in front of Annie, and skilled at staying aboard Tarzan even when he whirled around fast. A year of ups and downs, of kindnesses and catastrophes, and now here she was in southern Oregon, her California goal tantalizingly close.

The route you could trace with a finger—west along Highway 20, then south on 395 at Burns—would have her at the northern border of California in less than three hundred miles. If she and the boys could maintain a pace of about twenty miles a day, she could reasonably be in California in just over two weeks. Being unfamiliar with the vast country's geography, and certainly blessed with an optimistic turn of mind, Annie could be forgiven for thinking that soon enough, she'd be basking in sunshine.

The true joy of her journey, the whimsy, the serendipity, the *faith* she had in her father's maxim "Keep going and you'll get there" had served her well so far. It was likely the reason that she had attracted such a legion of fans across the nation. Just wandering had long been an American preoccupation, the essence of being free, but the world that was coming fast would, in fact, narrow people's perception of their choices, curtail their freedom to meander. America's wide-open spaces, which had seemed to beckon to the wanderer, would soon be replaced by a more efficient world of interstate highways, whose goal was to get you there. There was nothing efficient or planned or, frankly, even smart about heading along Highway 20 West on the cusp of winter, but had you seen Annie walking along in early November 1955, you might have envied her freedom.

Perhaps for the first time, however, Annie lacked a crucial piece of information, knowledge that had been learned the hard way by generations of California-bound pioneers. During the era of covered wagons, the season to pass into California on the California Trail started in late April and ceased in early October. During the winter, there were no passable routes in the north. You might be almost there—but you are not *actually* there until you make it through the Sierra Nevada—just ask the Donner Party. Annie, heading blithely west and south, apparently did not know this.

The area west of Boise and into Oregon had been settled mostly by Mormons, so for the first part of her trip along Highway 20, Annie had been hosted by Mormon families, who were happy to pass her along to a friend or relative a day's ride down the road. But not long after Juntura, Annie noticed that she was riding into mountains and that the houses were now few and far between. She started looking for a place to stay as soon as the noon hour hit—she'd stop and ask at the first house she saw, afraid she might not come across another before nightfall. As she was searching one day, a woman stopped to ask her where she was headed, then a few hours later came back and popped out of her car with a comb and a pair of scissors. She'd noticed that Annie's hair was flopping into her eyes and had figured she could use a trim. The woman cut Annie's hair right then and there into a neat pixie, after seating Annie on a rock. She'd also secured a place for Annie and the boys to spend the night, on a ranch about four miles down the road.

When Annie arrived at the Thienes ranch, she found a husband and wife and a house whose beautiful view encompassed an open valley. They had recently bought their dream ranch, and had only just finished building the house and barns. Mrs. Thienes led Annie to a brand-new bunkhouse and announced that she'd have the spacious spread to herself, as they hadn't hired any ranch hands yet. She instructed Annie to turn Tarzan and Rex out in the corral next to the ranch house with the other horses. Annie thought it was fenced—then, too late, after the horses trotted off down the hill, realized it was more of an open range.

She whistled for Tarzan and Rex, but the wind was blowing, and there were no horses in sight. Mrs. Thienes, however, told her not to worry—the horses would come back at dusk, when she gave them their grain. Annie did worry—the boys had run off before. But sure enough, at dusk, the entire herd came galloping back. Tarzan was right up in the lead as the band thundered up the hill, his tail floating on the breeze, the crest of his neck arched and his hooves flying with freedom and pride. And just in back of him, nose on his buddy's tail, was Rex. Behind them stretched a backdrop of ravishing pine-covered mountains, while off in the distance a stream meandered through the valley. Annie thought back to the first time she saw Tarzan, downtrodden, cast off, a bit thin. Now here he was galloping free, and in her heart, she knew he relished it as much as she did. Still, she was mightily relieved to see them.

She planned to depart the following morning, but the weather was not cooperating. For three days, Annie stayed put, hoping to outwait the relentless heavy rain. On the third morning, it stopped, and she was determined to head out during the break in the weather, in spite of the Thieneses' warning that they'd heard that heavy snows had fallen in the mountains. The way Annie looked at it, with every day that passed, she was just heading deeper into winter. She had to press on while she still could, at least to make it as far as Burns.

Annie was ready to depart just as the sun was rising. Mrs. Thienes had helped her load up, even as she'd begged her to reconsider. Annie could stay where she was as long as she wanted—all winter if need be, she said—but Annie was already feeling restless. The only way to get away from winter was to stick to her plan—and before long, she'd be in California, the land of sunshine.

The four travelers headed west toward Burns, and at first, as they descended toward the floor of the Drewsey Valley, the weather didn't seem too bad. The hills sheltered her from the wind, and the sun was bright and felt warm on her face. But as the day progressed and the road started to climb up into the mountains, a cold wind from the northeast cut right through her parka. By now, the knit gloves she had bought back in Laramie were raggedy and the thumbs had frayed off, and soon her hands began to go numb. Although Annie was planning to buy more warm clothes when she got to Burns, she didn't expect to arrive there until the following day. She tried to persuade Depeche Toi to ride under her parka to keep her warm, but he seemed to prefer standing on Tarzan's back with his nose pointing into the air, as if somewhere on that cold wind he could just catch a scent of California orange blossoms in the distance.

The weather steadily worsened as the day went on. Soon it was freezing cold, and an icy wind was blowing a stinging snow. No plow came by, nor a single car. She and her boys were the only things moving, and the snow was piling up fast. She'd saddled the horses over their blankets, and she'd even dressed Depeche Toi in the special dog blanket she'd received as a gift way back in New Hampshire. On her own body, she'd piled on every stitch of clothing she owned, but since she'd left her warmer things behind in Arkansas, she didn't have the kind of clothes

needed to withstand this kind of weather. She'd lost the fur-lined bonnet, the heavy anorak, the double layers of union suits, and the felt-lined
boots she'd worn the previous winter.

Even worse, the blinding snow was blowing so hard that she was having trouble keeping the boys on the road. In places, snow had drifted up
as high as the fences, so it was difficult to tell what was road and what
wasn't. The horses plodded forward, heads bowed, as Annie second-
guessed her decision to leave the safety of the Thieneses' ranch. They
couldn't have been more than five miles from Burns; around each bend
she expected to see the town come into view, but each time she was disappointed. She began to worry: What if they'd strayed from the main
road? What if they had turned off onto a side road without realizing it?
They'd been traveling for hours and had not seen a house, or a single
living soul.

It was almost dark and she was near frozen through when she finally
came to a lone house. She knocked on the door, and thankfully a woman
with a bright smile answered. When she saw the frozen woman and her
three snow-crusted animals, she called to her husband to get the horses
into the barn and made Annie come straight inside. Her name was Elsie
Eisenhower—"No relation," she quickly added while she stationed
Annie next to a warm kerosene stove, brought her a clean towel, a blanket, and a red flannel nightgown, and told her to get herself changed. "I
may not be related to the president," she informed Annie, "but he's in
charge of the nation and I rule this home. Now, get yourself out of those
frozen things and warm yourself up."

Once Annie was dried off and warm, Mrs. Eisenhower proceeded to
berate her for being out on a night like this and for putting herself and
her horses in danger. What had she been thinking? Annie had been
thinking she knew better than the local folks about how things were
going to work out, but evidently, even though she considered herself an
expert on snow, she didn't know a single thing about Oregon weather.
She did understand full well that she could have drifted off that road and
gotten lost out there, and then where would she and the animals be?

She'd made a mistake. A bad one. She had nothing to say in her own defense.

The next morning, it was seventeen below zero. The roads hadn't been plowed, the phone lines were down, and the snow was still falling. Elsie Eisenhower and her husband, Henry, sat Annie down over a cup of coffee and a hot bowl of oatmeal and they told her what she needed to do.

The thing to do, they said, was to wait until spring.

Spring? Annie didn't believe what she was hearing. She was so close to California, and it was only November. How could she possibly wait until spring?

But the Eisenhowers laid it out for her. There were nothing but mountain roads between here and California, and most of them would not be passable until after the snow melted. Annie listened, feeling more and more abashed. And when would the snow melt, she asked.

Maybe April, sometimes May, they said.

But they told her not to worry. She could stay right there in their house all winter. She could help with the housework and the care of the horses—take care of her own and help with the others—and they'd be pleased to have the company. She could stay as long as she liked, and maybe she'd like it so much, come spring she'd decide she'd traveled far enough.

Annie appreciated their kindness, but she couldn't imagine her journey coming to an end like that. She'd have no way to truly earn her keep, and she'd feel beholden. Even so, she could also see that she had ridden herself right into a trap—as much a dead end as that old end road in Maine she'd started out on. She might be from Maine, but it looked as if she was going to be defeated by the selfsame winter she'd been trying to flee. Socked in. And still not in California.

Annie insisted that if she was going to stay through the winter, she'd need to work to earn her keep, so the Eisenhowers found her a spot in a rooming house in Burns, where she could work doing odd jobs in exchange for her room and board. The horses stayed with the Eisenhowers.

Annie passed a melancholy second Thanksgiving alone in the Burns boardinghouse. She was too depressed to leave her room. It was just as cold here as Maine had ever been. Nevertheless, she tried her best to accept the situation. At least she was still breathing okay, and the horses were safe, and she had her best friend, Depeche Toi, to keep her company. She tried to count her blessings, but as she looked out the rooming house window at the unfamiliar, snowed-in landscape, California seemed farther away than ever.

Then suddenly her luck changed. The day after Thanksgiving, Elsie Eisenhower told her that a friend with a truck was going to try to make it through the mountains and he had room to take Annie and the critters along. Elsie warned Annie that even in a truck the route was risky—but Annie leapt at the chance. Once she stepped off that truck, she'd be in California.

Why don't you go on west to California?
There's work there, and it never gets cold.
Why, you can reach out anywhere and pick
an orange. . . . Why don't you go there?

—**John Steinbeck**

CHAPTER

25

A Long Road

A NNIE WOULD NEVER FORGET how the marching band had played "California, Here I Come" in her honor as she, Rex, Tarzan, and Depeche Toi had ridden along the parade route in Cheyenne. But never, in the twelve months and three weeks she'd been on the road, had she ever imagined that her entry into the Golden State would be quite like this.

Annie and the boys were not the only quartet heading to California in 1955. The screwball TV comedy *I Love Lucy* was in its fifth season, and several episodes throughout that year had been devoted to a road trip across America. In the first of these episodes, Ricky (at the wheel) and Lucy, beside him, with Fred and Ethel in the backseat, set off for the West Coast in a convertible gleaming with chrome. As they drive across the George Washington Bridge, the four of them belt out a jaunty rendition of "California, Here I Come."

"California, Here I Come" was written by Buddy DeSylva and Joseph Meyer. First performed by Al Jolson in 1921, the song had become the unofficial anthem of the Golden State long before Annie decided to head there, but the lyrics continued to encapsulate the American drive to reach California—a great westward migration that began in earnest in 1848 with the gold rush and accelerated with the 1869 placing of the "golden spike" at Promontory Summit, in the Utah Territory, completing the transcontinental railroad and opening up the West Coast not only to migrants but also to tourism. The Lincoln Highway Association rushed to finalize the new route from New York to San Francisco by 1915 in order to let motorists drive to California to attend two large fairs celebrating the opening of the Panama Canal—one in San Francisco and one in San Diego. The next major migration to the state happened during the 1930s, when the Great Plains were stricken by a combination of overcultivation and severe droughts. The blizzards of blowing topsoil created the conditions that led the area to be known as the Dust Bowl—and caused migrants to flee in large numbers to the West Coast.

The "bowers of flowers" and singing birdies extolled by Al Jolson were only more firmly enhanced in people's imaginations during the Golden Age of Hollywood, as studios pumped out films and fans avidly followed the lives of movie stars against the backdrop of a Southern California carefully curated to appear sunny and glamorous. The population of Los Angeles began to skyrocket during the 1920s, more than doubling in ten years. By 1950, California was the country's second most populous state.

Annie, Tarzan, Rex, and Depeche Toi rattled across the state line in the late afternoon of Saturday, November 26, 1955, in a big white truck. When the Eisenhowers' friend asked Annie where she wanted to be dropped off, she told him that in front of the county jail would do fine.

Just as she'd not understood how remote southeast Oregon would be, she looked around the tiny mountain town of Alturas, California, with surprise, and perhaps a small measure of disappointment. *Alturas* is Spanish for "heights," and the town sits astride the Pit River, high in the Great Basin mountain range in one of the state's more isolated regions. Situated on Route 395, it was on the way from nowhere to nowhere. The high elevation often made it inaccessible in winter. The closest large town, Redding, was some 150 miles southwest. Alturas, even today, has the honor of being the only incorporated town in California's remote northeast corner. Most of the county is made up of the Modoc National Forest, an area where black bears are common and bands of wild horses have roamed for at least 140 years. Alturas's motto is "Where the West Still Lives," and its old-fashioned downtown resembled many others Annie had passed along the way—but what it didn't look like was any kind of "California" Annie had imagined as a girl in Maine in deepest winter listening to her mother's stories of a land of perpetual sunshine.

Sitting at an elevation of over four thousand feet, Alturas has an average low temperature in November of twenty-two degrees. If Annie had been hoping for bowers of flowers, anything that might fit that description was still about six hundred miles to the south. It was beginning to sink in that in her second November on the road, she still had a lot of riding to do before she hit anything that felt like warm weather.

Not having sold any notecards to speak of since leaving Boise, and low on funds, Annie thought that sleeping at the jail would be her best option. Inside, she found a deputy sheriff. Turned out he'd heard she might head this way, but he said he hadn't been expecting her because he'd thought she was "hibernating up in Oregon."

"I was," Annie replied, "but the Eisenhowers arranged a truck for me."

The Eisenhowers! At that, the deputy sat up straight, picked up the phone, and hurriedly dialed the sheriff. "That woman from Maine just arrived from Oregon. The president of the United States arranged it! Yes! She doesn't want a hotel, she wants to stay here." Annie hastily explained that the Oregon Eisenhowers were no relation to the president, but the deputy remained just as impressed with his new visitor.

After she was settled in the empty cell, the deputy brought her fried eggs and bacon, hash browns, and coffee. He told her that word of her visit had spread fast. The chamber of commerce folks had heard she was in town, and they were out of sorts that she'd ended up at the jail—they'd hoped to put her up in a hotel. But Annie was weary. She'd already gotten settled, and the jail was just fine for her—the bed even had sheets and blankets—so she politely declined their offer.

So the folks from the chamber of commerce came up with another scheme. They'd read in the paper that Annie had never seen a motion picture—or, at least, not a "talkie." So the next day they took her to the movies, where a western was playing. She was enjoying it when she was interrupted in the middle of the film: someone had come into the theater to inform her that a reporter from the AP wire service was on the phone. She told the reporter all about her visit to the movie theater, then returned to her seat to watch the movie a second time.

Annie was planning to head from Alturas southwest to Redding, but a good look at her gas station map of California was sobering. To get to Redding she needed to wind her way out of the mountains, a trek of several weeks, and it was almost December. She'd be lucky to make it through without hitting another storm that closed the roads. On the other hand, from here on in, she'd be heading chiefly downhill, and along Route 299 the small towns were close together. Everyone told her that if she could make it to Redding, she'd leave winter behind; the trick would be to get there.

Hoping for the best—and, especially, relieved not be stuck up in Burns anymore—Annie packed up and set off the next morning. It took her two weeks to get down through the towns of Canby and Adin, Bieber and Nubieber, McArthur, Fall River Mills, and Burney, inching her way toward Redding, the greatest blessing being that every mile led them farther out of the mountains. For perhaps the first time along her journey, the weather cooperated. It was cold, and it snowed, but not so much that she couldn't keep going. The roads stayed open.

Annie rode into Redding on December 15, and the town was more than prepared for her arrival. She was offered a private room at the Golden Eagle, the town's fanciest hotel. By this point, she had only coins left in her pockets, so she insisted on being taken to the jail instead, but her protests were for naught. The mayor declared that his town would foot all of her bills. And no wonder. Annie had a very special visitor. Dick Pettit, a publicist who worked for television personality Art Linkletter, had been dispatched to Redding to meet Annie and present her with an official invitation to appear on Linkletter's popular prime-time TV show *People Are Funny*.

By 1955, Annie must have been one of the few Americans not to recognize the celebrity's name. Not every house had a television, but Linkletter had gotten his start in radio, then parlayed that name recognition and following into one of the largest television audiences of that era. Television shows that featured ordinary people doing stunts were common in the 1950s, but Linkletter's format—part interview, part game show—relied heavily on his own gifts as an interviewer. Although television critics found his "persona bland and his popularity unfathomable," American audiences loved him. He attributed his success to his ordinariness. Linkletter told the *New York Post* in 1965, "I'm like everybody's next-door neighbor, only a little bit smarter."

Like so many other people, Linkletter had started following Annie's journey in the newspapers, and had been won over. A quick look at his biography explains why he might have felt a connection. Abandoned at birth in Saskatchewan, Canada, and then quickly adopted, Art landed with a new father who was a one-legged itinerant evangelist. The family prayed and performed on street corners, with young Art playing the triangle.

Linkletter began working as a child, after his family relocated to what was then a small town, San Diego. When he graduated from high school he immediately took off, with only ten dollars in his pocket, to see the world. The way he described it, "Among other things, I learned to chisel rides on freight trains, outwit the road bulls, cook stew with the bindlestiffs and never to argue with a gun." In short, Linkletter cut his teeth in the grand American tradition: he was a hobo.

Linkletter immediately understood Annie's essential Americanness: her authority came precisely from the fact that her journey was neither choreographed nor staged. Here was a woman who was doing something just because she wanted to do it. She'd been capturing people's hearts all along her journey—but when she captured Linkletter's attention, she would win a bigger audience than she ever could have imagined.

Annie was, as usual, completely unruffled. She had a habit of treating everyone the same, and this wasn't the first time she'd been invited to appear on television. Besides, she had no sense of the difference between national and local coverage. So she figured out the distance between Redding and Los Angeles, calculated that it would take her about two months to travel the nearly six hundred miles, took Mr. Pettit's card, and promised to give him a call when she reached San Fernando, on the outskirts of L.A., so that he could arrange for her visit to the show.

She had been told that she'd be out of winter by the time she reached Redding, but she'd been told wrong. The last two weeks of December were cold and snowy, so Annie stayed put, right there in Redding, through Christmas, as a guest of the Golden Eagle Hotel. Finally, as 1955 turned to 1956, Annie and her boys hit the road again. They were heading south on California Highway 99, which ran right through the middle of the state, north to south. Destination: Hollywood.

There is a sacredness in tears.
They are not the mark of weakness, but of power.

—attributed to Samuel Johnson

1956

CHAPTER 26

Tough as Nails

T HE FOUR COMPANIONS HAD done it. They'd made it from Maine to California. This last leg of the journey promised to be easier. In anticipation of her appearance on his show, Linkletter's crew had done some advance filming of the travelers in and around Redding. For quite a while as Annie had worked her way across the more remote parts of the West, her exploits had been cataloged chiefly in small local newspapers from the towns where she stopped. But the rest of her trip would be covered in the national press, and Linkletter had promised to give her a place to stay once she reached Los Angeles. All she had to do was get there.

For Annie, 1955 had been a year of change, of firsts, of fears and challenges—and it had unrolled this way for most Americans, as well. Dramatic changes in transportation and communication were upending the old order and creating the impression that the world itself was rapidly shrinking. In 1954, the live broadcast of the Rose Parade had had fewer than two dozen local networks to transmit to. Just a year later, the parade broadcast spun out to a large network of local stations, bringing

California's wintertime dazzle to hundreds of thousands of new viewers. In 1955, General Motors became the first company worth $10 billion. Transatlantic passenger jets were just two years away. The giant wooden radio that families gathered around would soon become the pocket-sized transistor Sony TR-63, allowing listeners to bring newscasts, ball games, and music right along with them. And, more significant, 1955 was a pivotal year for the burgeoning civil rights movement. In January 1955, Marian Anderson became the first African American to sing at the Metropolitan Opera House. On May 17, 1954, *Brown v. Board of Education* had mandated the desegregation of schools throughout the land. On August 28, the brutal murder of fourteen-year-old Emmett Till shocked the nation, finally jarring the country's consciousness. When Annie left Minot, segregation was still the accepted law of the land. By the time she reached California, the civil rights era was beginning.

Annie had spent the past year on less-traveled roads and in small towns. From her own perspective on horseback, the country she had traveled across had seemed vast, yet still welcoming and friendly, a place where neighbors greeted each other in local diners and a visiting stranger would attract friendly notice. Annie still traveled at the speed of hoofbeats, but the world she had encountered, one of roadside diners on quiet byways, would soon become more obsolete than she could have imagined. In April 1955, Ray Kroc had opened the country's first McDonald's restaurant, creating a brand-new connection between dining and automobiles.

Heading south from Redding, the four travelers passed through Chico and Yuba City before reaching the state's capital, Sacramento. The horse folk of California had pretty much adopted Annie after learning of her journey on TV. She passed from one riding stable to the next, with people from the stables taking her home for a hot meal and a shower. When she arrived at the outskirts of the capital, a reporter from *The Sacramento Bee* caught up with her. He described her as being "the picture of health," and the two horses and dog as "in fine traveling condition." In response to his question about how it felt to be a woman on her own, she replied, "In these modern times, when women smoke like men, when they compete with men in the trades, and they serve in the armed forces, it is fitting that the last saddle tramp be a woman." When he asked what her plans were, Annie answered, in true form, "I'll ride until they bury me," though no longer did she seem to think that her death was imminent. She was feeling good.

The highway Annie was riding along, U.S. 99, was one of the country's major north-south thoroughfares. It began at the Canadian border, where it connected to Canada's Highway 99, and ran all the way south to Calexico, Mexico. Known as the Golden State Highway, it cut through the flat agricultural center of the state, making it a major thoroughfare for Dust Bowl refugees during the 1930s.

When naturalist John Muir first entered California's Central Valley, in 1868, he described it this way: "The valley of the San Joaquin is the floweriest piece of world I ever walked, one vast, level, even flower-bed, a sheet of flowers, a smooth sea, ruffled a little in the middle by the tree fringing of the river and of smaller cross-streams here and there, from the mountains." Less than a century later, the valley John Muir had seen was much changed. California's Central Valley (called the Sacramento Valley at its northern end and the San Joaquin Valley farther south) had become one of the major agricultural regions of the entire United States, and a place where industrial farming on a massive scale got an early start.

Highway 99's path through the Central Valley's middle was a major transportation route for truckers bringing agricultural products to the markets in Los Angeles and to the ports for shipping. Annie had spent parts of her travels along what were then "major highways," but even in 1956, California was ahead of the curve in terms of traffic volume. Not since she'd ridden along the truckers' route in New Jersey had she encountered so much traffic. Heavily laden agricultural trucks lumbered by with bone-shaking frequency, while speedy passenger cars zipped in and out between them. The sides of the road were littered with pieces of tire rubber and rusty cans, trash jettisoned from car windows, endless numbers of cigarette butts, yellowed newspapers, and pretty much anything that could fall off a truck or be tossed out a rolled-down window.

California's Central Valley was often covered by thick tule fog—named for the local tule grass wetlands known as *tulares*—which sometimes stretched in a long, thick, low cloud from south of Sacramento to the Tehachapi Mountains, in the southern part of the state. That January's weather was typically mild—in the upper fifties or low sixties—but when a tule fog hung over the valley, the sun couldn't penetrate the thick clouds, and the drizzle often froze into slick black ice. During tule fog season, massive pileups of vehicles were common because the visibility was so poor.

Tarzan hadn't gotten any better about trucks whizzing by. Each time one rattled past, he zigged sideways, with Depeche Toi clinging on for dear life and only Rex to help steady him, while Annie tried to keep hold of Tarzan's rope and not let him shake off any of his gear. By mid-February, they'd spent the last thirty days following Highway 99 south, passing through one small town after another. Each town had a motto. Turlock advertised itself as "the heart of the valley." Merced was "the gateway to Yosemite."

The four companions were near the town of Atwater, a few miles north of Merced. The sky was a pale bright blue traced with thin cirrus clouds, and the temperature hovered around sixty degrees—perfect weather for riding. The truck traffic hadn't been as heavy that day, and so Tarzan plodded along lazily, his lead rope slack, a comfortable half-length behind Rex. Depeche Toi had his chin resting on his folded paws, with his tail curled tightly around himself. He was so deep asleep that sometimes he would twitch—dreaming of chasing cats, Annie had no doubt. Rex marched along at a nice clip, his ears pointed forward, the slight breeze ruffling his mane. Annie rode with the reins in her left hand, her right hand holding Tarzan's rope, resting on her right thigh. She was wearing the broad-brimmed white hat she'd picked up back in Arkansas, and her hair, cut into a pixie up in Oregon, had grown out enough that it was curling around her ears. Even though it was still winter, Annie had acquired a deep tan, which set off the blue in her eyes. And it wasn't just the color in her eyes—maybe it was calling herself a saddle tramp that had done it, or maybe it was all the months she'd spent out west. When she'd left home in Maine, even if she hadn't realized it, she'd had a bit of an air of apology about her, a tendency to make herself smaller. Back then, she'd described herself as looking like a frog on a lily pad.

No more. Handsome Annie Wilkins rode with all of her sixty inches set straight in the saddle, her eyes and her heart roaming free and unfettered to distant horizons.

That day, her plan was to ride as far as Merced, where she'd been told there'd be a stable that would be happy to take her in. They had been making good time with the fine weather when they came across an obstacle. A load of wooden citrus crates had fallen off a truck, and the wooden slats lay scattered and splintered across the road. The crates must have been empty when they fell, as she didn't see any produce— just smashed box slats, some with their colorful citrus labels still attached.

Rex startled and planted his two front feet. Sleepy Tarzan almost bumped into him, and Depeche Toi, jolted awake and sensing that something was up, hopped off Tarzan's back to investigate. Annie slackened Tarzan's rope and let Depeche Toi run forward. He was small and nimble and dodged among the splintered crates with ease.

Annie looked to see if there was a way around the mess, but the sticks and broken crates were pretty well strewn across both lanes of traffic and on the shoulders as well. She examined the situation more closely. Although there was no clear path through, it looked as if she could pick her way across if she took her time. She loosened the reins and gave Rex a nudge with her heels. She figured he'd find his way across more easily if she gave him a free head. Rex stepped daintily, picking a path through the debris as if he were a girl carefully avoiding the lines in a game of hopscotch. Tarzan stumbled along lazily behind. Normally, Tarzan was the more vigilant of the two, but the debris on the road did not seem to particularly faze him. Depeche Toi trotted back to Tarzan, opened his mouth in a panting smile, waved his tail a few times, then spun around and trotted forward again, leaping over the fallen boards as if they were obstacles in the Grand National Steeplechase and he were a fleet Thoroughbred horse. That was enough to convince Tarzan to break into a jog. Annie gave him a little more rope. But Rex was not to be hurried. He raised his hooves cautiously and stepped carefully, avoiding the splintered boards and moving much more slowly than Tarzan and Depeche Toi.

Annie and the boys were almost all the way across the board-spangled asphalt when she heard it: first a vibration, then a rattle, and at last a roar. A car came barreling down the highway behind them, and instead of slowing as it hit the boards lying in the road, it just sped on by, making a racket as the tires crushed the broken boards. Rex, normally the placid one, was spooked. He jumped and twisted, nearly unseating Annie and spinning halfway around before springing forward toward his comrade Tarzan. In a moment, the car was out of sight, but Rex was trembling all over.

Something was wrong. She petted his neck and spoke soothing words, then slipped off him. He was holding his left hind foot aloft, and when she tried to lead him a bit farther off the road, she could see that he was lame. Looping the reins into the crook of her arm, she slid her hand along his left hind tendon, pinching slightly to encourage him to lift up his foot so she could take a look. Rex complied, and Annie could see what had happened. A splinter with a nail in it had wedged its way between his iron shoe and the sole of his hoof. Annie gently worried the splinter back and forth, hoping to dislodge it, although it was jammed tight. Rex waited patiently as she did this, and she was encouraged that the procedure didn't seem to be causing him any pain. At last, she managed to work it free. She led him forward a few steps, and he seemed okay, but when she clambered onto Rex's back, she could feel that he was still favoring his hind leg.

Annie waited until she found a wide part of the shoulder, then dismounted, rejiggered Tarzan's load to make room for herself on his back, and switched horses. She did not like to ride Tarzan along a roadway like this. With so many trucks, he was sure to be jumpy, but weighing the two options—riding Rex when he was lame or taking a risk on Tarzan—

she decided to ride the Morgan. If Tarzan started to misbehave, she'd lead both of them—it wouldn't be the first time she'd done it.

Before long, she came to the small town of Atwater and got directions to a nearby stable. Rex was still favoring the leg a bit, but it didn't seem too bad. She remembered arriving in Memphis with one of his shoes hanging halfway off and how patiently he'd endured that until she could get him a blacksmith a couple of days later. When she reached the stable, she told the owner that she needed a vet to come out and examine her horse. He replied that the best vet in the area was out of town, but that in the meantime, he'd see if he could help. He told her he was a vet, too— but Annie figured he was more like the kind of folk you'd see up in Maine: knew a lot about doctoring animals, but didn't have any kind of a license. Still, she'd appreciate it if he took a look.

He took hold of Rex's hind foot and, with a metal hoof pick, managed to pull out the broken-off tip that had still been caught between the hoof and the shoe.

"That ought to do it," he said, triumphantly showing her the little bit of broken nail.

Annie peered at it suspiciously. "When do you think that vet is going to get here?" she asked.

The man looked down at the hoof. "No, he'll be fine. I don't see a wound there—I think the nail was just stuck between the hoof and the shoe. I'll put some turpentine on it, just in case," he said.

The next morning, the stable owner told her he'd reached the out-of-town vet by phone. The vet was still on the road and wouldn't be able to come out, but he'd said she should put some carbolic acid on it and wait a day before hitting the road. The following morning, the same fellow looked Rex all over and checked the hoof again. He said he saw no infection, put a bit more carbolic acid on it, and declared that the horse was fine and didn't need a tetanus shot.

Annie pestered the man—he'd said he was a vet, but she wasn't so sure. "Can't you get that other vet over here to take a look?"

"He's got his hands full right now. He told me there was no reason to worry. Your horse will be fine."

"Are you sure it's safe to travel?" Annie asked.

"Absolutely," the stable owner replied. "There is nothing wrong with this horse."

Annie kept pressing him, in spite of the reassurances. "Are you sure?" she repeated. But, in fact, Rex did seem fine. Ever since the stable owner had pulled the last bit of nail from his shoe, he'd been walking normally, not favoring the leg at all. She thought about Tarzan when he'd drunk the poisoned water up in Colorado. When that vet had told her he'd pulled through and could travel on, she'd been unsure, but he'd been right. So now, even though she was unsure again, she decided to trust this man, too. And Rex really did seem fine.

The group set off south along Highway 99 again, heading toward Merced, then passed through Fresno. Rex showed no signs of lameness, and Tarzan was in good spirits. Her concerns about his injury faded away as the days passed. The farther south they rode, the more it started to hit her. At the rate they were going, she thought they might be in Los Angeles in less than two weeks. They were getting so close to their destination that for perhaps the first time on this long, long journey, Annie started to believe they were actually going to make it.

Almost two weeks after the stop in Atwater, the horses spent the night in a small stable near the town of Goshen, and in the morning, she noticed that Rex seemed a little bit agitated. But she didn't think much of it—a group of young boys had just run by, hooting and hollering, and she assumed that they'd unnerved the horses. The moment passed, and Rex and Tarzan both seemed like their usual selves when they set off south.

They were heading for the Tulare County Fairgrounds, where she'd been told she'd be able to find plenty of room to put up the horses for the night. As they reached the outskirts of Tulare, there was a good bit of traffic, and Annie noticed that Rex seemed unusually skittish. He kept wanting to jog ahead, and he danced from side to side when they reached intersections where they had to wait. She wondered what was making her normally placid horse so impatient. She found her way to the fairgrounds without much difficulty and rode the horses over to the stable, where she pulled up and began to unload her gear. While she was doing this, a friendly young man came up and offered to hold her bridle. He looked at Rex with concern and turned to Annie.

"How long has he been doing that?" he asked.

"Doing what?"

"Rolling his eyes," the man said.

Rolling his eyes? She remembered the moment when he startled at the boys running by, before they'd set off that morning. She thought about his odd behavior on the ride. Was something wrong? Annie's heart pounded in her chest. Her hands went cold.

"This horse needs a vet, and you're talking to one. Let's get him inside." The man took the lead rope and headed into one of the empty stalls, and Annie hurried along behind him, leading Tarzan. Inside the stall, the vet immediately started checking Rex over from top to tail.

"Has this horse been injured sometime in the last few weeks? A puncture wound? A piece of barbed wire or a rusty nail?"

Annie felt her blood run cold. She spilled out the story of the nail under the shoe, and the lameness, the turpentine and the carbolic acid. But, she explained, her heart full of hope, that had been almost two weeks earlier, and since then, he'd seemed fine. She could see the kindly vet's eyebrows furrow with concern and his eyes pinch with frustration.

Panic rose in Annie's throat. She explained the whole situation all over again, her words coming out in a nervous tumble—the nail under his shoe, the momentary lameness, the turpentine, the carbolic acid. The vet who'd told her not to worry. The miles they'd traveled without trouble since then.

"Lionel Brazil, DVM," the man said, introducing himself as he worked. "I don't know what kind of a vet told you not to worry," he said. "Your horse is very sick. He needs a tetanus shot, right now."

Annie's mouth dropped open in horror. *Tetanus.* She'd spent enough time on a farm to understand that tetanus was bad. At first glance, Rex appeared completely normal, but when the doctor clapped his hands loudly to startle the horse, and Rex lifted his head up at the sound, it looked as if the whites of his eyes were showing. The first sign of tetanus, the vet said brusquely.

Dr. Brazil left Annie alone. She was still holding on to Tarzan, and she had to snap herself out of her panic long enough to tend to her Morgan gentleman. There was no empty stall near Rex's, and she felt as if her heart was rent in two when Rex let out a pitiful whinny as she led Tarzan to an empty stall a short distance away. She gave one look to Depeche Toi, and her canine friend understood immediately. He cocked up one ear, then stayed put in front of Rex's stall to keep him company.

In a short time, Doc Brazil returned with a vet box. He extracted a hypodermic needle, drew up the serum, and pushed it into the base of Rex's neck.

By then, Annie had already secured a fresh bucket of water and a deep bed of clean straw, and she'd poured out oats and put out fresh hay. Then she'd returned to Tarzan and done the same, spreading the straw, carrying another sloshing rubber bucket of water, and hanging it with a snap. Tarzan whinnied at the rattling sound of grain falling into a bucket. He'd had a hard day's work too, and Annie tried to slow herself down and care for her old friend properly, even though her mind was racing.

She listened carefully as the vet gave her instructions. The next few days would be critical. The toxins were already circulating through Rex's body, and it might be too late for the tetanus shot to work. The rolling eyes were a sign that his nerves were already affected, but there was hope. The vet tried to reassure her. Rex might just pull through yet. But Annie could read the look on the earnest young veterinarian's face. He wasn't dishing out any false promises, and she didn't believe any.

Annie explained earnestly that she didn't have any money. She'd arrived in Tulare with less than a dollar in her pocket. She'd figured she'd start selling some notecards and then things would come out right; she'd thought she had time.

Tramp of fate. That was what she had called herself, when she'd set out. An old lady—and a foolish one, people said—who thought five coin tosses could show her the universe's opinion on the matter.

Now she was standing in a dusty fairgrounds, destitute, alone but for her four-footed comrades, and one of them needed her help, right now, not at some hazy point farther along their path where prosperity was supposed to grow on trees, just like in the old hobo anthem that promised paradise was just down the road, free for the taking—on the Big Rock Candy Mountain. Annie had been on the road for more than a year, and she'd never seen any cigarettes growing on trees or soda water fountains, and all the mountains she'd encountered had been made of real rock, not rock candy, and yet she'd just kept taking it all on faith, believing that things had a way of working themselves out. How many times had she cavalierly told a reporter that she didn't care where she was buried. The statement had been true, but it had never included her horses. In the words of Saint Francis of Assisi, "Not to hurt our humble brethren is our first duty to them, but to stop there is not enough."

That was where Annie stood right now. She was the embodiment of *not enough*. Not enough sense to tell the first vet to give Rex a tetanus shot. Not enough money to ensure that she could pay this new one.

She thought back to the moment when the people near Charlotte had presented him to her, proudly giving her a bill of sale, valuing Rex at the kingly sum of eight hundred dollars. She'd done nothing to deserve him. She'd not earned him. He had arrived to her as a gift, and, ever faithful, asking nothing of her, he'd followed her willingly, alongside highways, through deserts, over mountains, always her humble servant. Never a word of complaint.

She had let him down.

All this rushed through her mind as she looked at the vet, whose rugged, sympathetic face hadn't changed much when she'd said she didn't have any money.

He grunted by way of reply and said he hadn't figured she did. Annie wanted to cry or hug that young man right there on the spot, but being a New Englander, she just nodded and said, I'll pay you as much as I can.

The vet didn't even answer her, because by now he had turned all of his attention back to Rex and it was as if Annie didn't exist at all. In its way, that was comforting. She didn't know anything about Doc Brazil.

She didn't know he'd spent his whole life right around Tulare, that he was born and bred a farmer and had always had an affinity for stock. That he'd gotten himself an education at the University of California, Davis, the best veterinary school in the state, and he wasn't even thirty yet, and was constantly frustrated with the older folks in the area, some of whom called themselves vets even though they had no formal education and were stuck in the old ways when new ways of helping animals had greatly improved in recent years. Annie didn't need to know any of that. She could tell by his gentle hands, by the way he closed his eyes and listened deeply through the stethoscope, by the thorough and precise and methodical way he worked his way around her sick companion that her horse was in good hands. She had gotten Rex to this point—and for this she felt that she was at fault. But somehow providence had at least landed her here, with this compassionate man who knew how to help.

Brazil had explained that there was nothing to do now but watch and wait. It was hard to know if Rex had gotten the antitoxin serum in time. In some cases, the shot could reverse the course of the illness. Other times, you'd see the horse start to stiffen up, the tail extended, the limbs tight, and eventually the jaw frozen shut—hence the disease's nickname, lockjaw—which made it so that a horse could no longer eat or drink.

He'd be around to check on the horse every day, he promised. Soon, it was dark in the stable, with just the sounds of the rustling straw and the animals moving around. Normally, Annie found this atmosphere peaceful and companionable, but that night she couldn't sleep. She could only hope, and pray, and vow to do everything she could to ease his journey, whatever that journey might be—just as her good friend Rex had done for her.

For the next two weeks, Annie never left his side. She and Depeche Toi sat next to him in the stall. Annie refilled his bucket with fresh water, trying to tempt him to take a sip, and held grain, and pieces of hay, and bits of carrot and sugar she scrounged from a box next to the coffee-maker in the stable office. Doc Brazil came around every day as promised, and often more than once. He didn't say much, but he informed Annie about the small changes he noted. Not that Annie needed him to tell her which way they were heading. She could see Rex's gait getting stiff, his tail getting high. Each day he lipped up less and less food. One day, he couldn't eat anymore and she had to dribble water into his mouth with a syringe.

Doc gave her time. He didn't press. He could no doubt see that a tight circle, an invisible silver thread, connected these four beings, Tarzan and Depeche Toi, Annie and Rex. The two other animals were disconsolate about their comrade. Tarzan wasn't eating much either; Depeche Toi clung close to Annie most of the time but trotted down to check on Tarzan every twenty minutes, regular as a cop on a beat.

Annie couldn't have told you how many days had passed since she'd arrived in Tulare. Her whole world had telescoped down to this one place. People brought her hot cups of coffee, and she drank them, and sandwiches, and she ate them, but none of it meant anything to her. The sky could have been bright orange outside. The world could have turned to ash. She would not have noticed.

But one morning in late February, Rex lay flat out on the straw and wouldn't get up.

Doc Brazil placed a hand on Annie's shoulder. He looked at her. She nodded. *Not to hurt our humble brethren is our first duty to them, but to stop there is not enough.*

She sat with Rex's head in her lap, stroking his neck, and before long she heard Tarzan calling out from down the line, letting out a low, mournful call, like no sound she'd ever heard him make before. He knew. Animals know.

When Rex was gone, she bowed her head into his mane and wept. She wept a torrent of tears to match the mighty Mississippi, which they'd crossed together, to match the frozen snows of the Rockies, to match every drop of the blue Pacific Ocean, which still lay out to the west of them, and which Rex would never see.

When she left the stall, Depeche Toi ran straight to Tarzan and whined until Annie swung the door open, and Annie followed behind. Now it was just the three of them again. Three wanderers from the state of Maine. Strangers far from home. All they had was each other.

*One's destination is never a place but rather
a new way of looking at things.*

—Henry Miller

—

CHAPTER

27

The Golden State

ANNIE WAS SO LISTLESS that she couldn't seem to come up with a plan. George Bell, an old horse trainer who worked on the fairgrounds, had taken a liking to her, and as a horseman himself, he understood how much she was grieving. She could stay as long as she wanted, he told her. His wife insisted that she join them for meals in the trailer they lived in on the grounds.

Annie didn't know what to do. She had no money, for one thing. She'd paid the vet the last dime in her pocket. She had not one cent left.

After weary days of doing nothing, she forced herself to saddle up Tarzan and ride into town to sell a few notecards. Her spirits had sunk so low that she could hardly bring herself to smile at people. For the first time on her journey, she felt like a beggar.

She hadn't been out there for more than about ten minutes when a young woman came up and requested a notecard. When she asked how much, Annie replied that people usually gave her a dime. But the woman reached down into her pocket and pulled out a ten-dollar bill. Buy some bones for your dog, she said. Annie was so moved she could barely stutter out a word of thanks.

When she got back to the stable, she kept thinking that it was all a mistake. She was so sure that she'd see Rex's handsome head looking over the stall's half door, his white star shining on his forehead, his brown eyes bright. Passing the empty stall door set her back all over again.

But the Bells wouldn't give up on her. George and his wife kept inviting her over for dinner in their trailer. George regaled her with stories about his days driving a sulky in harness races. His wife cooked delicious meals to tempt her appetite, always setting aside a generous portion for Depeche Toi. George visited with Tarzan, and pointed out that he sure did have the look of a good old-fashioned Morgan, and debated the finer points of old-timey racers versus newer ones. And gently, they tried to persuade Annie that she might think about going on along to Los Angeles. After all, Art Linkletter was waiting.

But there was no mistaking it. The heart had gone out of the trip for Annie. For nearly a year and a half, she'd been buoyed along by a sense of some kind of purpose, a sense of destiny. All that was gone now. She'd run out of gumption. She was only 180 miles short of her destination. She'd decided to be a tramp of fate, and now fate had persuaded her that it was time to give up.

When she'd arrived in Tulare it had been mid-February, and now it was March. The newspapers were running stories about Rex's death, and pretty soon, people started calling the fairgrounds, offering to give her another horse. George Bell kindly insisted on squiring Annie around to look at each one—volunteering his professional opinion. But Annie had an excuse about all of them. Too big, too small, too skittish, too slow, too old. She knew in her heart, however, that they all suffered from the same problem: too not Rex.

Then one day she got a call informing her that she was to go out to the ranch where a local congressman lived. Art Linkletter had found another horse for her. His name was King. Annie felt a faint flutter of hope when she heard the name. *Rex,* she'd been told, was the word for "king" in Latin. Maybe this was a sign.

Sure enough, the horse was a real beauty. He was big like Rex, about twelve years old, and he was a bona fide parade horse. He could ride in traffic all day long. He loved nothing more than crowds and flags, loud noises, big trucks. What's more, Depeche Toi seemed to like him. Her dog ran right up, tail waving in the air, and crouched as if to play, and King acted as if he already knew him—reached down and blew him a hot-breathed horse kiss. Annie felt a little surge of happiness, swiftly followed by a stab of sorrow. It should be Rex here with them. But that was not to be. Annie hoped they could find a little spot in their bruised hearts to let their new companion in.

She spent several more days reading and rereading the letters she carried with her, letters from people she'd met along the way. There was Nellie Bennett from Maine, who never seemed to tire of helping people, and Jean Lane, the restless racer of dogs and horses. There was Mina Titus Sawyer, who traveled the world by writing to people, and who had never stopped sending Annie letters and postcards to encourage her, and telling her to come for a visit and stay awhile whenever she got back to Maine. There were the Roses in Trenton, with their monkeys and ponies and dalmatians and house full of joy, and the Eisenhowers in Burns, who'd taken her in on a cold and snowy night, and, of course, there was the lonely Wyoming sheep farmer and his open-ended invitation. Like the postcards and letters she carried in her saddlebags, she'd carried a little piece of each of them, and a promise that they could ride along with her in spirit. For herself, Annie no longer cared about reaching her destination, but she realized that she owed it to everyone who had ever believed in her. She had that one thing left to offer. She could refuse to quit.

ON MARCH 25, 1956, after traveling close to five thousand miles, Annie, Tarzan, Depeche Toi, and the newcomer, King, arrived in San Fernando. The three citizens of Maine had been together from the start at the top of Woodman Hill; their fourth traveler, King, had only just joined, and yet they had welcomed him into the fold, while still holding a place in their hearts for their comrade Rex. He was with them in spirit. They had crossed an entire country, and now they had arrived at the northern end of the San Fernando Valley, which led to Los Angeles. As

Henry Miller said, "Los Angeles gives one the feeling of the future more strongly than any city I know of." It was the place that Dorothy Parker called "seventy-two suburbs in search of a city," a place that in 1956 was, more than anyplace else in America, the most extreme example of the full conquest of the automobile. In just three months, on June 29, 1956, President Eisenhower would sign the National Interstate and Defense Highways Act, and a new era would officially begin.

When Annie and her companions walked into the town of San Fernando, she reached deep into her pocket and pulled out the smudged card she'd been saving. She looked for a pay phone and dialed the number. She told Art Linkletter that she was fifteen miles north of Hollywood, and she was ready.

TARZAN AND KING WERE put up in the Hudkins Bros. Stables in North Hollywood, a legendary location. This was the very place that had supplied Silver for the Lone Ranger and Trigger for Roy Rogers, as well as most of the other bucking, whirling, jumping, and galloping horses that were shown on TV and in the movies in the 1950s. For Annie and Depeche Toi, there was a suite of rooms in a garden hotel nearby. Annie had never seen such luxury. She was like Lucy and Ethel when they arrived in a modern hotel in Hollywood at the end of their TV road trip. Annie admired every inch of it: the mid-century modern furniture, all gleaming and clean, the wall-to-wall carpeting on the floors, the bright red geraniums in the window boxes. The refrigerator, the rotary phone, the shower and bathtub. Never had she ever, when she'd set off from Minot, Maine, imagined herself in a place like this.

On April 15, 1956, Annie appeared on Art Linkletter's popular game show *People Are Funny*. She was supposed to enter the studio with both Tarzan and King, but Tarzan hadn't forgotten his fear of trucks, and at the last minute he decided he didn't want to load up. So it was just Annie and King—and, of course, Depeche Toi.

Annie was wearing her riding clothes: the men's dungarees cinched at the waist with a leather belt, a button-down shirt, and her broad-brimmed white hat. King and Depeche Toi weren't fazed at all by any of it—not the hot white lights, not the men with cameras, not the studio audience. King strutted and posed like a movie star, but at first Annie felt frozen and tongue-tied. Pretty soon, though, she forgot about the lights and the cameras and warmed up to telling the friendly TV host her story, interspersed, as always, with a good chunk of her personal philosophy of life. At the end of the segment, he told her to buy herself a saddle and handed her a check. Annie looked at the number written on it: it was more money than she'd ever seen before—enough for her to live easy for several years. She'd done it. She'd never have to worry about starving alone on a Maine hilltop again.

In May 1956, Annie Wilkins, Tarzan, King, and Depeche Toi were the honored guests at the annual banquet of Equestrian Trails Incorporated, an organization that had been founded to help preserve California's bridle trails in a time when much of the state's open land was being subdivided and developed into vast housing tracts. The organization presented Annie with a giant trophy and a letter of commendation for promoting the equestrian lifestyle. In October 1956, she appeared on national television again—this time on Groucho Marx's show *You Bet Your Life*.

Perhaps Art Linkletter captured Annie best when he explained why he'd felt an immediate kinship when he met her: "Not only was her calm assurance infectious, but she also transmitted to our audience the quiet strength of her personal philosophy—that happiness comes only to those who participate in the adventure of life, and that true security is, in essence, a state of mind."

You could think about everything Annie lacked: No parents, no children, not much health. No insurance, no bank account, no home. But she chose to focus on what she did have: Courage. Loyalty. Love in abundance. New friends throughout the country. A belief that she should just keep going. A sense of humor. A tolerance for meager things—jail cell cots, straw-bale mattresses, thin soups.

And more than anything, Annie had trust. When she set off, she was sure she was going to find the same America she'd grown up believing in: A country made up of one giant set of neighbors. People who'd be happy to give you a helping hand. People spread out far and wide, from sea to shining sea, with different accents, and different favorite dishes, and different kinds of houses, people who lived with dust or traffic, snowstorms or tornadoes, on mountains or flatlands, in cities or small towns. People who liked Eisenhower or couldn't stand him, people who were fundamentally decent and, deep down, the same.

When she rode off that hill in Minot, Maine, she brought her heart, her soul, her hopes and aspirations with her, but most important, she brought her animals. They never questioned whether her harebrained scheme was a good idea. They never suggested that she get her head examined, or told her to fill up her bank account, or demanded that she get a map and plan out a logical route. They never asked her if what she was trying to do was flat-out impossible. Theirs was love and trust, freely given, demanding nothing in return.

Love, loyalty, gratitude. Rex, Depeche Toi, and Tarzan. Four-footed guides in a rocky world. From them, Annie learned every lesson she needed on her journey.

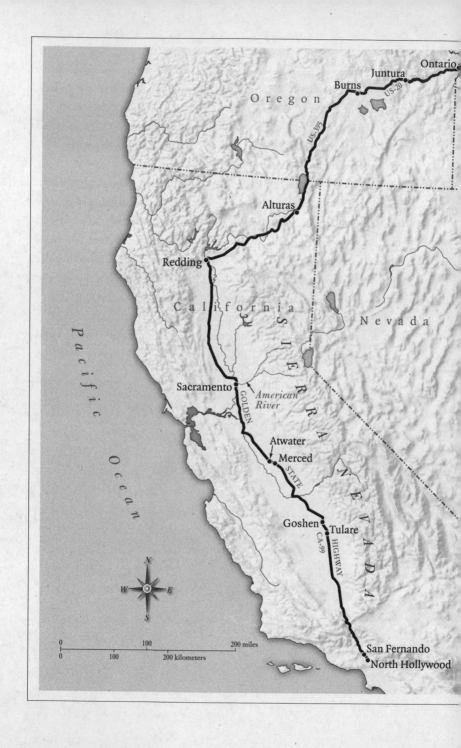

POCATELLO, ID
to
NORTH HOLLYWOOD

se

Idaho

I-90

e River

MASSACRE
ROCKS
STATE PARK

Pocatello

Wyoming

Utah

Colorado

New
Mexico

Arizona

Epilogue

ANNIE DIED ON FEBRUARY 19, 1980, in Whitefield, Maine, at the age of eighty-eight, approximately twenty-six years after she was given two to four years to live. Not long after arriving in California, she achieved her goal of seeing the Pacific Ocean. She and Tarzan traveled from North Hollywood to Long Beach, where she rode him along the shore accompanied by the Long Beach Mounted Patrol. Sadly, Tarzan did not live to see Maine again. Without his friend Rex to steady him, he injured a leg when he spooked at traffic while Annie rode him along the coast toward Santa Barbara in 1957. She nursed him for five months before losing him. She never rode long-distance again. Deciding that King would be better off staying in California and continuing his career as a parade horse, she sold him to a good home through her connection to Equestrian Trails Incorporated. King had a happy life and continued to appear in Southern California parades for many years. Depeche Toi never left Annie's side. When her riding days were over, she returned to Maine by bus.

Not much is known about Annie's later years, but after she left California, she never really settled down. She lived in New York City, in Harlem, for a few years, and she dreamed of someday owning a little trailer that she'd park out in an empty field somewhere, but she never did. She didn't move back to Minot, although she did go for a visit once, and the townsfolk noticed that she was all decked out in a dress and heels and carrying a handbag—proud as can be. She kept in touch with many of the people she'd met along her journey, especially Mina Titus Sawyer, the woman who'd helped get word of her travels out to the newspapers in the first place, and Jean Lane (she'd remarried and was now called Jean Bryar), who'd given her both encouragement and the idea to sell notecards along the way. Jackass Annie had the last laugh, because now Annie Wilkins is considered one of Minot's most famous citizens. She is buried in the Libby plot in the Maple Grove Cemetery in Mechanic Falls, Maine. Engraved on her headstone: LAST OF THE SADDLE TRAMPS.

Author's Note

———

IN 1967, ANNIE WILKINS SPENT several months living in the home of her old friend Mina Titus Sawyer, the reporter who had kept in touch with her throughout her journey. When Annie had left home in November 1954, she'd taken with her a sixty-cent diary to keep her company on the road. As she rode across the country, she kept on writing— not just in a succession of diaries but also sending a steady stream of postcards to friends back home as well as to people she'd met along the way. Annie had a sixth-grade education. Her handwriting was cramped, her spelling creative, her grammar rudimentary, but her story was compelling.

For several months during the spring of 1967, Annie sat with Mina, who, as a reporter, had specialized in human-interest stories and pieces about Maine. Together, with the help of Annie's diaries (there were six in total, though two had been lost during the flash flood in Wyoming), the postcards Mina had received from Annie during her trip, and Annie's twelve-year-old memories, they reconstructed her story. Annie's meeting with Art Linkletter, and his sponsorship of the final leg of her journey, had created a lasting connection between the two of them. Mina Titus Sawyer got in touch with an associate of Linkletter's, a literary agent in Los Angeles, and they managed to sell Annie's story in book form. This led to the culmination of two dreams: Annie's to get her story on paper and Mina's to publish a real book.

Writing an account about an older woman for a family audience in

1967, however, required Mina to sand off many aspects of Annie's real story: she excised the two failed marriages, Annie's short stint in vaudeville, the fact that her "uncle" was not blood kin, and the truth about her farm—that she had lost it to back taxes. To accept Annie as a likable character, readers of that era needed to see her as God-fearing, brave, unwilling to accept charity, self-reliant, and moral. All of these things were fundamental to Annie, but they weren't the whole story. Interestingly, as she traveled across the country, she was portrayed more honestly in local newspaper accounts than in national ones. When a story about Annie went out on the wire services, she was almost always referred to as a widow. But in local articles, she shared truths—about her marriages, her hardships, her money problems. She had nothing to hide.

In 2017, I pulled up to a modest white frame house in a small town in Maine. I had an appointment to meet eighty-seven-year-old Crystal Decker. Mrs. Decker was Mina Titus Sawyer's daughter. She shared her memories of her mother: a remarkable woman who got a college education in 1912; who, as a single woman, adopted a daughter from an orphanage during the Great Depression; who adored animals; and who maintained an extensive correspondence with pen pals all over the world, even though she never left her native state of Maine. Crystal Decker searched through her mother's papers for me, hoping that she might have saved Annie's old diaries—but they were gone, and so was the correspondence between the two women. She also shared Mina's photo albums, which had some personal pictures of Annie and her mother, and her own memories of Annie, and she was kind enough to grant me full permission to use Annie's memoirs to tell this story.

As I uncovered more of the real story, I found many missing links. Crystal Decker remembered her mother and Annie trying to piece together parts of the story from ragged scraps of paper with hard-to-read scribbles on them. Annie was an ordinary person, leading an ordinary life, and except for the numerous newspaper articles that recounted her journey, most parts of her life had left barely a trace. I had to rely on my experience as a historian and researcher to pull together her true life story from census data and official documents, like title deeds and marriage and death certificates, and the memories she shared with different people as she made her way across the country.

I call her Annie, instead of the name she called herself, Mesannie (or sometimes Mes-Annie). I could find no explanation of why she started to refer to herself that way. She had no birth certificate, but on all the official documents I could find, her name was just plain Annie. I suspected that perhaps she'd added the prefix during her vaudeville days; nevertheless, an exhaustive search into the B. F. Keith archives turned up no sign of an Annie or a Mes-Annie. I suspect she just gussied up "Annie" for the fun of it. She loved to sign her entire name: Annie Mabel Libby Stuart Wilkins. The one name she never included was Robinson, the surname of her first ex-husband, the horse thief. Whatever she may have lived through during that difficult marriage to the ex-convict, she never spoke of it. She erased his name, if not his memory, entirely from her life.

Using Annie's memoirs as a guide, I dug into the archives of small-town libraries and historical societies all across America, locating newspaper articles and scrapbooks that included old clippings and postcards that Annie had sent back from the road. I was even able to find people who remembered their childhood encounters with Annie when she came to stay in their family home. When they shared their stories with me, I always asked the same question: What would have made your father or mother or grandparent open their home to a stranger? Everyone answered the question a somewhat different way, but it all came back to the same thing: Because that was the way they treated everyone.

Most of the time, I could find a newspaper account that told me the real names of the people involved and provided information about the events that had occurred in an individual town; in some cases, unfortunately, I was unable to do so. In those cases, I've gone with the names Annie used in her memoirs; these are indicated in the endnotes. As for the rancher in Wyoming: a thorough search in the area did not reveal a rancher by the name of Harvey Kelsey, so I hunted for a man born in the right year, in the right county, who was a sheep rancher—and I did find one, divorced, right age, right area. I suspected that I had found my man, but there was one biographical detail that differed: Annie's rancher said he'd been born in Pennsylvania, and the man I found had been born in Wyoming. Perhaps Annie had misremembered this one detail, but because of that, I decided not to rely on my own speculation and instead went with the name she called him in her memoirs.

I drove more than ten thousand miles while researching this book. Navigating mostly with 1950s vintage gas station maps, I traveled through small towns and down the sorts of back roads the average contemporary traveler never sees. I avoided the interstates. Using old black-and-white photos, I had fun locating old motor courts that had been converted to other uses, and everywhere I went, I began to recognize buildings that had once been filling stations or roadside diners. The old America is still there; you just have to know how to look for it.

I grew up in Southern California in the 1960s and 1970s. I was born into the world of cars and freeways, of strip malls and giant parking lots. Probably because of this, I've always had a deep fascination for the American landscape, for the epic road trip, for the romance of back roads and small towns. As I traveled, I never knocked on a door and asked for a place to stay, but I knocked on many doors—of libraries and historical societies, and in search of people who could tell me something about Annie. To all of them who went out of their way to help me, thank you for reassuring me that Annie's America is still out there, and it is ours.

Acknowledgments

————

I N FEBRUARY 2020, I took off for my final leg of research, one of the many long road trips I took while writing this book. Little did I know that a global pandemic was hovering just around the corner. For much of the time that I was writing about Annie's great journey, I was, like so many other people, trapped in my own home. Lucky for me, Annie's story took me all across America, but I never could have reconstructed her journey without the help of people in small towns all across Annie's route.

As always, I'm indebted to my editor, Susanna Porter, who has a brilliant understanding of how stories work, which she imparts with unstinting generosity. And thanks also to her assistant, Emily Hartley, who graciously helps me with all kinds of problems, large and small. I am eternally grateful to the wonderful team at Ballantine, Jennifer Hershey, Kara Walsh, Kim Hovey, and Lindsey Kennedy, the world's best cheerleaders for books, readers, and writers, whose boundless enthusiasm never seems to flag. Thank you to production editor Steve Messina, who takes a bunch of words and turns them into a flawless book, and copy editor Bonnie Thompson, who double-checked the many distances, names, and locations in this book with great patience and a zeal for accuracy. For the radiant cover and beautiful interior design, thank you to Victoria Allen, Robbin Schiff, and Barbara Bachman.

It gives me great pleasure to thank my agent, Dorian Karchmar, who is not just brilliant and perceptive, but also kind, funny, and understanding.

I owe a special debt of gratitude to Crystal Decker, daughter of Mina Titus Sawyer, the co-author of Annie Wilkins's memoir, *Last of the Saddle Tramps*. Many people in and around Minot were incredibly generous with their time, and these people were absolutely invaluable in helping me understand Annie's world. Thank you to the Minot Maine Historical Society, especially the late Eda Tripp, who shared the memories and materials she collected about Annie and her life. Her knowledge of Minot history was extensive, and her desire to share that knowledge was strong. She was ill during the time that I interviewed her, and I will be ever cognizant of her kindness and generosity to me—a complete stranger—even when she was suffering from cancer. I was sorry to learn that she passed away just a few months after I visited her. I also am grateful to Ben Conant, Lucille Hemond Hodsdon, and Hester Gilpatric for sharing memories of Annie and of the area around Minot during her time. I loved hearing so many details about the incredible resourcefulness of people who lived in a small Maine farming community, especially those who lived through the Great Depression. And I noted from all the residents of Minot a well-deserved pride in their beautiful town and in one of its most famous citizens, Annie Wilkins.

I tip my hat to Kathryn Kelly, genealogist extraordinaire, who tracked down more details about Annie and her family than I ever could have found on my own, and whose deep knowledge of Maine history was extremely helpful in putting those documents into context. Thank you to Penny Loura of the Windham Historical Society; Lisa Walker, Cheatham County historian; Cheryl Baker, Modoc County librarian; Carl Hallberg, Wyoming State Archives; Eric Petty, Woodford County Historical Society; Jason Fenimore, Louis B. Goodall Memorial Library; Harland Eastman, Sanford-Springvale Historical Society; and Samantha Beckwith, SeaCoast Pony Club. Thank you to the incredibly helpful and generous Brookfielders, equestrian Mary Tamburri, and Kate Simpson from the Merrick Public Library. Thanks to Tennesseans Robert Hicks, Michael Curcio, and Lucinda Dyer for helping me try to track down the elusive origin of Rex. Many thanks to Carrie Niederman, DVM, for walking me through equine tetanus, and to Paige Relyea

Lehman for connecting me to Carrie. Thank you to Lynne Holland of the University of Maine Cooperative Extension for teaching me about cucumber growing in Maine. Many thanks to Morgan horse enthusiast Jill Smith for sharing her resources and knowledge of the breed. Thank you to Bonnie D'Ignazio, Eleanor Blaisdell, Russell Foster, and Brenda Bradley for sharing memories of Annie's visits. Their families exemplify the principle of showing kindness to strangers. Thank you to Mike Kassel, curator of Wyoming's Frontier Days Old West Museum, for teaching me all about Cheyenne's historic rodeo. Thank you to fellow historian Gail Hogan Lucia for her expertise about ice harvesting and her knowledge of Springfield, and thank you to Julie Bryar Porter and Lindsay Bryar Bliznik for memories of their glamorous grandmother Jean Lane Bryar. Thank you to Lloyd Bennett for sharing his memories of his incredible mother and father, Nellie and Laurence Bennett, perhaps my favorite people that Annie met along her journey. Thank you to Mills Rose for sharing her many detailed memories of her parents and of Rose's Riding Academy, and to Mike Brazil, who shared memories of his father. As always, Fran Jurga is my go-to expert for all things related to hooves and shoeing. Special thanks to my assistant, Katrina Spivek, who kept me organized in many different ways, and to Giovanna Perricone, whose expert research assistance was invaluable in putting together this book.

Writing is a lonely process, but my writer friends are endlessly available to discuss the endless minutiae of the business of writing, and without them, I don't know what I'd do. Thanks especially to Jon Clinch, Renée Rosen, Darcie Chan, Danielle Younge-Ullman, Karen Dionne, Keith Cronin, Lauren Baratz-Logsted, Kelly Mustian, and Sachin Waikar. Thanks to my dear friends Tasha and Andrew Grant, who graciously hosted me no fewer than five times on their Wyoming ranch as my research kept me crisscrossing the back roads of our country.

There would be no writers if not for readers, and there would be no readers were it not for the dedication of librarians and booksellers. I'd like to thank the many booksellers who have supported me, hand-selling copies of my books, always seeming to know who needs an uplifting horse story and pressing it into another reader's hands. You change lives every single day. In particular, I'd like to thank Pages: A Bookstore in Manhattan Beach, California, for their support and for getting signed copies of my books to my readers. And a special word to all librarians: You are the custodians of our past, and the beacons to our future. I never cease to be amazed at the helpfulness of librarians and the extraordinary resources to be found in even the smallest of our nation's public libraries.

I'd like to give a nod to John Steinbeck and William Least Heat-Moon, writers of two of my favorite books about American road trips, whose books *Travels with Charley* and *Blue Highways* inspired me to retell the story of Annie's amazing journey.

As always, I'm grateful to my family.

Notes

INTERVIEWS AND CORRESPONDENCE

Lloyd Bennett	(LB)
Eleanor Blaisdell	(EB)
Mike Brazil	(MB)
Ben Conant	(BC)
Crystal Decker	(CD)
Bonnie D'Ignazio	(BD)
Steve Foster	(SF)
Hester Gilpatric	(HG)
Lucille Hemond Hodsdon	(LHH)
Lynne Holland	(LH)
Mike Kassell	(MK)
Gail Hogan Lucia	(GHL)
Carrie Nicderman, DVM	(CN)
Julie Bryar Porter	(JBP)
Millie Rose	(MR)
Eda Tripp	(ET)
Lisa Walker	(LW)

Unless otherwise noted, dialogue is taken from *Last of the Saddle Tramps*, by Mesannie Wilkins with Mina Titus Sawyer, and is used by permission of Mina Titus Sawyer's estate.

PROLOGUE

3   **joined the circus:** "Historical Resume of the Town of Minot, Maine," Minot Maine Historical Society, sites.rootsweb.com/~meandrhs/minot/history/history .html.

CHAPTER 1: LIVING COLOR

7   **Two state-of-the-art NBC television cameras:** Jack Gould, "Tournament of Roses Parade Is Sent over 22-City Network," *New York Times,* January 4, 1954.

8   **Some three thousand miles away:** For my impressions of Minot, Maine, and its environs during Annie's time, I interviewed Hester Gilpatric, Lucille Hemond Hodsdon, the late Eda Tripp, and Ben Conant, and consulted resources available from the Minot Maine Historical Society and the Maine Memory Network.

9   **Originally, Minot had been settled by Anglo-Saxons:** Interview, LHH, November 20, 2019. For an excellent history of Minot, Maine's colonial past, see Alan Taylor, *Liberty Men and Great Proprietors.* For information about Androscoggin County's Franco-American community, see Mary Rice-DeFosse and James Myall, *The Franco-Americans of Lewiston-Auburn.*

CHAPTER 2: LIVE RESTFULLY

12   **Minot, Maine, was not really a single town:** Geo J. Varney, "History of Minot, Maine," in *A Gazetteer of the State of Maine* (Boston: B. B. Russell, 1886).

16   **Her grandfather's big square farmhouse:** Interviews, ET and HG. "Miss Annie Wilkins, 63, en Route to California," *Sanford Tribune and Advocate* (Maine), November 18, 1954.

CHAPTER 3: TAX MONEY

19   **The economy that favored small Maine farms:** For a good overview of Maine's economic history and how it affected small farms, see "A Different Place: 1945–1970," Maine Memory Network, www.mainememory.net.

19   **Benjamin Tibbetts, who was interviewed in 1877:** Alan Taylor, *Liberty Men and Great Proprietors,* "Introduction: Back Country Resistance." For a good overview of the economy of Lewiston-Auburn, see Douglas Hodgkin, *Lewiston Politics in the Gilded Age.*

20   **By 1954, the old corn factory had shut down:** Interview, ET, for the importance of the corn industry to Maine's rural economy. See also Paul B. Frederic, *Canning Gold: Northern New England's Sweet Corn Industry: A Historical Geography* (Lanham, Md.: University Press of America, 2002).

21   **The cucumber seed packs came in the mail:** Interview, LH, Southern Maine Agricultural Extension, for all information about pickling cucumbers and growing them in Maine.

22 **Almost no one had everything they needed:** Interview, BC.

22 **These Boston variety seedlings:** Interview, LH.

24 **In 1950, twenty million Americans lived on family farms:** "Agriculture 1950: Changes in Agriculture 1900–1950."

24 **highway workers constructing the extension:** "History," www.maineturnpike .com/About-MTA/History.aspx.

CHAPTER 4: THE SEARCH

27 **"Looking for a tough horse":** Mesannie Wilkins with Mina Titus Sawyer, *Last of the Saddle Tramps*, 12.

28 **"Saddle horses for sale at all times":** Classified ad, *Lewiston Evening Journal*, October 6, 1954, 10.

30 **a little thin:** "Maine Widow's Horse in Good Shape, Doctors Decide," *Springfield Union*, December 3, 1954.

CHAPTER 5: LEAVING HOME

40 **By the early part of the nineteenth century:** Daniel Chipman Linsley, *Morgan Horses*, 24.

40 **The Libby Family in America:** Charles T. Libby, *The Libby Family in America*, 16.

40 **In the early years of the republic:** See Alan Taylor, *Liberty Men and Great Proprietors*, for an excellent explanation of the rebellious attitudes of settlers in Maine and the importance of holding a title deed to the land.

41 **The long stone walls:** For an overview of the significance of New England's stone walls, see Susan Allport, *Sermons in Stone*. For an overview of the settlers' impact on the land in New England, I recommend William Cronon, *Changes in the Land*. See also Jean-Manuel Andriote, "The History, Science and Poetry of New England's Stone Walls," *Earth*, May 19, 2014.

41 **Figure, the original Morgan:** Jeanne Mellin, *The Complete Morgan Horse*, 8–18.

CHAPTER 6: CARS

44 **Animal husbandry expert:** M. E. Ensminger, *Horse Husbandry*, 1.

48 **In 1954, there was only one stretch:** "History," www.maineturnpike.com/About -MTA/History.aspx. For a wonderful read about the development of the Interstate Highway System, I recommend Earl Swift, *The Big Roads*, and Tom Lewis, *Divided Highways*.

48 **Prior to World War I, the areas of Androscoggin:** Interview, BC, for an understanding of the agricultural way of life in the area of Androscoggin County in the mid-twentieth century.

48 **One Minot resident remembered:** "Historical Resume of the Town of Minot,

Maine," Minot Maine Historical Society, sites.rootsweb.com/~meandrhs/minot/
history/history.html.

49 **As the first superhighway:** "History," www.maineturnpike.com/About-MTA/
History.aspx.

CHAPTER 7: STRANGERS

52 **The word "tramp":** For information about the history of tramps in America, I
relied on Todd DePastino, *Citizen Hobo.*

54 **The Libbys had helped settle Maine:** One of Annie's cherished family stories
was about how her ancestors had helped haul the mast of John Paul Jones's warship. For more information about Maine pines and warship construction, see
Samuel F. Manning, *New England Masts and the King's Broad Arrow.*

55 **The Christian theologian Richard R. Niebuhr:** Richard R. Niebuhr, "Pilgrims
and Pioneers," *Parabola* (Fall 1984): 7.

57 **Anyone who knew Nellie Bennett:** Interview, LB. See also Francis Sayward,
"Livest Man in the Room: Family, Faith Help Windham Doctor Beat Handi-
cap," clipping dated April 1955, from the author's personal collection, courtesy
of Lloyd Bennett.

CHAPTER 8: JAILBIRDS

64 **Police stations had long offered overnight lodging:** Todd DePastino, *Citizen Hobo,*
12, quoting Eric H. Monkkonen, *Police in Urban America, 1860–1920* (Cambridge, U.K.: Cambridge University Press, 1981).

65 **a frog on a lily pad:** "Cross-Country Rider Takes Week-End Rest Here." Undated newspaper clipping from scrapbook. Courtesy of Windham Historical
Society.

67 **On the surface, Mina Titus Sawyer:** Interview, CD, for all information about the
life of Mina Titus Sawyer and her friendship with Annie Wilkins.

67 **She chuckled at the fact that Annie:** "Call of the West—Farm 'Girl' Hits Open
Road," *Spokane Chronicle,* November 12, 1954.

69 **As one observer described it:** Samuel Rezneck, "Unemployment, Unrest, and Relief in the United States During the Depression of 1893–97," *Journal of Political
Economy* 61, no. 4 (1953): 325–44; retrieved from www.jstor.or/stable/1826883.

70 **In 1900, only about half:** Kermit S. Nickerson, *150 Years of Education in Maine.*

70 **The life of a New England girl:** For a fascinating look at the lives of female textile
workers in the nineteenth century, see Thomas L. Dublin, ed., *Farm to Factory.*

70 **At twenty-one, Annie found herself in Windsor:** I pieced together Annie's early
life and her marriage to Peter Robinson, as well as her work history, from census
data and marriage and divorce certificates. In 1921, she was listed as employed by
the town of Grafton, New Hampshire, as a member of a crew shoveling snow to
clear roads. On Robinson's jailing for horse thievery, see "Maine Woman's
Horseback Trek Discounts Theories of 'Weaker Sex,'" *Times-News* (Twin Falls,
Idaho), October 11, 1955.

70   **Three years later, Peter Robinson:** "Miss Annie Wilkins, 63, en Route to California," *Sanford Tribune and Advocate* (Maine), November 18, 1954.

CHAPTER 9: VETERANS

73   **Like the American-made Timex watches:** "The Timex Story," timex.com/the-timex-story/.

73   **"looked like Buffalo Bill's wife":** Mesannie Wilkins with Mina Titus Sawyer, *Last of the Saddle Tramps, 33.*

74   **Eleven-year-old Eleanor:** Interview, EB, for all information about Annie's visit with the Blaisdell family.

76   **A woman who lived on a farm:** Priscilla Fowler Thomas, "Childhood Memories: The 1930s," Rochester, New Hampshire, Historical Society, rochesterhistoricalnh .org/2015/07/25/childhood-memories/.

CHAPTER 10: FACE IN A BOX

81   **"You flagg'd walks of the cities!":** Walt Whitman, "Song of the Open Road," quoted from the Poetry Foundation, poetryfoundation.org/poems/48859/song -of-the-open-road.

81   **In the early nineteenth century, Samuel Blodget:** For a history of Manchester, see Grace Everlina Holbrook Blood, *Manchester on the Merrimack: The Story of a City.*

82   **Russell Foster was driving down High Street:** Interview, SF, for all information about Annie's visit with the Foster family.

85   **That year had been a special one for the city's traditional.** "History of Veteran's Day," www.va.gov/opa/vetsday/vetdayhistory.asp.

86   **When Annie came by:** Interview, SF.

87   **"the cheerful voice":** "Song of the Open Road," quoted from the Poetry Foundation, poetryfoundation.org/poems/48859/song-of-the-open-road.

87   **"I've got on two union suits":** "Widow on Horseback Is Due Tomorrow," *Springfield Union,* December 1, 1954.

CHAPTER 11: HORSE PEOPLE AND DOG PEOPLE

90   **It turned out they had much in common:** "Jean Bryar Obituary," Sled Dog Central, June 4, 2012, sleddogcentral.com/obituaries/Bryar_jean.htm, and Jean Emerson, "Jean Bryar, 87, Dies," United States Trotting Association, June 16, 2012. Also from correspondence with JBP and Lindsay Bryar Bliznick.

91   **more than any kind of training:** John Rendel, "Husky from the Arctic: Work, Devotion and Experience Needed to Develop Top-Flight Sled Dog," *New York Times,* February 27, 1964.

91   **"Thinking," attributed to:** Not much is known about the author of this poem, but it is usually attributed to Walter Wintle. Its first known publication was in the *Unity* magazine, published by the Unity Tract Society, 1905.

93 **"She's a wonderful woman"**: "Maine Woman Takes Buggy," *Springfield Union,* November 28, 1954.

94 **Meanwhile, all of her doings had been reported**: "Mrs. Wilkins' Friends Slowing Her Pace," *Springfield Union,* December 3, 1954.

94 **But that mean-spirited opinion hadn't dampened**: "Maine Woman, Horse, Dog, Leave City," *Springfield Union,* December 4, 1954.

CHAPTER 12: THE CHECKERED GAME OF LIFE

96 **While Bradley's Checkered Game of Life**: Jill Lepore, "The Meaning of Life: What Milton Bradley Started," *New Yorker,* May 21, 2007.

97 **The story had caught the eye**: "Mrs. Wilkins Rides On Again, but at Ease in an Automobile," *Springfield Union,* December 5, 1954.

98 **Fortunately, Joe Bolduc of nearby Chicopee**: Ibid.

98 **Peter Hogan, however, still had a stable full of horses**: Interview, GHL, for all information about the Hogan family and the fascinating history of ice harvesting in Springfield.

98 **Soft music seemed to be seeping out of the walls**: Highland Hotel promotional materials, 1955, from the author's personal collection.

105 **The next day, the headlines about Annie blared**: "Maine Widow's Horse in Good Shape, Doctors Decide," *Springfield Union,* December 3, 1954.

105 **"Mrs. Annie Wilkins of West Minot, Maine"**: "Mesannie Wilkins' Life Story One of Courage, Work," *Springfield Union,* December 4, 1954.

CHAPTER 13: ODDS

108 **"He who hears the rippling of rivers"**: Henry David Thoreau, *A Week on the Concord and Merrimack Rivers.*

109 **Located roughly halfway between Springfield**: "Windsor Locks History: A Project of Windsor Locks Library," windsorlockshistory.org/.

110 **The U.S. Army selected**: Diane Church, "A Look at 'The History of Bradley Field,'" *Hartford Courant,* September 17, 2014.

110 **The largest undeveloped piece of property**: Howard J. White, *Meet Noden-Reed Park.*

111 **That evening, Gertrude Austin and Chester Reed**: "Windsor Locks Welcomes Woman on Horseback," *Hartford Courant,* December 5, 1954.

CHAPTER 14: PARTY TIME

115 **The two-lane Bear Mountain Bridge**: "Bear Mountain Bridge History," New York State Bridge Authority, www.nysba.net/bridgepages/BMB/BMBpage/NYSWeb_bmb_page_NoLogo.htm.

116 **Over her shoulder, she saw**: "California, Here We Come on Horseback," *Journal-News* (Rockland County, N.Y.), December 13, 1954.

119   **but a high-profile murder trial:** "Sheppard Murder Case," Encyclopedia of Cleveland History, case.edu/ech/articles/s/sheppard-murder-case.

120   **New Jersey has been called:** *History of Trucking in New Jersey—NJMTA 100th Anniversary* (video), May 23, 2014, www.youtube.com/watch?v=yoOz8oLtcec.

121   **Earlier in the day, two young patrolmen:** "Woman, 63, Crossing Country on Horse, Marks Birthday in Wayne," *News* (Paterson, N.J.), December 14, 1954, and "Riding Horseback to Coast," *Morning Call* (Paterson, N.J.), December 13, 1954.

122   **"My name is Millie Rose":** All information about the Rose family and Rose's Riding Academy came from my interview with MR.

CHAPTER 15: THE CLOVER LEAF INN

128   **A local paper mourned:** "Retired to Limbo," *Intelligencer Journal* (Lancaster, Pa.), April 1, 1952.

130   **one of America's celebrated "auto trails":** "The Auto Trails: America's Predecessor to Numbered Highways," *Forgotten Railways, Roads & Places* (blog), www.abandonedraillines.com/2020/03/the-auto-trails.html.

131   **Cloverleaf intersections were considered:** Hugo Martin, "A Major Lane Change," *Los Angeles Times*, April 7, 2004.

132   **Bonnie D'Ignazio, ten years old:** Interview, BD.

133   **In Media, the local newspaper:** Doris D. Wiley, "The Lady on Horseback Visits County," *Delaware County Daily Times* (Chester, Pa.), January 4, 1955.

134   **Annie was traveling along a road:** "History of Chadds Ford Township," chaddsfordpa.gov/index.asp?SEC=62EFD49F-BD73-49BF-B9FF-DD2177703556 &Type=B_BASIC.

135   **A couple seated in the corner:** Laura Fraser, "Miss Annie Wilkins from Maine," from the Oral History Collection of the Chadds Ford Historical Society.

138   **But the first person she ran into:** "Coast to Coast Rider Visits Area," *News-Journal* (Wilmington, Del.), January 6, 1955, and "Woman Riding Horseback Across U.S. Visits Kennett," *Morning News* (Wilmington, Del.), January 8, 1955.

141   **the Pennsylvania Turnpike, one of the early marvels:** Pauline Shieh and Kim Parry, "The Building of the Great Pennsylvania Turnpike," Pennsylvania Center for the Book, pabook.libraries.psu.edu/literary-cultural-heritage-map-pa/feature -articles/building-great-pennsylvania-turnpike.

CHAPTER 16: LOG CABINS

142   **On January 10, 1955, after spinning:** "Woman, Horse, Dog Are Given Van Lift to Lexington, Ky.," *Morning News* (Wilmington, Del.), January 10, 1955.

142   **Her driver's final destination was a Thoroughbred farm:** "Former Vaudeville Girl, 63, Riding Horse to California," *Lexington Leader* (Ky.), January 10, 1955.

143   **On the very day Annie arrived:** Ibid.

148   **In 1894, a New York entrepreneur:** "The Story of Lincoln's Birthplace Cabin," lincolncollection.tumblr.com.

150 **On that day, the local paper reported:** "Local Area Hit by Cold Weather," *Glasgow Daily Times* (Ky.), February 17, 1955.

150 **Meanwhile, a city council member:** "Coast to Coast Woman Resumes Trip in Mid-State," *Nashville Banner,* February, 15, 1955.

150 **According to the newspaper, she was:** "California Woman Makes Stop Here," *Franklin Favorite* (Ky.), February 10, 1955.

151 **He introduced himself as Dr. Carter Moore:** "Coast to Coast Woman Resumes Trip in Mid-State," *Nashville Banner,* February, 15, 1955.

151 **Annie told a reporter of the Scottsville *Citizen-Times:*** "Horseback Woman Enjoys Stay," *Citizen-Times* (Scottsville, Ky.), February 12, 1955.

CHAPTER 17: A NEW FRIEND

153 **The jail turned out to look more like a hospital:** Bill Jones, "Robertson County Jail—Through the Years," www.robertsoncountyconnection.com/news/robertson-county-jail---through-the-years/article_848f9339-4e93-557f-88b8-291631a1bfac.html.

154 **They were walking along Route 49:** "Cross Country Rider Takes Weekend Rest Here," undated clipping from *The Ashland City Times,* courtesy of the Cheatham County Historical and Genealogical Association.

155 **Bradley's daughter Bonnie:** Personal communication, LW, Cheatham County historian.

157 **The townspeople were friendly:** The account of Annie being presented with Rex comes from her memoir, *Last of the Saddle Tramps,* 94–98. See also "Mrs. Wilkins Has a Tennessee Walker," *Country Courier* (West Brookfield, Mass.), March 24, 1955, and "She Trades Horses in the Middle of Trip," *Arkansas Gazette,* April 14, 1955. Annie had only one horse when she left Ashland City, and she had two by the time she got to Waverly, Tennessee. She variously described the place where she got Rex as "near Ashland City," Dickson, or Charlotte, but I was unable to identify the exact location. Annie referred to the people who found Rex for her as the Richardses, but it's not clear if this was their real name.

163 **She was headed to the home of Mrs. Casey Jones:** All information about Casey Jones and his widow is courtesy of the Casey Jones Home & Railroad Museum, in Jackson, Tennessee.

163 **Mary Jones was in her nineties:** "Casey Jones Met Death: Anniversary Tribute to Widow," *Jackson Sun,* April 29, 1955.

CHAPTER 18: LOST

170 **Annie was east of Forrest City:** "Carl's Court," promotional materials, from the author's personal collection, and "Mrs. Wilkins Has News for Winchell," *Country Courier* (West Brookfield, Mass.), April 14, 1955.

170 **Whereas Annie's approach to her journey:** Devine traveled around the country for more than a decade. For more about his travels, see, for example, "Two

Wheeler," *Charlotte News,* December 29, 1967; "Bike Rider Covering Hemisphere," *Courier-Journal* (Louisville), December 31, 1960; and "Hoping to Pedal 52,000 Miles, Devine Stops in Westmoreland," *Manhattan Mercury* (Kans.), January 30, 1955.

171 **She was mounted upon Rex:** "Traveling in Arkansas," *St. Louis Post-Dispatch,* April 9, 1955, and "Horse, Bicycle Riders Decry Highway Menace," *Nashville Banner,* April 8, 1955.

172 **About midnight, she was awakened:** "Mrs. Wilkins Has News for Winchell," *Country Courier* (West Brookfield, Mass.), April 14, 1955.

CHAPTER 19: MAPS

179 **The first road map for drivers:** For a good resource about the American road map, see Douglas A. Yorke, Jr., and John Margolies, *Hitting the Road: The Art of the American Road Map.*

180 **The major distinction on a 1955 gas station map:** One of my favorite road trip books, *Blue Highways,* by William Least Heat-Moon, is named for the blue routes.

182 **Residents were given instructions:** Donald L. Stevens, Jr., "Deforestation and the Rise of Modern Recreation," *A Homeland and a Hinterland: The Current and Jacks Fork Riverways,* Historic Resource Study, Ozark Scenic National Riverway (National Park Service Midwest Regional Office, 1991), www.nps.gov/parkhistory/online_books/ozar/hrs9.htm.

183 **Route 66 passed right through its downtown:** Christina Crapanzano, "A Brief History of Route 66," *Time,* June 28, 2010.

184 **In 1880, Marshfield was the site:** "Marshfield and the Cyclone That Nearly Blew the Town Away," *Ozarks Alive!* (blog), April 18, 2017, ozarksalive.com/marshfield-cyclone-nearly-blew-town-away/.

185 **A film produced by:** American Road Builders' Association, *We'll Take the High Road* (video), 1955, available on YouTube: youtube.com/watch?v=9SD3nLr7M_c.

185 **Disney had modeled Disneyland's Main Street:** "Marceline," waltdisneymuseum.org/marceline/.

186 **"In the period of the 1950s and 1960s":** Quoted in Nathan Masters, "How Disneyland's Main Street, USA, Changed the Design and Preservation of American Cities," kcet.org/shows/lost-la/how-disneylands-main-street-usa-changed-the-design-and-preservation-of-american-cities. The quote is from Vincent Scully, foreword to Beth Dunlop, *Building a Dream: The Art of Disney Architecture* (New York: Abrams, 1996).

187 **But unbeknownst to Annie:** Bill Hatch, "Stray Bits," *Springfield Union,* September 29, 1955.

188 **Disney declared that Main Street U.S.A.:** Bob Thomas, "Disneyland Park Is Rising in California," *Standard-Examiner* (Ogden, Utah), May 8, 1955.

CHAPTER 20: LAST OF THE SADDLE TRAMPS

189 **Annie, Tarzan, Rex, and Depeche Toi arrived:** "She Rests Herself and Horses Here on a Cross-Country Trek," *Kansas City Times,* May 30, 1955.

194 **Traveling through Jim Crow America:** For an excellent recent examination of car travel in Jim Crow America, see Gretchen Sorin, *Driving While Black: African American Travel and the Road to Civil Rights* (New York: Liveright, 2020).

195 **Having made it as far as Swope Park:** "She Rests Herself and Horses Here on a Cross-Country Trek," *Kansas City Times,* May 30, 1955.

195 **In a note she wrote to a friend back east:** "Letter," Mes-Annie Wilkins to Mrs. Merton Rowe, August 13, 1955, Minot Maine Historical Society.

196 **Annie had spread out a map of Kansas:** "Maine to California: Horsewoman Spanning Nation," *Manhattan Mercury* (Kans.), June 10, 1955, and "Visits Waconda Springs on Horseback Trip Across Nation," *Salina Journal* (Kans.), June 26, 1955.

CHAPTER 21: POISON

204 **For the next few days, Annie headed north:** "Last Saddle Tramp Stops at Wray, Is Crossing Nation," *Wray Gazette* (Colo.), July 21, 1955.

207 **Cheyenne was a city of about thirty thousand:** "The Founding of Cheyenne" and "The Holy City of the Cow," Wyoming Tales and Trails, wyomingtalesandtrails .com/photos7.html.

207 **In 1873, the British traveler Isabella Bird:** Isabella Bird, *A Lady's Life in the Rocky Mountains* (London: John Murray, 1879), archive.org/details/inrocky ladyslifeoobirdrich/page/n10/mode/2up.

208 **Cheyenne's Frontier Days celebration:** Interview, MK.

210 **The Lincoln Highway Association:** James Lin, "The Origins of the Lincoln Highway Association," lincolnhighwayassoc.org/history/.

212 **"Cars from 47 states":** "Good Attendance," *Billings Gazette* (Mont.), July 28, 1955.

214 **Racing teams hauling the clunky wagons:** "Bucking Horses Keep Ambulance Crews Busy at Cheyenne Rodeo," *Billings Gazette* (Mont.), July 28, 1955.

216 **Annie and her companions passed through the tiny town of Buford:** "Mrs. Wilkins, Idaho-Bound, Asks Governor to Have 'Potatoe' Ready for Her Arrival," *Country Courier* (West Brookfield, Mass.), August 25, 1955.

CHAPTER 22: MOLEHILLS AND MOUNTAINS

218 **Out of Laramie, Annie had two choices for her route:** John Richard Waggener, *Snow Chi Minh Trail.*

220 **Homesteader Elinore Pruitt Stewart rode across Wyoming:** "Letters of a Woman Homesteader," *Atlantic Monthly,* October 1913.

221 **First built in the 1870s as a wagon road:** "The Snowy Range Scenic Byway,"

Laramie, History & Adventure: That's WY, VisitLaramie.org/brochure-snowy
-range-scenic-byway.

CHAPTER 23: THE RED DESERT

227 **When she told the store man what had happened:** In a later interview, she said
that a Mexican American family had rescued her and been so kind that they'd
asked their children to sleep on the floor so she could rest on the bed after she'd
been caught in the flood. "Maine Saddle Tramp Insists That U.S. Is 'Goodly,'"
Boston Herald, April 7, 1967.

229 **Covey's Little America was located:** Steve Sanger, "Queen of the Highways,"
American Heritage, April–May 2005; see also "Lincoln Highway Photos,"
wyomingtalesandtrails.com/littleamerica.html.

230 **Instead, she headed off the main road:** In her memoir, she refers to him as Harvey Kelsey, but this is not his real name. Annie never revealed it.

235 **"I celebrate myself":** Walt Whitman, "Song of Myself," quoted from the Poetry
Foundation, poetryfoundation.org/poems/45477/song-of-myself-1892-version.

CHAPTER 24: WINTER AGAIN

238 **The approach to town led through a tunnel:** "Female Paul Revere Takes Rest in
City," *Idaho State Journal* (Pocatello), October 29, 1955.

239 **It was mid-October when:** "Maine Woman's Horseback Trek Discounts Theories of 'Weaker Sex,'" *Times-News* (Twin Falls, Idaho), October 11, 1955.

240 **When Annie registered for a camping spot:** Mesannie Wilkins with Mina Titus
Sawyer, *Last of the Saddle Tramps,* 179.

240 **The governor had been expecting her:** "Maine Woman on Horse Trip West
Stops in Idaho," *Marion Star* (Ohio), October 25, 1955, and "Makes Progress
on Horse Ride," *Indiana Gazette* (Pa.), October 25, 1955.

242 **As John Bidwell, a covered-wagon pioneer settler:** John Bidwell, "The First
Emigrant Train to California," in Charles L. Barstow, ed., *The Western Movement* (New York: Century, 1920), 133.

247 **Annie insisted that if she was going to stay through the winter:** "Letter from
Annie," *News* (Paterson, N.J.), December 30, 1955.

CHAPTER 25: A LONG ROAD

252 **So the folks from the chamber of commerce:** "Maine Woman Sees Western
Movie Here After 2700 Mile Ride," *Modoc County Record* (Calif.), December 1,
1955.

252 **Annie rode into Redding:** Art Linkletter, *Women Are My Favorite People,* 152.

252 **Annie had a very special visitor:** Ibid.

253 **Linkletter told the *New York Post* in 1965:** William Grimes, "Art Linkletter, TV
Host, Dies at 97," *New York Times,* May 26, 2010.

253   **A quick look at his biography:** Ibid.

253   **"Among other things, I learned to chisel rides":** Ibid.

CHAPTER 26: TOUGH AS NAILS

256   **When she arrived at the outskirts of the capital:** William Lythgoe, "Maine Woman Reaches Capital on Maine–LA Horseback Trip," *Sacramento Bee,* January 31, 1956.

257   **When naturalist John Muir first entered:** John Muir, *A Thousand-Mile Walk to the Gulf,* ed. William Frederic Badè (Boston: Houghton Mifflin, 1916), 190.

258   **The four companions were near the town of Atwater:** "Stalled by Sick Horse," *Hartford Courant,* February 29, 1956, and "Sick Horse in Tulare Threatens End of Long Ride from State of Maine," *Tulare Advance-Register* (Calif.), February 28, 1956.

263   **"He needs a tetanus shot":** For information about the course of tetanus in equines, I consulted CN. For information about Lionel Brazil, I relied on an interview with MB.

CHAPTER 27: THE GOLDEN STATE

268   **Annie was so listless:** "Mrs. Wilkins Can't Mount but Her Troubles Do," *Tulare Advance-Register* (Calif.), March 8, 1956.

269   **But the Bells wouldn't give up on her:** Ibid.

269   **Art Linkletter had found another horse for her:** "Horse-Riding Visitor May Soon Be on Her Way," *Tulare Advance-Register* (Calif.), March 3, 1956.

271   **"Los Angeles gives one":** Henry Miller, *The Air-Conditioned Nightmare* (New York: New Directions, 1945).

271   **"seventy-two suburbs in search of a city":** According to Adrienne Crew, this quote is frequently attributed to Dorothy Parker, but that may be a misattribution. See Adrienne Crew, "Misquoting Dorothy Parker," LA Observed, August 22, 2013, laobserved.com/intell/2013/08/misquoting_dorothy_parker.php.

272   **In May 1956, Annie Wilkins:** "Woman on Horse Sees U.S.," *Valley Times* (North Hollywood, Calif.), September 9, 1956, and "Look Out Groucho! It Won't Be Easy," *Country Courier* (West Brookfield, Mass.), June 28, 1956.

272   **"Not only was her calm assurance":** Art Linkletter, preface to *Last of the Saddle Tramps,* by Mesannie Wilkins with Mina Titus Sawyer, v.

EPILOGUE

277   **Without his friend Rex to steady him:** "Mesannie Wilkins, 'Last of the Saddle Tramps,' Writes Letter; Friends Trying to Get Her on TV," *Country Courier* (West Brookfield, Mass.), October 24, 1957.

Bibliography

"Agriculture 1950: Changes in Agriculture 1900–1950." *1950 Census of Agriculture*. Vol. 2, *General Report*. Washington, D.C.: Government Printing Office, 1952.

Allport, Susan. *Sermons in Stone: The Stone Walls of New England and New York*. Woodstock, Vt.: Countryman, 2012.

Anderson, M. "Images of Nineteenth Century Maine Farming in the Prose and Poetry of R. P. T. Coffin and C. A. Stephens." *Agricultural History* 63, no. 2 (1989), 120–29. Retrieved from jstor.org/stable/3743507.

"Annie Given Shelter with Horse Tarzan." *Hartford Courant*, November 15, 1954.

Annual Report of the Selectmen and Treasurer of the Town of Grafton. Franklin, N.H.: Towne & Robie, 1921.

Annual Report of the Selectmen and Treasurer of the Town of Grafton. Canaan, N.H.: Reporter Press, 1922.

"As They Continue Their Trip." *St. Louis Globe-Democrat*, November 15, 1954.

"Back on Her Horse." *Kansas City Times*, June 1, 1955.

Beston, Henry. *Northern Farm: A Chronicle of Maine*. Waterville, Maine: Thorndike Press, 1979.

"Bike Rider Covering Hemisphere." *Courier-Journal* (Louisville), December 31, 1960.

Blood, Grace Everlina Holbrook. *Manchester on the Merrimack: The Story of a City*. Manchester, N.H.: Manchester Historic Association, 1975.

"Bucking Horses Keep Ambulance Crews Busy at Cheyenne Rodeo." *Billings Gazette* (Mont.), July 28, 1955.

"California-Bound Rider." *Hartford Courant*, December 5, 1954.

"California Here I Come." *Daily Inter Lake* (Kalispell, Mont.), December 2, 1954.

"California, Here We Come on Horseback." *Journal-News* (Rockland County, N.Y.), December 13, 1954.

"California Woman Makes Stop Here." *Franklin Favorite* (Ky.), February 10, 1955.

"Call of the West—Farm 'Girl' Hits Open Road." *Spokane Chronicle*, November 12, 1954.

Carlton Coes, Elizabeth. "Mrs. Wilkins, Tarzan and Hurry-Up Pass Here on Way to See Folks Who Live 'Round by the Back Door." *Country Courier* (West Brookfield, Mass.), December 2, 1954.

"Casey Jones Met Death: Anniversary Tribute to Widow." *Jackson Sun,* April 29, 1955.

"Coast-to-Coast on Horseback." *Boston Globe,* November 11, 1954.

"Coast-to-Coast Rider Snowed In in Tennessee." *Burlington Free Press* (Vt.), February 15, 1955.

"Coast to Coast Rider Visits Area." *News-Journal* (Wilmington, Del.), January 6, 1955.

"Coast to Coast Woman Resumes Trip in Mid-State." *Nashville Banner,* February 15, 1955.

Crapanzano, Christina. "A Brief History of Route 66." *Time,* June 28, 2010.

Cronon, William. *Changes in the Land: Indians, Colonists, and the Ecology of New England.* New York: Farrar, Straus and Giroux, 2011.

"Cross Country Horse Dies." *Burlington Free Press* (Vt.), March 3, 1956.

"Cross Country Rider Takes Weekend Rest Here." *Ashland City Times* (Tenn.), undated newspaper clipping. Courtesy of Windham Historical Society.

Delbanco, Andrew, ed. *Writing New England: An Anthology from the Puritans to the Present.* Cambridge, Mass.: Belknap Press/Harvard University Press, 2001.

DePastino, Todd. *Citizen Hobo.* Chicago: University of Chicago Press, 2003.

"A Different Place: 1945–1970." Maine Memory Network. www.mainememory.net.

Dublin, Thomas L., ed. *Farm to Factory: Women's Letters, 1830–1860.* New York: Columbia University Press, 1993.

"Eisenhower's State of the Union Address, 1954." pbs.org/wgbh/americanexperience/features/eisenhower-state54/.

Emerson, Jean. "Jean Bryar, 87, Dies." United States Trotting Association, June 16, 2012. ustrottingnews.com/jean-bryar-87-dies/.

"En Route to California." *Courier-News* (Bridgewater, N.J.), November 15, 1954.

Ensminger, M. E. *Horse Husbandry.* Danville, Ill.: Interstate Printers and Publishers, 1951.

"Female Paul Revere Takes Rest in City." *Idaho State Journal* (Pocatello), October 29, 1955.

Forest Trees of Maine. Augusta, Maine: Department of Agriculture, Conservation and Forestry, 2008.

"Former Vaudeville Girl, 63, Riding Horse to California." *Lexington Leader* (Ky.), January 10, 1955.

Freeland, Joe. "Saddle-Sore Maine Woman Arrives Here Headed West." *Jackson Sun* (Tenn.), March 13, 1955.

"Goin' Cross Country: Woman Dismounts to Visit Smylie." *Idaho State Journal* (Pocatello), October 25, 1955.

"Good Attendance." *Billings Gazette* (Mont.), July 28, 1955.

Gould, Ralph Ernest. *Yankee Boyhood: My Adventures on a Maine Farm Seventy Years Ago.* New York: Norton, 1950.

"Go West, Young Lady." *Monroe News-Star* (La.), March 28, 1955.

Grimes, William. "Art Linkletter, TV Host, Dies at 97." *New York Times,* May 26, 2010.

Halberstam, David. *The Fifties.* New York: Fawcett Columbine, 1994.

Hanchett, Leland J., Jr. *Connecting Maine's Capitals by Stagecoach.* Falmouth, Maine: Pine Rim, 2017.

"Hard Cold Halts Widow Riding to California." *Hartford Courant,* November 28, 1954.

Hatch, Bill. "Stray Bits." *Springfield Union,* September 29, 1955.

Heat-Moon, William Least. *Blue Highways: A Journey into America.* 1982. Reprint, Boston: Little, Brown, 2012.

Hodgkin, Douglas. *Dear Parent: A Biography and Letters of Edward Little.* Auburn, Maine: Androscoggin Historical Society, 2017.

——. *Lewiston Politics in the Gilded Age, 1863–1900.* Douglas I. Hodgkin, 2015.

Hodsdon, Lucille Hemond, and Noella Hemond, compilers. *Bakerstown Births— Minot, Early Poland, Auburn & Mechanic Falls, 1750–1950 or So.* Norway, Maine: privately published by Lucille Hemond Hodsdon, 2008.

"Hoping to Pedal 52,000 Miles, Devine Stops in Westmoreland." *Manhattan Mercury* (Kans.), January 30, 1955.

Hopkins, Lorraine. "Windsor Locks Welcomes Woman on Horseback Trip." *Hartford Courant,* December 4, 1954.

"'Horseback Annie' Reaches Kentucky." *Berkshire Eagle* (Pittsfield, Mass.), January 10, 1955.

"Horsebacks Across U.S." *News-Messenger* (Fremont, Ohio), March 27, 1956.

"Horseback to California." *Cincinnati Enquirer,* November 28, 1955.

"Horseback Woman Enjoys Stay." *Citizen-Times* (Scottsville, Ky.), February 12, 1955.

"Horse, Bicycle Riders Decry Highway Menace." *Nashville Banner,* April 8, 1955.

"Horse-Riding Visitor May Soon Be on Her Way." *Tulare Advance-Register* (Calif.), March 3, 1956.

"Horsewoman Arrives in New Hampshire." *Hartford Courant,* November 12, 1954.

"Jean Bryar Obituary." *Sled Dog Central,* June 4, 2012, sleddogcentral.com/obituaries/ Bryar_jean.htm.

Jensen, Tim. "Flashback Friday: Windsor Locks History with Mel Montemerlo." Patch.com, March 24, 2017.

Keith, B. F. "The Vogue of Vaudeville." *National Magazine* 9, November 1898.

Kelly, Kathryn. "Ancestors of Annie Mabel Mesannie Libby Stuart." November 15, 2017 (personal communication).

Ladd, William, Esq. "Annals of Poland, Bakerstown, and Minot." *Collections of the Maine Historical Society,* vol. 2. Portland, Maine: The Society, 1847.

"'Last of Saddle Tramps' Reaches Her Goal on Horseback Journey Across United States." *Florence Morning News* (S.C.), March 25, 1956.

"Last Saddle Tramp Stops at Wray, Is Crossing Nation." *Wray Gazette* (Colo.), July 21, 1955.

Leamon, James S. *Historic Lewiston: A Textile City in Transition.* Auburn, Maine: Central Maine Vocational Technical Institute, 1976.

Lepore, Jill. "The Meaning of Life: What Milton Bradley Started." *New Yorker,* May 21, 2007.

"Letter." Annie Wilkins to Mrs. Merton Rowe, March 5, 1955. Courtesy of Minot Maine Historical Society.

"Letter." Annie Wilkins to Mrs. Merton Rowe, May 9, 1955. Courtesy of Minot Maine Historical Society.

"Letter." Mes-Annie Wilkins to Mrs. Merton Rowe, August 13, 1955. Courtesy of Minot Maine Historical Society.

."Letter from Annie." *News* (Paterson, N.J.), December 30, 1955.

Lewis, Tom. *Divided Highways: Building the Interstate Highways, Transforming American Life.* Ithaca: Cornell University Press, 2013.

Libby, Charles T. *The Libby Family in America, 1602–1881.* Portland, Maine: B. Thurston & Co., 1882.

Linkletter, Art. *Women Are My Favorite People.* New York: Doubleday, 1974.

Linsley, Daniel Chipman. *Morgan Horses: A Premium Essay on the Origin, History, and Characteristics of This Remarkable American Breed of Horses, Tracing the Pedigree from the Original Justin Morgan* [. . .]. New York: C. M. Saxton, Barker, 1860. Reprint, Shelburne, Vt.: National Museum of the Morgan Horse, 2000.

"Local Area Hit by Cold Weather." *Glasgow Daily Times* (Ky.), February 17, 1955.

"Long Trip on Horseback." *Brookville American* (Ind.), May 26, 1955.

"Look Out Groucho! It Won't Be Easy." *Country Courier* (West Brookfield, Mass.), June 28, 1956.

Loving, Nancy S. *Go the Distance: The Complete Resource for Endurance Horses.* Shropshire, U.K.: Kenilworth Press/Quiller, 1997.

Lythgoe, William. "Maine Woman Reaches Capital on Maine–LA Horse Trip." *Sacramento Bee,* January 31, 1956.

"Maine Horsewoman Riding Horse Coast to Coast." *Southern Illinoisan,* January 10, 1955.

"Maine Horsewoman Taking Back Roads to Dodge Pen Fans." *Springfield Union,* November 25, 1954.

Maine Invites You. 19th ed. Portland, Maine: Maine Publicity Bureau, 1953.

"Maine Rider Slow Piling Up Miles but Friends Snowball." *Springfield Union,* November 24, 1954.

"Maine Saddle Tramp Insists That U.S. Is 'Goodly.'" *Boston Herald,* April 7, 1967.

"Maine to California: Horsewoman Spanning Nation." *Manhattan Mercury* (Kans.), June 10, 1955.

"Maine Widow's Horse in Good Shape, Doctors Decide." *Springfield Union,* December 3, 1954.

"Maine Woman, Horse, Dog, Leave City." *Springfield Union,* December 4, 1954.

"Maine Woman on Horse Trip West Stops in Idaho." *Marion Star* (Ohio), October 25, 1955.

"Maine Woman Riding Horse to California." *Atlanta Constitution,* November 11, 1954.

"Maine Woman Sees Western Movie Here After 2700 Mile Ride." *Modoc County Record* (Calif.), December 1, 1955.

"Maine Woman's Horseback Trek Discounts Theories of 'Weaker Sex.'" *Times-News* (Twin Falls, Idaho), October 11, 1955.

"Maine Woman, 63, Hits Trail Again to California by Horse." *Boston Globe,* November 15, 1954.

"Maine Woman Still on Trail: Is Riding Horse to California." *Billings Gazette* (Mont.), November 12, 1954.

"Maine Woman Takes Buggy." *Springfield Union,* November 24, 1954.

"Makes Progress on Horse Ride." *Indiana Gazette* (Pa.), October 25, 1955.

"Ma Kettle Herself!" *Cincinnati Enquirer,* May 23, 1955.

Maner, Gene. "Former Vaudeville Girl, 63, Riding Horse to California." *Lexington Leader* (Ky.), January 10, 1955.

Manning, Samuel F. *New England Masts and the King's Broad Arrow.* Somersworth: New Hampshire Printers, 1979.

"Mel-Annie Wilkins' 'Tramp of Fate' Heard From." *Country Courier* (West Brookfield, Mass.), December 30, 1954.

Mellin, Jeanne. *The Complete Morgan Horse.* Shelburne, Vt.: American Morgan Horse Association, 1995.

"Mesannie Wilkins in Sterling, Mass., on Horseback Trip." *Burlington Free Press* (Vt.), November 24, 1954.

"Mesannie Wilkins, 'Last of the Saddle Tramps,' Writes Letter; Friends Trying to Get Her on TV." *Country Courier* (West Brookfield, Mass.), October 24, 1957.

"Mesannie Wilkins' Life Story One of Courage, Work." *Springfield Union,* December 4, 1954.

Mickelson, Sig. *The Decade That Shaped Television News: CBS in the 1950s.* Santa Barbara, Calif.: ABC-Clio, 1998.

"Minot Horsewoman Nears Halfway Mark." Undated clipping from scrapbook, courtesy of Windham Historical Society.

"Miss Annie Wilkins, 63, en Route to California," *Sanford Tribune and Advocate* (Maine), November 18, 1954.

Mogensen, Maxwell. *Legendary Locals of Androscoggin County.* Mount Pleasant, S.C.: Arcadia, 2013.

"More Word Comes from Mrs. Wilkins." *Country Courier* (West Brookfield, Mass.), January 20, 1955.

"Mrs. Wilkins About to Cross Mississippi." *Country Courier* (West Brookfield, Mass.), April 7, 1955.

"Mrs. Wilkins Can't Mount but Her Troubles Do." *Tulare Advance-Register* (Calif.), March 8, 1956.

"Mrs. Wilkins Expects 'Some Silly Thing.'" *Country Courier* (West Brookfield, Mass.), March 8, 1956.

"Mrs. Wilkins' Friends Slowing Her Pace." *Springfield Union,* December 3, 1954.

"Mrs. Wilkins Has a Tennessee Walker." *Country Courier* (West Brookfield, Mass.), March 24, 1955.

"Mrs. Wilkins Has News for Winchell." *Country Courier* (West Brookfield, Mass.), April 14, 1955.

"Mrs. Wilkins, Idaho-Bound, Asks Governor to Have 'Potatoe' Ready for Her Arrival." *Country Courier* (West Brookfield, Mass.), August 25, 1955.

"Mrs. Wilkins Rides On Again, but at Ease in an Automobile." *Springfield Sunday Republican,* December 5, 1954.

"Mrs. Wilkins Says Her Courage Is Still Good." *Country Courier* (West Brookfield, Mass.), February 10, 1955.

Nickerson, Kermit S. *150 Years of Education in Maine.* Augusta: State of Maine Department of Education, 1970.

"1950 Census of Population: Preliminary Counts." *Population of Oregon, by Counties.* U.S. Department of Commerce, 1950.

"Obituary, Lionel Brazil." *Fresno Bee* (Calif.), September 12, 2007.

The Old Maps of Androscoggin County, Maine in 1873. Philadelphia: Sanford and Everts, n.d.

"One Old-Fashioned H. P." *Dayton Daily News* (Ohio), January 11, 1955.

Pastry, Joe. "A Brief History of Home Canning." July 23, 2008, joepastry.com/2008/a_brief_history_of_home_canning_1/.

Penney, John William, and Minnie Penney. *Eighty-eight Years on a Maine Farm*. Camden, Maine: Down East, 1973.

"People and Animals." *Pampa Daily News* (Tex.), January 19, 1955.

Pringle, Laurence. *Ice! The Amazing History of the Ice Business*. New York: Calkins Creek, 2012.

Rendel, John. "Husky from the Arctic: Work, Devotion and Experience Needed to Develop Top-Flight Sled Dog." *New York Times*, February 27, 1964.

"A Restful Day Was Spent." *Kansas City Times*, May 30, 1955.

"Retired to Limbo." *Intelligencer Journal* (Lancaster, Pa.), April 1, 1952.

Rice-DeFosse, Mary, and James Myall. *The Franco-Americans of Lewiston-Auburn*. Mount Pleasant, S.C.: Arcadia, 2015.

"Riding Horseback to Coast." *Morning Call* (Paterson, N.J.), December 13, 1954.

Sanger, Steve. "Queen of the Highways." *American Heritage*, April–May 2005.

Sargent, David A. *Remembering Lewiston-Auburn on the Mighty Androscoggin: River Views*. Mount Pleasant, S.C.: History Press/Arcadia, 2010.

Schacht, Beulah. "Take It from Beulah: Annie Doesn't Make Excuses." *St. Louis Globe-Democrat*, May 25, 1955.

"Seeing the Country." *Monroe Morning World* (La.), April 9, 1955.

"She Rests Herself and Horses Here on a Cross-Country Trek: A Jackson County Couple Aids a 63-Year-Old Maine Woman Lost in Swope Park—Now She Seeks Services of Blacksmith." *Kansas City Times*, May 30, 1955.

"She Trades Horses in the Middle of Trip." *Arkansas Gazette*, April 14, 1955.

"Sick Horse in Tulare Threatens End of Long Ride from State of Maine." *Tulare Advance-Register* (Calif.), February 28, 1956.

"Stalled by Sick Horse." *Hartford Courant*, February 29, 1956.

Steinbeck, John. *Travels with Charley: In Search of America*. New York: Penguin Books, 2012.

Storms, Aarene. *Endurance 101: A Gentle Guide to the Sport of Long-Distance Riding*. Arlington, Wash.: Triangle Ranch Communications, 2012.

Swift, Earl. *The Big Roads: The Untold Story of the Engineers, Visionaries, and Trailblazers Who Created the American Superhighways*. Boston: Houghton Mifflin Harcourt, 2011.

"Taking a Breather." *Salina Journal* (Kans.), June 26, 1955.

Taylor, Alan. *Liberty Men and Great Proprietors: The Revolutionary Settlement on the Maine Frontier, 1760–1820*. Chapel Hill: University of North Carolina Press, 1990.

Taylor, P., and A. Loftis. "The Legacy of the Nineteenth-Century New England Farmer." *New England Quarterly* 54, no. 2 (1981): 243–54. doi:10.2307/364972.

Thomas, Bob. "Disneyland Park Is Rising in California." *Standard-Examiner* (Ogden, Utah), May 8, 1955.

Thoreau, Henry David. *A Week on the Concord and Merrimack Rivers.* Boston: James Munroe, 1849, online-literature.com/thoreau/concord-and-merrimack/.

Thorson, Robert M. *Stone by Stone: The Magnificent History in New England's Stone Walls.* New York: Bloomsbury, 2009.

Titus, Dorothy M., and Percy Hobart Titus, eds. *Titus Family in America: Eleven Generations of the Direct Line from Robert Titus.* Boston: privately published by the editors, 1943.

Tomko, Gene, and Paul Garon. *What's the Use of Walking If There's a Freight Train Going Your Way? Black Hoboes & Their Songs.* Chicago: C. H. Kerr, 2006.

"'Tramp of Fate' Claims New Title." *Country Courier* (West Brookfield, Mass.), July 28, 1955.

"Traveling in Arkansas." *St. Louis Post-Dispatch,* April 9, 1955.

"Two Wheeler." *Charlotte News,* December 29, 1967.

Van der Veer, Judy. *Hold the Rein Free.* New York: Scholastic Book Services, 1968.

———. *November Grass.* Santa Clara, Calif.: Santa Clara University, 2001.

"Visitor's Horse Dies." *Tulare Advance-Register* (Calif.), March 2, 1956.

"Visits Waconda Springs on Horseback Trip Across Nation." *Salina Journal* (Kans.), June 26, 1955.

"Voters to Consider 22-Acre Gift." *Hartford Courant,* January 20, 1974.

Waggener, John Richard. *Snow Chi Minh Trail: The History of Interstate 80 Between Laramie and Walcott Junction.* Wheatland: Wyoming State Historical Society, 2017.

Ward, Lynd, and Ruth Adams Knight. *Brave Companions.* New York: Doubleday, Doran, 1945.

"Wayne's Visitor of Year Ago Reaches End of Her Odyssey." *Herald-News* (Passaic, N.J.), December 29, 1955.

White, Elwyn Brooks. *One Man's Meat.* 1942. Reprint. Thomaston, Maine: Tilbury House, 1997.

White, Howard J. *Meet Noden-Reed Park.* Windsor Locks, Conn.: Windsor Locks Historical Society, 1991.

"Widow on Horseback Is Due Tomorrow." *Springfield Union,* December 1, 1954.

"Widow on Horseback Near California Destination." *Hartford Courant,* January 4, 1956.

"Widow on Horseback Sees Need of Smithys." *Hartford Courant,* March 25, 1955.

"Widow, 63, Riding Horse from Maine to California." *Tampa Tribune* (Fla.), March 25, 1955.

Wiley, Doris D. "The Lady on Horseback Visits County," *Delaware County Daily Times* (Chester, Pa.), January 4, 1955.

Wilkins, Mesannie, with Mina Titus Sawyer. *Last of the Saddle Tramps.* Englewood Cliffs, N.J.: Prentice-Hall, 1967.

Wilmot, Sydney. "Use of Convict Labor for Highway Construction in the North." *Proceedings of the Academy of Political Science in the City of New York,* 4, no. 2 (1914): 6–68.

"Woman, Horse, Dog Are Given Van Lift to Lexington, Ky." *Morning News* (Wilmington, Del.), January 10, 1955.

"Woman on Horse Sees U.S." *Valley Times* (North Hollywood, Calif.), September 9, 1956.

"Woman Rides Horse from East to Coast." *Arizona Republic* (Phoenix), December 29, 1955.

"Woman Riding Horseback Across U.S. Visits Kennett." *Morning News* (Wilmington, Del.), January 8, 1955.

"Woman, 63, Crossing Country on Horse, Marks Birthday in Wayne." *News* (Paterson, N.J.), December 14, 1954.

Woodard, Colin. *The Lobster Coast: Rebels, Rusticators, and the Struggle for a Forgotten Frontier.* New York: Penguin Books, 2004.

Yorke, Douglas A., Jr., and John Margolies. *Hitting the Road: The Art of the American Road Map.* San Francisco: Chronicle, 1996.

Index

Note: Page numbers in **bold** reference maps.

ELIZABETH LETTS is the #1 *New York Times* bestselling author of *The Eighty-Dollar Champion* and *The Perfect Horse*, which won the 2017 PEN Center USA Literary Award for research nonfiction, as well as three novels, *Finding Dorothy, Quality of Care,* and *Family Planning.* A former certified nurse-midwife, she also served in the Peace Corps in Morocco. She lives on a horse ranch in rural Wyoming and in Northern Michigan.

elizabethletts.com

Facebook.com/ElizabethLettsAuthor

Twitter: @ElizabethLetts

Instagram: @elizabethletts